The Official Guide to the MCAT® Exam

Fifth Edition

By the staff of the
Medical College Admission Test
Association of American Medical Colleges

The Official Guide to the MCAT® Exam, Fifth Edition

Published by:

Association of American Medical Colleges
655 K Street, NW, Suite 100
Washington, DC 20001-2399

Any and all AAMC and MCAT fees, policies, and procedures may change without notice at any time. Up-to-date MCAT fees, policies, and procedures are available at **aamc.org/mcat** or you may contact the AAMC Services Contact Center at mcat@aamc.org.

AAMC®, Association of American Medical Colleges®, AMCAS®, American Medical College Application Service®, MCAT®, Medical College Admission Test®, MSAR®, and related marks are trademarks of the Association of American Medical Colleges. Other trademarks used in this publication are the property of the respective owners.

ISBN: 978-1-57754-173-8

How This Guide Is Structured

The Official Guide to the MCAT® Exam was developed under the direction of Medical College Admission Test (MCAT) staff and with the help of many contributors from the Association of American Medical Colleges (AAMC). It provides an overview of the Medical College Admission Test (MCAT) exam. We are pleased to offer this resource to some 85,000 examinees who have historically taken the exam each year. To help guide you through this material, we divided the content into two parts:

Part I. The first part of the book provides extensive information on procedural aspects of the MCAT exam. Here, for example, you will find a description of the exam's overall format, an explanation of the registration process and test-day procedures, and an extensive discussion about MCAT scores.

Part II. The second part of the book concentrates on the exam content itself and focuses on the foundational concepts, content categories, scientific inquiry, critical analysis, and reasoning skills that tomorrow's doctors will need to know. Part II provides details about the format and focus of each exam section as well as abundant practice questions and tips to help you fine-tune your approach.

The contents pages outline these parts in detail.

CONTENTS

Part II: Preparing for the MCAT® Exam

Tables and Charts

Fifth Edition
The Official Guide to the MCAT® Exam
    xi
MCAT® is a program of the
Association of American Medical Colleges

FOREWORD

An Open Letter to Premed Students

Dear Aspiring Physician:

Let me be among the first to congratulate you on considering a career in medicine!

While this is an exciting time, you may be asking yourself many questions: What will the health system of the future look like? What kind of physicians will it require? Although no one can answer these questions precisely, important shifts are underway that will require tomorrow's doctors to be prepared to care for a growing, aging, increasingly diverse population and to work within a changing health care system.

For 90 years, the Medical College Admission Test® (MCAT®) has been one of the first steps on the journey to becoming a physician. An important predictor of students' academic success in medical school, the MCAT exam is designed to measure the competencies that medical school faculty think are the most important for entering students to demonstrate. Updated in 2015, the exam tests students' knowledge of the natural, social, and behavioral sciences and assesses critical analysis and reasoning skills, including the ability to apply knowledge to practice in diverse settings.

The AAMC has many resources available to help you prepare for the MCAT exam. I encourage you to take advantage of this guide and the flashcards, practice exams, and other resources on the AAMC website that will provide you with valuable insight into the structure of the exam and help you identify areas for further study and practice (aamc.org/mcat).

Becoming a doctor is one of the most rewarding career paths I can imagine, and the AAMC is here to be a resource for you. We wish you great success as you continue on your journey.

Sincerely,

Darrell G. Kirch, MD
President and CEO
AAMC

PART I:

Inside the MCAT Exam

Chapter 1

The MCAT Exam: An Overview

You're reading this book because you want to know more about the MCAT® exam. As the developers and administrators of the test, we're here to serve as a resource. From basic information about the MCAT exam to practice questions and tips for doing well, we have a lot to share with you—including practice questions with detailed solutions and tips for getting the right answers, all written by the test developers.

To get started, here are a few things we want you to know:

- **There are no secrets.** Searching online or talking with friends, you may have the sense that doing well on the MCAT exam is a mystery. However, in reality, that isn't the case. There are no secrets, and there is no way to "game" the test. All the test-taking strategies you can find can't substitute for this fundamental fact: *You can do well on the MCAT exam by knowing the concepts and applying the skills it tests*. And that's the truth.

- **Be prepared.** There's plenty you can do to prepare for the exam and potentially strengthen your performance. First, you need to know the test basics—how to register, what to know about test day, and how to read and understand your scores. Second, you need to get comfortable with how the test is structured and the types of questions it asks. This book will help you prepare.

- **It's part of a journey.** The MCAT exam is a crucial step for getting into medical school, but it's only one part of the admissions process. As we'll discuss later on, the MCAT exam is part of a comprehensive, holistic admissions process that medical schools have designed to find the students who can best fit with their programs and succeed as physicians.

The truth of the matter is that the MCAT exam is challenging, as is the path to getting into medical school. But if you're considering a career in medicine, you're probably the type of person who looks to embrace a challenge. Keep this in mind as you prepare for test day.

So sit back. Take a deep breath. Relax for a moment. Let us share some information and insights that can help you prepare to take the MCAT exam.

MCAT INSIDER: Just starting to think about medical school?

If you are just starting to think about a career in medicine, other AAMC resources can help. Start with the AAMC guidebook, *The Official Guide to Medical School Admissions* (available in print or as an ebook—see aamc.org/msar), the most authoritative guide to preparing for and applying to U.S. medical schools. Also visit the MCAT exam website: aamc.org/mcat.

What Is the Purpose of the MCAT Exam?

The MCAT exam is a standardized test that has been a part of the medical school admissions process for 90 years. Taken by roughly 85,000 students each year, it provides medical school admissions officers with valuable information about the readiness of their applicants to handle the rigors of medical school. Admissions officers look not only for students whose base knowledge of concepts in the natural, social, and behavioral sciences will serve as a strong foundation in the early years of medical study, but also for those with strong scientific problem-solving and critical-analysis skills. The exam helps identify which applicants are most likely to succeed in medical school and in medical careers. MCAT scores are unique in being the only measures of academic readiness for medical school that have the same meaning for all applicants. Unlike undergraduate grades, MCAT scores have the same meaning no matter where you went to school and what courses you took.

The MCAT exam has a long track record of identifying students who can succeed in medical school. Historically, the exam has added substantial value to the prediction of performance in all four years of medical school. MCAT scores do a good job of predicting medical students' grades, licensing exam scores, and graduation rates.

Proven and effective, MCAT scores are required of applicants by virtually every medical school in the United States and many in Canada.

How Is the MCAT Exam Structured?

The MCAT exam is taken on a computer and has four multiple-choice test sections:

- Chemical and Physical Foundations of Biological Systems

- Biological and Biochemical Foundations of Living Systems

- Psychological, Social, and Biological Foundations of Behavior

- Critical Analysis and Reasoning Skills

The first three sections in that list are organized around foundational concepts, or "big ideas," in the sciences. They reflect current research about the most effective ways for students to learn and use science, emphasizing deep knowledge of the most important scientific concepts over knowledge of many discrete scientific facts.

Leaders in science education say that some of the most important foundational concepts in the sciences ask students to integrate and analyze information from different disciplines. In that vein, questions in those three sections will ask you to combine your scientific knowledge from multiple disciplines with your scientific inquiry and reasoning skills. You will be asked to demonstrate four different scientific inquiry and reasoning skills on the exam:

- Knowledge of scientific concepts and principles

- Scientific reasoning and problem solving

- Reasoning about the design and execution of research

- Data-based and statistical reasoning

These four skill areas are discussed in depth in Part II of this guide.

The fourth section of the MCAT exam, Critical Analysis and Reasoning Skills, will be similar to many of the verbal reasoning tests you have taken in your academic career. It includes passages and questions that test your ability to comprehend and analyze what you read. The Critical Analysis and Reasoning Skills section asks you to read and think about passages from a wide range of subjects in the social sciences and humanities, including ethics, philosophy, studies of diverse cultures, and population health. Passages are followed by a series of questions that lead you through the process of comprehending, analyzing, and reasoning about the material you've read. This section is unique because it has been developed specifically to measure the analytical and reasoning skills you'll need to be successful in medical school. Again, you can find more detail in Part II.

The chart below provides an overview of the exam as it is administered on test day.

MCAT Exam Structure		
This chart gives an overview of how long each section of the MCAT exam takes and a general sense of how much "seat time" you should plan for.		
Test Section	**Number of Questions**	**Time**
Test-Day Certification	--	4 minutes
Tutorial *(Optional)*	--	10 minutes
Chemical and Physical Foundations of Biological Systems	59	95 minutes
Break *(Optional)*	--	10 minutes
Critical Analysis and Reasoning Skills	53	90 minutes
Midexam Break *(Optional)*	--	30 minutes
Biological and Biochemical Foundations of Living Systems	59	95 minutes
Break *(Optional)*	--	10 minutes
Psychological, Social, and Biological Foundations of Behavior	59	95 minutes
Void Question	--	3 minutes
Satisfaction Survey *(Optional)*	--	5 minutes
Approximate Content Time	--	**6 hours, 15 minutes**
Approximate "Seat" Time	--	**7 hours, 30 minutes**
NOTE: Total time does not include arrival at the test center or check-in times.		

The structure of the MCAT exam and the content in each section are grounded in a wide base of evidence. They reflect data gleaned from surveys of medical school faculty and administrators, residents, and medical students and recommendations from national panels and advice from national experts in medicine and medical education about the competencies that entering medical school students need to have. It also takes into account analyses of past examinees' results as well as data from medical school applicants.*

* For more information, see Schwartzstein RM, Rosenfeld GC, Hilborn R, Oyewole SH, Mitchell K. Redesigning the MCAT exam: balancing multiple perspectives. Academic Medicine 2013;88(5):560-567.

Summary of MCAT Exam Sections

Chemical and Physical Foundations of Biological Systems

This section asks you to combine your knowledge of foundational concepts in the chemical and physical sciences with your scientific inquiry, reasoning, research methods, and statistics skills to solve problems that demonstrate your readiness for medical school.

Understanding the mechanical, physical, and biochemical functions of tissues, organs, and organ systems is important to the study of medicine. You will be tested on your knowledge of the basic chemical and physical principles that underlie the mechanisms operating in the human body and your ability to apply an understanding of these general principles to living systems.

Critical Analysis and Reasoning Skills

This section asks you to critically analyze information from a wide range of social sciences and humanities disciplines. Specific knowledge of these disciplines is not required for this section; all the information you will need appears in the passages provided. Content is drawn from several areas, including (but not limited to) ethics, philosophy, studies of diverse cultures, and population health.

Biological and Biochemical Foundations of Living Systems

This section asks you to combine your knowledge of foundational concepts in the biological and biochemical sciences with your scientific inquiry, reasoning, research methods, and statistics skills to solve problems that will demonstrate your readiness for medical school.

Understanding the processes unique to living organisms, such as growing and reproducing, maintaining a constant internal environment, acquiring materials and energy, sensing and responding to environmental changes, and adapting, is important to the study of medicine. You will be tested on your knowledge of how cell and organ system processes within an organism act both independently and together, as well as your ability to reason about these processes at various levels of biological organization within a living system.

Psychological, Social, and Biological Foundations of Behavior

This section asks you to combine your knowledge of the concepts in psychology, sociology, and biology with your scientific inquiry, reasoning, research methods, and statistics skills. Demonstrating that you can do this well provides a solid foundation for learning about the behavioral and sociocultural determinants of health and health outcomes in medical school.

Understanding the behavioral and sociocultural determinants of health is important to the study of medicine. You will be tested on your knowledge of the ways that psychological, social, and biological factors influence perceptions and reactions to the world; behavior and behavior change; what people think about themselves and others; the cultural and social differences that influence well-being; and the relationships among social stratification, access to resources, and well-being.

MCAT Exam: A Better Test for Tomorrow's Doctors

Science advances rapidly, transforming the delivery of health care to an increasingly diverse patient · population. Tomorrow's doctors need to be prepared for this transformation, which will play a major role in shaping what students need to know when they start medical school and what they learn in medical school.

To meet evolving needs, the MCAT exam has changed significantly five times since 1928, with the current iteration of the test launching in 2015. The current version followed a comprehensive review of the MCAT exam by many experts and reflects extensive research, including surveys of more than 2,700 baccalaureate and medical school faculty, residents, medical students, and medical school admissions and academic affairs officers. The changes preserved what worked in the last edition of the exam while enriching the test's content with concepts tomorrow's doctors will need to know.

As an example, the natural sciences sections now reflect the latest research in biology, general and organic chemistry, biochemistry, and physics. The addition of a section on social and behavioral sciences recognizes the importance of sociocultural and behavioral determinants of health and health outcomes. These sections ask examinees to use their scientific reasoning, research methods, and statistics skills to solve problems in the same ways that natural, behavioral, and social scientists do. A section on critical analysis and reasoning reflects the value that medical schools place on those skills.

In essence, students taking the current MCAT exam are a part of a next-generation approach in · helping gauge how well potential medical students are prepared for their studies.

What Does the MCAT Exam Measure?

The different sections of the MCAT exam are carefully designed to test the concepts and skills most needed by entering medical students.

The Biological and Biochemical Foundations of Living Systems and the Chemical and Physical Foundations of Biological Systems sections are designed to:

- Test introductory-level biology, organic and inorganic chemistry, and physics concepts

- Test biochemistry concepts at the level taught in many colleges and universities in first-semester biochemistry courses

- Test cellular (Biological and Biochemical Foundations of Living Systems section only) and molecular biology topics at the level taught in many colleges and universities in introductory biology sequences and first-semester biochemistry courses

- Target basic research methods and statistics concepts described by many baccalaureate faculty as important to success in introductory science courses

- Require you to demonstrate your scientific inquiry and reasoning, research methods, and statistics skills as applied to the natural sciences

The Psychological, Social, and Biological Foundations of Behavior section is designed to:

- Test your knowledge and use of the concepts in psychology, sociology, and biology that provide a solid foundation for learning in medical school about the behavioral and sociocultural determinants of health

- Target concepts taught at many colleges and universities in first-semester psychology and sociology courses

- Target biology concepts that relate to mental processes and behavior that are taught at many colleges and universities in introductory biology

- Target basic research methods and statistics concepts described by many baccalaureate faculty as important to success in introductory science courses

- Require you to demonstrate your scientific inquiry and reasoning, research methods, and statistics skills as applied to the social and behavioral sciences

The Critical Analysis and Reasoning Skills section is designed to:

- Test your comprehension, analysis, and reasoning skills by asking you to critically analyze information provided in reading passages

- Include content from ethics, philosophy, studies of diverse cultures, population health, and a wide range of social sciences and humanities disciplines

- Provide in the passages all the information you need to answer the questions

---

MCAT FAQ: Does the MCAT exam test knowledge or reasoning skills?

There is a friendly debate between those who think the MCAT exam is principally a test of your mastery of a full range of science topics and those who claim it is designed to evaluate your ability to solve problems. The truth is much broader than either of those narrow perspectives: The MCAT exam tests foundational concepts, content categories, and scientific inquiry and reasoning skills that tomorrow's doctors will need to know. The goal of the exam is not just to test what students know, but to test how well they use what they know.

Timeline for Application and Admission to Medical School

Use this general guide to help prepare for the medical school application and admissions process. Be sure to talk to your prehealth advisor to create a schedule that works best for you.

COLLEGE YEAR 1	<ul><li>Talk with an academic advisor about selecting courses</li><li>Make an appointment with a prehealth advisor to introduce yourself, discuss the best way to sequence your classes, and get acquainted with campus resources</li><li>Attend prehealth meetings on campus and make sure you're on email lists to get relevant updates and information</li><li>Seek opportunities to volunteer and get medically related experience and, if interested, identify research opportunities on your campus</li><li>Develop relationships with faculty, advisors, and mentors on your campus</li><li>Explore the AAMC's Considering a Medical Career resources (aamc.org/aspiringdocs)</li><li>Identify summer volunteer, paid, research, and leadership opportunities related to medicine</li><li>Apply to summer enrichment programs (services.aamc.org/summerprograms) or research programs (aamc.org/members/great/61052/great_summerlinks.html)</li><li>Complete first-year premedical coursework and other school-specific degree requirements</li></ul>
SUMMER FOLLOWING COLLEGE YEAR 1	<ul><li>Work or volunteer in the medical field; consider internships or research and leadership opportunities on campus or in your local community</li><li>Participate in summer enrichment or research programs</li><li>Take summer courses through a university if desired or necessary</li></ul>
COLLEGE YEAR 2	<ul><li>Check in with your prehealth advising office; attend all prehealth meetings, and make sure you're still on email lists to receive information and updates</li><li>Pursue meaningful clinical experiences, medically related activities, opportunities to volunteer, research positions, and/or leadership roles</li><li>Continue to develop relationships with faculty, advisors, and mentors on your campus</li><li>Apply for summer research, internship, or enrichment programs such as the Summer Health Professions Education Program (shpep.org)</li><li>Consider returning to your previous summer position, or apply for a new summer volunteer, paid, or research position related to medicine</li><li>Complete second-year premedical coursework and other school-specific degree requirements</li></ul>
SUMMER FOLLOWING COLLEGE YEAR 2	<ul><li>Work or volunteer in the medical field; consider internships, research opportunities, and leadership positions on campus or in your local community</li><li>Participate in summer enrichment, research, or internship programs</li><li>Take summer courses through a university if desired or necessary</li><li>Investigate:<ul><li>Medical school application process (aamc.org/students/applying)</li><li>Medical College Admission Test® (MCAT®) (aamc.org/mcat)</li><li>AAMC Fee Assistance Program (aamc.org/fap)</li></ul></li></ul> *(continued on next page)*

COLLEGE YEAR 3	<ul><li>By this time, you should have a well-established relationship with a prehealth advisor and should be actively participating in prehealth activities</li><li>Identify and pursue leadership opportunities within the prehealth organizations on your campus</li><li>Consider the relationships you've developed with faculty, advisors, and mentors on your campus to determine who you'll approach to write letters of evaluation for your applications</li><li>Continue participating in meaningful clinical experiences or other medically related activities such as volunteering, doing research, and/or taking on leadership roles on campus; if possible, consider taking on a more substantial role</li><li>Investigate:<ul><li>Medical schools in the United States and Canada (services.aamc.org/30/msar/home)</li><li>The Minorities in Medicine website to get information on groups underrepresented in medicine (aamc.org/students/minorities)</li></ul></li><li>Meet with your prehealth advisor to:<ul><li>Strategize about your application timeline, whether you'll apply immediately following graduation or after one or more gap years</li><li>Discuss your schedule for completing the remaining premedical coursework and other school-specific degree requirements</li><li>Identify the best time for you to take the MCAT exam; visit the MCAT website to find the best options for test dates and locations (aamc.org/mcat)</li><li>Discuss letters of evaluation and prehealth advisor committee letters (if applicable)</li><li>Review your medical education options</li></ul></li><li>If you're prepared and ready, take the MCAT exam in the spring</li><li>If you're considering a gap or bridge year, investigate a meaningful paid or volunteer medically related experience to complete during that time</li><li>Familiarize yourself with medical school application services:<ul><li>The American Medical College Application Service® (AMCAS®)</li><li>Texas Medical and Dental Schools Application Service (TMDSAS) (utsystem.edu)</li><li>Association of American Colleges of Osteopathic Medicine Application Service (AACOMAS) (aacom.org/become-a-doctor/applying)</li><li>Ontario (Canada) Medical Schools Application Service (OMSAS) (ouac.on.ca/omsas)</li></ul></li><li>Research medical school curricula and joint-, dual-, and combined-degree programs</li><li>Complete third-year premedical coursework and other school-specific degree requirements</li></ul>
SUMMER FOLLOWING COLLEGE YEAR 3	<ul><li>Continue your involvement with meaningful paid, volunteer, internship, medically related research, and leadership experiences</li><li>If applying to begin medical school following your senior year:<ul><li>Complete your application</li><li>Work on secondary applications</li><li>Ask instructors, mentors, and advisors to write letters of evaluation for you</li></ul></li><li>If you haven't already done so, take—or, if necessary, retake—the MCAT exam</li></ul>

(continued on next page)

COLLEGE YEAR 4	<ul><li>You should be regularly consulting with your prehealth advisor to:<ul><li>Discuss letters of evaluation and prehealth advisor committee letters (if applicable)</li><li>Review your progress toward completing prerequisites for medical schools— it may be appropriate to consider a postbaccalaureate premedical program (students-residents.aamc.org/postbacc)</li><li>Discuss the status of your applications and the admissions process for schools to which you've applied</li></ul></li><li>If you're applying for enrollment immediately following senior year:<ul><li>Complete supplementary application materials for schools to which you've applied</li><li>Prepare for your interviews and campus visits at medical schools</li><li>Become familiar with applicant responsibilities (aamc.org/applicantprotocols)</li></ul></li><li>If you've applied for enrollment immediately following senior year:<ul><li>Receive acceptances!</li><li>Make decisions about your medical school choices</li><li>Notify medical schools that you will not be attending on or before the deadline given</li><li>Ensure that all Internal Revenue Service (IRS) and financial aid forms are completed and submitted as early as possible</li></ul></li><li>Complete undergraduate degree requirements and graduate</li></ul>
SUMMER FOLLOWING GRADUATION	<ul><li>If enrolling immediately following senior year:<ul><li>Purchase books and equipment and make appropriate living arrangements</li><li>Attend orientation programs and matriculate into medical school</li></ul></li><li>If applying for enrollment following a gap or bridge year(s):<ul><li>Complete your application</li><li>Work on secondary applications</li><li>Ask instructors, mentors, and advisors to write letters of evaluation for you</li></ul></li></ul>
GAP AND BRIDGE YEAR(S)	<ul><li>If you haven't done so, study for and take the MCAT exam</li><li>Seek meaningful employment, education, and/or experience</li><li>Pay down credit card and/or undergraduate debt as much as possible</li><li>Continue to consult regularly with your prehealth advisor throughout the process</li><li>Complete supplementary application materials for schools to which you've applied</li><li>Interview and take campus tours at medical schools</li><li>Become familiar with applicant responsibilities (aamc.org/applicantprotocols)</li></ul>
ONCE ACCEPTED INTO MEDICAL SCHOOL	<ul><li>Make final decisions about medical school choice</li><li>Notify medical schools that you will not be attending on or before the deadline given</li><li>If you haven't already done so, ensure that all IRS and financial aid forms are completed and submitted as early as possible</li><li>If you haven't already done so, purchase books and equipment and make appropriate living arrangements</li><li>Attend orientation programs and matriculate into medical school</li></ul>

Chapter 2

Register for and Schedule the Test: MCAT Fundamentals

In addition to thinking ahead and studying for scientific principles and skills that the MCAT® exam tests, part of your success hinges on how well you understand the *logistics of taking the test*.

Well before you show up on test day, you will want to make sure you fully understand details such as how to register, how to schedule an appointment, when and where to take the test, and, if necessary, how to find information about test accommodations and financial aid. This section walks you through those basics.

Important information you need to know is updated regularly on the AAMC's MCAT website—aamc.org/mcat. There, you will find schedules, facts, and tips, including specifics on the:

- Exam schedule

- Registration system

- Scheduling deadlines

- Score release schedule

- Testing-center locations

Who Can Take the MCAT Exam?

First things first: Confirm that you are eligible to take the MCAT exam.

Eligibility

You may sit for the MCAT exam if you are preparing to apply to health professions schools. These include (but are not limited to) the following types of schools: MD-granting, DO-granting, podiatric, and veterinary medicine.

Special Permissions

You must apply for special permission to take the MCAT exam under these two circumstances:

- You wish to take the test for any reason other than applying to a health professions school.

- You are a currently enrolled medical student.

To apply for special permission, please send an email request to mcat@aamc.org stating the reason(s) you wish to take the exam. The MCAT office will attempt to review and respond to your request within five business days, although heavy volume may delay our ability to reply within this timeframe.

We ask that you be mindful of registration deadlines because staff cannot extend those dates for any reason.

International Students

If you are an international student, you are welcome to take the MCAT exam, provided you meet the eligibility requirements described above. If you are in an MBBS (bachelor of medicine/bachelor of surgery) degree program or hold the MBBS degree, you may register for the MCAT exam without seeking special permission.

When Should I Sit for the MCAT Exam?

You should take the MCAT exam when you're ready. As a general rule, you should plan to take it 12 to 18 months before your expected entry into medical school—but not before you have completed basic coursework and are comfortable with your knowledge of general biology, inorganic chemistry, organic chemistry, first-semester biochemistry, general physics, introductory psychology, and introductory sociology. Many medical schools prefer that applicants take the MCAT exam in the spring because of the short time between the availability of late summer scores and school application deadlines. (Taking the exam in the spring also allows time for students to retake the test later in the summer, if necessary.) For additional guidance, please see your prehealth advisor.

If you plan to test with accommodations (see separate section in this chapter), be sure to allow enough time between submitting your accommodation application and your registered test date to get a response to your accommodation application before your registered test date.

How Do I Register for an MCAT Exam?

There are a few steps you must complete before scheduling an MCAT exam.

Register for an AAMC ID

Before you can log into the MCAT Registration System, you must create an AAMC account and obtain an AAMC identification (ID) number (aamc.org/students/applying/mcat/reserving). This number is an eight-digit identifier assigned automatically to your personal information. The number will be used to uniquely identify you. **You will need this ID and the username and password you create throughout your relationship with the AAMC, including when you register for the MCAT exam, receive your scores, and apply to medical school and residency.**

Fifth Edition
The Official Guide to the MCAT® Exam
14
MCAT® is a program of the
Association of American Medical Colleges

MCAT INSIDER: Protect Your AAMC Account

It is your responsibility to protect and secure your AAMC account information. It is important that you do not share your password, because the AAMC cannot reverse any actions taken by another party logged into your account. Review the AAMC Terms of Use at aamc.org for more information.

Check Your ID!

The first, and most important, information you will enter is: your name. Your first and last names in the Registration System (apps.aamc.org/mrs) must exactly match how they appear on the ID you will bring with you on test day. If your name on your registration does not match the one on your ID, you will not be allowed to enter the test center on test day. (Middle names are not verified on test day. If they appear on your ID, you may choose to enter them.)

MCAT INSIDER: Make Sure We Know How to Reach You

Every so often, we have to reschedule a very small percentage of examinees due to inclement weather and facilities issues such as power outages. Therefore, we must be able to contact you. We do this by phone and email. Make sure your email address is correct in your AAMC account and your email account is set to receive email from the AAMC ("aamc.org" and "aamcsurveys.org") and Pearson VUE ("pearson.com") so our messages aren't sent to your spam folder.

Answer the Registration Questions

In the MCAT Registration System, you will need to answer a variety of questions before you schedule your exam. These questions ask for biographic information, self-identification, and your education background. Additionally, you will agree to the necessary consents, including the Examinee Agreement in the *MCAT Essentials*. Be sure to read these very carefully. They have critical policies that all MCAT examinees are required to adhere to. Finally, the MCAT Registration System is where you opt into (or out of) the MCAT Recruiting List, the Medical Minority Applicant Registry (Med-MAR), and releasing your MCAT scores to your health professions, or prehealth, advisor.

What are some common ID errors?

The "Last Name" field in the Registration System will allow you to enter two names. If you have two family names, or surnames, on your ID but you have entered only one on your registration, you will not be allowed to test. Another common error is entering a shortened version of your first name in the registration when your ID includes your full first name.

MCAT INSIDER: Providing a "Release to Alternate Contact" Consent

To protect your private information, we will only correspond with you about your exam details. If you would like to grant us permission to speak with another person (such as a parent) about your MCAT exam, you must designate that person in the "Release to Alternate Contact" consent on the "Use of Personal Info" page during registration. Please note that we will not reveal certain details, such as MCAT scores or other personal information, to third parties without your consent. (A separate release is required if you are applying for accommodations and would like the MCAT Office of Accommodated Testing to correspond with medical professionals or others on your behalf.)

How Do I Schedule an MCAT Exam?

Once you have completed your MCAT registration, you are ready to schedule your MCAT exam. This section provides information to help you as you review your test date and location options.

How Do I Select an Appropriate Test Date?

The MCAT exam is administered many times each year from January through September. Specific dates are posted on the MCAT website at aamc.org/students/applying/mcat/reserving.

Although the AAMC selects exam dates to ensure that scores are available to meet most medical school application deadlines, we recommend that you check the specific scheduling requirements of the school(s) of your choice, provided in the Medical School Admission Requirements™ website school profiles (aamc.org/msar) for MD-granting schools. Once you have determined your preferred test date, you can find the registration schedule for that particular exam session on the MCAT Scheduling Deadlines and Score Release Schedule, also posted online at students-residents.aamc.org/applying-medical-school/taking-mcat-exam/register-mcat-exam.

MCAT INSIDER: Have Backups and Be Patient

Seats are limited on each test day and in each test center. If you have a few possible test dates and testing locations in mind, you will have a better chance of finding a date and location that work for you. If you cannot find a seat, be sure to check back around scheduling deadlines because seats may become available.

When Should I Schedule My MCAT Exam?

Once you have determined which date you prefer, you can find the scheduling timeframes online (see aamc.org/students/ applying/mcat/reserving). There, you will learn when the scheduling period opens (and closes!) as well as the date we expect scores to be released.

The MCAT scheduling fee structure rewards well-prepared students who plan in advance. Students who plan early have more flexibility in choosing their testing locations and dates.

There are three scheduling zones for each testing date—Gold, Silver, and Bronze. For each exam administration date, the fees are lowest in the Gold Zone. You will encounter increased costs as you move into the Silver and Bronze Zones. All deadlines for these zones occur a set number of days before the exam. These deadlines take effect at 7:59 a.m. local, test center time. For example, if your MCAT exam is scheduled for August 9, 2018, in Los Angeles, California, your Bronze Zone scheduling deadline is 7:59 a.m. PT on August 1, 2018.

Benefits for examinees who plan early and schedule during the Gold Zone include:

- More flexible options for testing dates and locations
- Lower fees for examinees who need to reschedule testing dates or locations
- Partial refunds for examinees who need to cancel their reservations

Scheduling Zones for Each Test Date		
GOLD Zone	**SILVER Zone**	**BRONZE Zone**
Deadline: 29 days before the exam	Deadline: 15 days before the exam	Deadline: 8 days before the exam
Benefits	**Benefits**	**Benefits**
• More flexibility for dates and locations • Can reschedule exam date and/or location for the lowest fee • Can cancel reservation and get a partial refund	• Same registration fee as Gold Zone • Can reschedule exam date and/or location but for a higher fee • Can cancel reservation but without a refund	• Late fee attached to scheduling • Can cancel reservation but without a refund

How Do I Select a Test Center?

The MCAT exam is offered at hundreds of locations throughout the United States, Canada, and the world, with multiple sites available in most major U.S. and Canadian cities. You will select a specific test center through the online scheduling system. The process is relatively simple: you enter an address or location to find the nearest test centers, select an exam date, and select "search." If the test time appears next to a test center, that means there is a seat available. Select the time to reserve the seat and advance through to the payment screen.

How Do I Pay for the MCAT Exam?

The scheduling fee associated with the MCAT exam covers the cost of the test itself as well as the distribution of your scores. This section provides more information about fees.

Scheduling Fees

The MCAT scheduling fee is subject to change. To find the current fee, visit aamc.org/students/applying/mcat/reserving.

Additional Fees

Please note there are additional fees for changing the date or location of your exam and testing at international test locations. Charges associated with changing your date or site are determined by the scheduling zone you are in when you submit your request (Gold, Silver, or Bronze). Basically, you should know that convenience decreases and your costs increase as you move from the preferred Gold Zone to the Bronze Zone for scheduling.

You may be required to pay applicable sales tax, value-added tax, goods and services tax, or similar taxes required by law in the country or locality in which you are testing. If taxes are applicable, they will be collected at the time of scheduling. For up-to-date information, please review Pearson VUE's Tax FAQs (pearsonvue.com/taxfaqs).

Payment Methods

The MCAT Registration System accepts VISA and MasterCard, including debit cards with the VISA or MasterCard logos. We regret we are unable to accept other forms of payment at this time.

Is Financial Aid Available to Help With the MCAT Scheduling Fee?

The AAMC believes the cost of applying to medical school should not be a barrier to people interested in becoming physicians. The AAMC Fee Assistance Program assists MCAT examinees who, without financial assistance, would be unable to take the MCAT exam.

It's important to apply for fee assistance well in advance of when you are planning to schedule your MCAT exam because processing times can vary. Be sure to:

- Review the Fee Assistance Program Eligibility Guidelines and Benefits (see aamc.org/fap).
- Complete the online Fee Assistance Program application.
- If requested, upload the required supporting documentation and signed cover letter.

For further information and updates, visit aamc.org/fap.

> **MCAT INSIDER: Fee Assistance Program Application**
>
> You must receive Fee Assistance Program approval before you schedule your exam or you will be charged the full MCAT fee. Additionally, if you are using a previous Fee Assistance Program approval, it must not have expired at the time of registration.

How Do I Change or Cancel My MCAT Exam Appointment?

If you need to change your MCAT exam date or location, certain rules apply.

What if I Need to Change My Test Location or Date?

Whether you are permitted to change your test date or location—or both—and the fee for doing so hinges on the scheduling zone. If you need to make a change, you should do it as early as you can but at least by the Bronze Zone scheduling deadline to give us sufficient time to notify the test center (see aamc.org/mcat/changes). During the Gold Zone, you can reschedule and cancel for a partial refund; however, during the Silver Zone, the reschedule fee increases, and no refund is provided for cancellations. The reschedule option is not available within the Bronze Zone. The Bronze Zone deadline is the last day to cancel your appointment, and you will not receive a refund.

If you make a change in both test date and center simultaneously, a single charge will be levied; if you make separate changes, you will be charged individually for each change. Please make your change(s) through our online Registration System at apps.aamc.org/mrs.

MCAT INSIDER: Know Your Limits!

Unfortunately, you cannot reschedule into a future testing (calendar) year.

What if I Need to Cancel My Test Appointment?

If you decide not to sit for the exam after you have scheduled it, you will be eligible for a partial refund if you cancel before the Gold Zone scheduling deadline. Additional fees for international appointments or other changes are not refundable. You may cancel your appointment without a refund until the Bronze Zone scheduling deadline. Please cancel your appointment online by the appropriate scheduling deadline through apps.aamc.org/mrs. You may not cancel your appointment after the Bronze Zone scheduling deadline.

What if I Don't Make It to the Test, and How Would That Affect My Testing Limits?

Failing to appear for your scheduled appointment or not cancelling your appointment by the Bronze Zone scheduling deadline will result in a "No Show" status. A "No Show" will count toward your testing limits. You may only test three times in one year, you may not test more than four times within the span of two testing years, and there is a lifetime limit of seven attempts beginning in April 2015. If you feel you will be unable to test on your scheduled date, be sure to reschedule or cancel your appointment as soon as possible. See the *MCAT Essentials* at aamc.org/mcat for specific details about testing limits.

MCAT INSIDER: Voiding Your Exam

If you "void" your exam on test day, you will not receive a score on your exam, but your testing attempt will count toward the number of times you may test in a given time period. For more information, see the *MCAT Essentials* at aamc.org/mcat.

Can I Take the MCAT Exam More Than Once?

The short answer is "yes," but there are factors to consider, such as the limits on how many times you may test in a given time period. For more information on testing-limit policies, see the *MCAT Essentials* at aamc.org/mcat.

Taking the MCAT Exam With Accommodations

The AAMC is committed to giving everyone the opportunity to demonstrate their proficiency on the MCAT exam. This includes ensuring access to people with disabilities, in accordance with relevant law.

If you have an impairment or condition you believe requires an adjustment to the standard testing conditions, we encourage you to apply for accommodated testing. A decision about most requests is made within 60 days after the receipt of all your documentation.

What Types of Conditions or Impairments Might Warrant Accommodations?

Examples of conditions and impairments that may warrant accommodations in accordance with the Americans with Disabilities Act (ADA) include:

- Learning disabilities
- Vision impairments
- Attention deficit hyperactivity disorder
- Psychiatric impairments such as major depression or generalized anxiety disorder
- Physical impairments
- Chronic medical conditions such as diabetes or Crohn disease

In some cases, an individual may qualify for an accommodation if he or she has a temporary medical condition that requires an adjustment to the standard testing conditions. Examples of such conditions include:

- A recent injury
- Pregnancy

Keep in mind that not all impairments or conditions require accommodations. A determination about the need for accommodations on the MCAT exam is based on a comprehensive review of the available documentation, including evidence of the diagnosis and the associated functional limitations.

MCAT FAQ: How Do I Know if I Need Accommodated Testing?

You should apply for accommodations on the MCAT exam if you have a physical or mental impairment that warrants a modification to standard testing conditions.

What Kinds of Accommodations Are Available?

Some examinees with disabilities may qualify for accommodations such as extended time or testing in a separate room. Individuals with physical or mobility impairments may need such accommodations as a height-adjustable workstation or an adaptive computer mouse. Individuals with vision impairments may need font enlargement.

MCAT INSIDER: Even Orange Juice Counts!

On occasion, an examinee will arrive at the test center with medical supplies or even a small container of orange juice—only to learn that the particular item is not permitted in the standard test room without prior approval. Please know that even the seemingly most minor deviation from standard test conditions may be considered an accommodation that requires preapproval. Examinees who are unsure whether their item requires preapproval should contact the MCAT Office of Accommodated Testing Services at accommodations@aamc.org.

Again, it is important to remember that each application receives a careful and individualized review. Examinees who are found to be eligible are granted accommodations that are determined to be the most appropriate for their individual needs and the demands of the current MCAT exam.

How to Apply: MCAT Accommodations Online

MCAT Accommodations Online (MAO) is a web-based application system that allows individuals seeking testing accommodations for the MCAT exam to submit and track the status of their applications (see aamc.org/mcat/accommodations).

For more detailed information, please see the MCAT Accommodations homepage at aamc.org/mcat/accommodations.

Time Frame for Your Accommodation Request

Your first request for accommodations on the MCAT exam is considered an initial application. The review cycle for an initial application may take up to 60 days. Therefore, you will want to submit a complete application no later than 60 days *before* the Silver Zone registration deadline associated with your preferred test date. This allows time for the review cycle and the time needed to confirm your accommodations.

> **MCAT INSIDER: Begin the Accommodations Process Early**
>
> The MCAT Office of Accommodated Testing Services may require up to 60 days to process your request for accommodations. You should submit your request and related documentation as far in advance of your desired test date as possible.

Chapter 3

Prepping for the Test Itself

Much of your preparation for medical school comes in the form of academic development, which includes your undergraduate coursework and mastery of scientific principles and skills. Your undergraduate coursework should help you develop an understanding of the concepts and practice the skills that you'll be responsible for knowing and applying on the MCAT® exam.

Good preparation can help you improve your performance on the exam. How you do that depends on you. The most important thing is to invest some time and thought into planning your personal strategy for taking the MCAT exam.

Since you can't tackle everything at once, you may find it useful to break your studying into chunks to get a sense of how much time you'll need to study specific topics and how much time you want to devote to answering practice questions. Breaking your studying into smaller units may make it more manageable.

There is no definitive research or data indicating that one approach to test preparation is better than another, so we don't offer a prescribed path to test preparation. But we *do* offer some pointers and general advice. With that in mind, here are some things to focus on as you get ready to take the test.

Familiarize Yourself With the Exam

We can't emphasize enough how important it is to plan well for taking the MCAT exam. Here are some elements of good planning.

Know the Logistics

As in so many other aspects of life, details matter when it comes time to take the MCAT exam. Imagine, for example, getting lost on the way to the test because you failed to map the location. Or forgetting to bring the right form of identification. Or being too hungry to focus because you didn't plan for the length of the test. You need to take steps to make sure you plan for all the logistics of taking the MCAT exam.

Part of your planning should be to fully understand the test logistics that we talk about elsewhere in this book—things like how to register for the test, what to bring (and not bring) on test day, and when to arrive at the test center. Review those sections of the book carefully. Refer to our checklist in Chapter 4 and then make your own list to make sure you have a good grasp of test logistics.

The *MCAT® Essentials,* which is required reading for examinees, provides exhaustive information on registration, test-day policies, and scoring details; lists of contacts and services; and other helpful information. This resource is available on the AAMC's website (students-residents.aamc.org/mcatessentials).

Don't underestimate the importance of these details. No matter how well you study for the test content, not knowing a logistical detail may add additional stress that could affect your performance on test day.

Think Broadly About What the MCAT Exam Tests For

Think carefully about the scientific principles and skills that the MCAT exam asks you to demonstrate. The exam is designed to assess a range of competencies. For example, while it tests your understanding of entry-level concepts in disciplines such as biology, chemistry, physics, and biochemistry, it also tests your knowledge of the psychology, sociology, and biology concepts that are foundational to what you'll learn in medical school about behavioral and sociocultural determinants of health. The MCAT exam asks you to demonstrate your skill in scientific reasoning and your understanding of research methods and statistics because that indicates your ability to analyze critically and apply your knowledge in interdisciplinary, real-world situations. To perform your best on test day, you need to be comfortable in all these areas.

Here's an example: While having ready recall of the definition of *prejudice* might help you perform well on the MCAT exam, you might also need to know how to use that knowledge to solve a problem about the relationship between prejudice and discrimination. Recall knowledge alone will not be sufficient to solve all the problems presented in the questions on the exam.

In terms of the concepts that the MCAT exam covers, there should be no surprises on test day: Everything you need to know about the foundational concepts covered on the exam is readily available to you beforehand.

Much of the content knowledge you'll need for the MCAT exam will derive from your undergraduate coursework. It's up to you to assess how well-prepared you feel. Have you completed all the coursework associated with the MCAT exam content? Do you feel confident in all content areas? Are there some content areas where you feel you need further study or practice? Do you know the concepts in enough depth to apply this knowledge to solve problems, especially in interdisciplinary contexts?

The What's on the MCAT Exam? interactive tool on the AAMC website helps you explore all four sections of the exam: the foundational concepts, content categories, topics, and scientific inquiry and reasoning skills (students-residents.aamc.org/mcatexam). Review each section, then figure out the areas you've covered as well as the areas you have yet to cover. This is a good first step to understanding what's tested on the MCAT exam. Part II of this book offers a detailed description of the foundational concepts, content categories, topics, scientific inquiry and reasoning skills, and critical analysis and reasoning skills you will be responsible for knowing on test day.

Also visit the How Is the MCAT Exam Scored? resource on the AAMC website for explanations of scaled scores and percentile ranks (aamc.org/howisthemcatscored). The resource addresses frequently asked questions and provides links to current and historical percentile rank information.

Get to Know the Look and Feel of the Test

To help you acclimate to what you'll see on the computer in the testing center, you can start exploring the free Practice with the Exam Features online tool on the AAMC website. This tool allows you to practice the *highlight, strikethrough,* and *flag-for-review* features on the exam so you won't have to worry about learning those details on test day.

In addition, all AAMC MCAT prep products, discussed in the next few pages, replicate the format, features, and functionality found on the actual exam. These practice materials will also help you familiarize yourself with the look and feel of the exam format while you're practicing how to review and answer practice questions.

For MCAT prep products and resources, be sure to check the AAMC's Prepare for the MCAT Exam page at students-residents.aamc.org/mcatprep. The MCAT prep team at AAMC publishes information on new products and resources as they become available.

Figure Out What You Know and What You Don't Know

Once you've become familiar with the content and format of the exam, you should establish a baseline to inform your studies and preparation ahead.

Assess Yourself

Consider taking a full-length practice test to get a sense of how much content you've covered so far and where your strengths and weaknesses are. The AAMC offers a low-cost, full-length Sample Test, written by the same people who write the MCAT exam, that you can use for this initial baseline.

After taking the Official MCAT® Sample Test, you can review your results without scaled scoring to assess your performance in each of the exam sections as well as the foundational concept, content category, scientific inquiry and reasoning skill, and discipline of each of the questions. Combine this information with the information you cataloged from the What's on the MCAT Exam? interactive tool to determine what areas you need to study.

Create a Study Plan

Once you have an outline of the areas you need to study, create a study plan. The AAMC offers a free, downloadable guide to creating a study plan at aamc.org/mcatstudyplan.

For additional hints and advice from students on creating a study plan, visit How I Prepared for the MCAT® Exam on the AAMC website (aamc.org/howipreparedforthemcat). This is a compilation of study tips and approaches used by students who performed well on the MCAT exam. Each student profile includes scores, study schedules, strategies, personal challenges, and "dos and don'ts" as narrated by the students themselves.

Although there's no one-size-fits-all approach, these steps can help you identify areas to focus your studying on. Use the insights you gain from this initial review and assessment to inform your studies and help you plan the best use of your time.

Gain Understanding, and Study

After you've identified the areas you need to study and created a study plan, you can gather resources to study those content areas.

Consult All Your Resources

You can tap into a rich collection of tools and resources that help you study for the MCAT exam. Use all the support that's available to you. Here are some places to start.

- The free, online Khan Academy MCAT Collection, which includes more than 1,100 videos and 3,000 review questions on all areas of the exam, created by Khan Academy with support from the AAMC and the Robert Wood Johnson Foundation (khanacademy.org/test-prep/mcat)
- Your classes, textbooks, labs, class notes, and research experience
- Your friends and family
- Libraries and bookstores
- Local or online study groups focused on preparing for the MCAT exam
- Other free and open-access textbooks
- The Roadmap to MCAT Content in Psychology and Sociology Textbooks, a free, downloadable AAMC resource that lists open-source and low-cost textbooks that cover all the foundational concepts and content categories in the Psychological, Social, and Biological Foundations of Behavior section of the exam (aamc.org/MCATpsychsoc)
- The Roadmap to MCAT Content in Biochemistry Textbooks, a free, downloadable AAMC resource that lists open-source and low-cost textbooks that cover all the biochemistry-related foundational concepts and content categories in the exam (students-residents.aamc.org/biochemresource)
- Free online learning resources and classes
- Web portals such as the National Science Digital Library and Open Education Resources Commons
- Prehealth advisors and professors at your school
- Student support offices at your school
- Paid tutors, courses, and other resources

Study Actively

When you're studying for the exam, don't just read content or passively watch videos—make time to restate, summarize, or analyze what you reviewed. Discuss the content with peers, integrate the content across disciplines, and check for understanding.

Practice

Know that old saying "practice makes perfect"? We can't guarantee that you'll perform to your satisfaction on the MCAT exam, but practicing for the test really does make a difference. Here are some practical tips.

Practice Effectively—Monitor Yourself

Spend time answering questions and practicing the scientific inquiry and reasoning skills, not just reviewing content. Apply various learning strategies such as concept maps, compare-and-contrast charts, and review sheets that synthesize information.

Pay attention to what's going on in your own mind. In addition to focusing on content and skills, a good habit to develop is self-monitoring. Education experts call this *metacognition* or *"thinking about thinking."* After you complete the practice questions, carefully review your answers and treat each incorrect response as a learning opportunity. Figure out why you got the question right or wrong and what piece of knowledge you need to learn or skill you need to improve to get a similar question right in the future. Spending time thinking about your own process of learning and solving problems may help you identify patterns in your thinking. For example, do you doubt your first answer and frequently change it? Is your first answer generally right or wrong? Do you respond too quickly so that you miss what the question is asking?

All of the AAMC's online MCAT prep products come with a useful feature called "Why Did I Miss This Question?" It's a review tool that helps you track your reasons for selecting incorrect answers in the practice products: you guessed incorrectly, accidentally selected a wrong option while knowing the correct answer, misunderstood the question, etc. Reviewing the reasons you selected a wrong answer will help you analyze patterns, if any, that emerge as you practice. If you took the Sample Test as a baseline earlier in your preparation, you can use this review tool to help you assess your test-taking strategies while you're identifying gaps in your content knowledge.

The AAMC offers several online products to help you practice for the exam. Among them, the AAMC MCAT® Section Bank and six Official MCAT® Question Packs offer more than 1,000 questions in total, covering all the disciplines on the exam. These products, as well as other online AAMC MCAT prep products, allow at least five "starts," or opportunities to start and complete the practice questions. The products offer an unlimited number of opportunities to review the results of those starts. Additionally, the Official MCAT® Flashcards offer another 150 discrete questions in biochemistry, biology, chemistry, physics, psychology, and sociology (aamc.org/mcatstudymaterials).

How I Prepared for the MCAT® Exam

Check out how 21 other students prepared for the MCAT® exam on the How I Prepared for the MCAT® Exam feature online: aamc.org/howiPreparedforthemcat. You can read first-hand accounts of how students managed their time, resources, and challenges to achieve a satisfying score on the exam.

The preparation materials offer many features that mirror accommodated testing features. All of our online products offer customization, including extended time, stop-the-clock breaks, and ZoomText compatibility. The preparation materials offer many features that mirror accommodated testing features. All of our online products offer customization, including extended time, stop-the-clock breaks, braille and print versions, and screenreader (JAWS) and ZoomText compatibility. (If you have any questions about accommodations, please visit our MCAT Exam with Accommodations page.)

Practice for the Exam-Day Experience

As you approach exam day, take full-length practice tests to gauge how you might perform on the actual exam. The AAMC currently offers Practice Exams 1, 2, and 3, which are 230-question full-length practice tests written by the same people who write the MCAT exam. All three practice tests provide scaled scores and have the same features, format, and functionality as the actual exam. Simulate the test-day experience by setting aside a full day and following test-day logistics, timing, and other details.

You can also ask your advisor to help you conduct a mock exam day for you and your peers. The AAMC provides informational resources to help you and your advisor plan this day (students-residents.aamc.org/mockexam).

Do remember that you may need to make adjustments to your study plan or exam date depending on how you do on your full-length practice test. If you don't perform the way you had hoped to, take some time to collect your thoughts and reexamine your plan.

Khan Academy MCAT Collection

Created with support and funding from the AAMC and the Robert Wood Johnson Foundation, this collection offers more than 1,100 videos and 3,000 review questions covering all the content that's tested on the MCAT exam, free of charge.

Visit aamc.org/khanacademymcat.

Free Resources

Earlier in this chapter, we explained how you can use free AAMC resources to help you study content areas, create a study plan, and practice online questions. You can find all these resources on the AAMC website.

- **What's on the MCAT Exam? interactive tool**
  (students-residents.aamc.org/mcatexam)

  An online resource that describes the structure and content of the exam. Includes detailed information on the sections, foundational concepts, content categories, scientific inquiry and reasoning skills, and disciplines.

- **How to Create a Study Plan** (aamc.org/mcatstudyplan)

  A downloadable guide that provides guidance on creating your own study plan for the exam.

- **Khan Academy MCAT video collection** (aamc.org/khanacademymcat)

  Includes more than 1,100 video tutorials and 3,000 review questions covering all the content tested on the exam.

- **Roadmap to MCAT Content in Psychology and Sociology Textbooks** (aamc.org/MCATpsychsoc)

  A free, downloadable guide to psychology and sociology textbooks that cover the foundational concepts and content categories tested on the exam and are available free or at low cost.

- **Roadmap to MCAT Content in Biochemistry Textbooks**
  (students-residents.aamc.org/biochemresource)

  A free, downloadable guide to open-source and low-cost textbooks that cover all the biochemistry-related foundational concepts and content categories on the exam.

- **How I Prepared for the MCAT® Exam student testimonials**
  (aamc.org/howipreparedforthemcat)

  A showcase of study tips and approaches used by students who performed well on the MCAT exam. Each student profile includes study schedules, strategies, personal challenges, and dos and don'ts as narrated by the students themselves.

Low-Cost Products

The AAMC also offers many low-cost products for purchase online. Combined, the products include more than 2,200 unique practice questions. All of the questions were written by the same people who write the MCAT exam and are annotated with the foundational concepts and content categories that each question tests. These products are available on the AAMC website: aamc.org/mcatstudymaterials.

- **MCAT® Practice Exams One, Two, and Three**

  Full-length, 230-question practice tests with scaled scores

- **Official MCAT® Sample Test**

  Full-length, 230-question practice test without scaled scores

- **MCAT® Section Bank**

  300 practice questions in the natural, behavioral, and social sciences; emphasizes biochemistry, psychology, and sociology

- **Six MCAT® Question Packs** (Biology volumes 1 and 2, Chemistry, Physics, and Critical Analysis and Reasoning Skills volumes 1 and 2)

  120 passage-based and discrete questions in each pack; six different packs available

- **Online Practice Questions from the Official Guide**

  Online version of the 120 questions in the Official Guide

- **MCAT® Flashcards**

  150 discrete questions total, in biochemistry, biology, chemistry, physics, psychology, and sociology (25 questions per discipline)

- **MCAT® Prep Complete Bundle**

  All 14 current MCAT prep products (2,210 questions) at a significant discount

- **MCAT® Prep Online-Only Bundle**

  All 12 current online-only prep products (2,060 questions) at a significant discount

- **MCAT® Question Pack Bundle**

  All six packs (720 questions) at a significant discount

The AAMC Fee Assistance Program provides MCAT prep product benefits and discounted registration fees to those needing financial assistance. Please visit the Fee Assistance Program website at aamc.org/fap for information on eligibility, benefits, and application processes if you're in need of assistance.

Stay Well

You are the most important thing that you will bring to the MCAT exam. For that reason, taking care of yourself is an important step in test preparation. Make sure you're prepared mentally, emotionally, and physically so that when you take the test, you will be calm, focused, and confident.

A little anxiety about the test is normal—and may even help you stay alert during the test. But too much anxiety can be counterproductive. Whether you exercise, practice relaxation techniques, visualize yourself doing well on the test, or follow any number of other helpful methods, only you know how to best manage your emotions and mentally prepare to take the MCAT exam. The important thing is that you remember to take the time to prepare.

Maintaining familiar routines may also serve you well. Suddenly changing your sleeping and eating habits or taking on new and unfamiliar activities may expose you to risks that could derail your plans. With all that is going on as you prepare for the test, remember to take some time to take care of yourself.

Contact Us

The MCAT prep team at the AAMC wishes you the best of luck in preparing for the exam. If you have questions about the AAMC's MCAT prep products and resources, there are several ways to contact us.

General questions

Email mcatprep@aamc.org or call 202-828-0600 from Monday through Friday, 9 a.m.–7 p.m. ET. Our Services Contact Center is closed 3–5 p.m. on Wednesdays.

Fee Assistance Program

Email fap@aamc.org or call 202-828-0600 Monday through Friday, 9 a.m.–7 p.m. ET.

Challenges to MCAT prep product items

Email mcatprep@aamc.org.

Questions about your MCAT prep products order

Email AAMCstore@aamc.org or call 202-828-0416 Monday–Friday, 9 a.m.–5 p.m. ET.

Chapter 4

Taking the MCAT Exam: Test-Day Procedures and Security

As you plan to take the MCAT® exam, you should be studying, reviewing sample questions, and practicing. But don't forget to plan for test day itself! This chapter will help you with what might be called the "nuts and bolts" of the MCAT exam.

From time to time, testing policies change. Please visit the MCAT website for the most current information: aamc.org/students/applying/mcat/taking.

For more details about test day, be sure to read the AAMC publication *MCAT Essentials* (aamc.org/mcat).

Before Arriving at the Test Center

Some of the basics for planning for test day involve common sense. In the weeks building up to the test, you will want to eat well, exercise, and get plenty of sleep. In other words, as you prepare mentally, you will want to make sure you are prepared physically. Avoid excess in the weeks before the test—try to be as consistent as possible about sleeping, eating, exercising, and relaxing.

As you think about actually taking the MCAT exam, you'll want to keep in mind and plan for some specific items. Please read this chapter carefully, consult our checklist, and make your own list of things to do to prepare for test day.

What Should I Bring to the Test Center?

The only personal item you may bring into the testing room is your ID. No other items are permitted unless approved by the AAMC.

A Valid Identification (ID)

Your ID is critical for admission to the MCAT exam and must be a current, valid government-issued ID. To be considered valid, your ID should not be expired and it should include your photo and signature, which you must be able to reproduce on test day. The first and last name(s) on the valid ID must match your registration exactly. The test center cannot accept employee IDs, library cards, school IDs, temporary (paper) IDs, or other similar forms of identification, even if issued by a government-sponsored institution. If you have special circumstances that you wish to discuss (e.g., initials in place of your first name or having a single, or mononymous, name), please contact AAMC Services at aamc.org/contactmcat or 202-828-0600.

MCAT® is a program of the
Association of American Medical Colleges

> **MCAT INSIDER: The Number One Concern on Test Day? Identification!**
>
> The most common error is when a test taker fails to bring an ID that matches his or her registration *exactly*.

The test administrator will admit only those examinees who can be positively identified through valid forms of identification. Your ID may be electronically swiped to check its validity, and a scanned image of the ID may be captured.

> **MCAT INSIDER: Providing Current Identification**
>
> If you are unable to provide the required identification or if you have any concern that your identification may not be acceptable, you MUST contact AAMC Services no later than the Silver Zone scheduling deadline. Email aamc.org/contactmcat or call 202-828-0600.

The following items and behaviors are prohibited during the MCAT exam and during breaks:

 Electronic devices, including cellular phones.

 Recording equipment of any kind.

 Books, notes, water bottles, or study materials of any kind.

 Disruptive or abusive behavior. Talking in the testing room with anyone other than a proctor. Talking about or discussing the exam.

The Test Center Will Provide . . .

The test center will provide you with a noteboard (a whiteboard that can't be erased), a marker, foam wireless earplugs, and a storage key for a locker or other storage solution for your personal belongings. No other testing aids are allowed.

Personal Medical Items

In general, you may not bring any personal items into the testing room other than your ID. However, certain medical devices and items are permitted without prior approval. Common items that do not require prior approval include:

- Medication (removed from its container)
- A cast
- A prosthetic device
- An inhaler
- Crutches

Other personal medical items may be brought to the test center, stored in your locker or other storage solution, and accessed on breaks without prior approval.

If you need immediate access in the testing room to a medical item not included on the list of items not requiring prior approval, you will need to apply for accommodations. The application review period for requesting personal medical items in the testing room is 30 days. Please make sure to submit your application as soon as possible, and no later than 30 days before the Silver Zone deadline associated with your exam date.

If you are requesting other accommodations—for example, extra time—in addition to a personal medical item, you must follow the MCAT Accommodations Online procedures described in Chapter 2.

For more information, please see our accommodations website, aamc.org/mcat/accommodations.

What Should I Wear to the MCAT Exam?

Be sure to dress comfortably and come prepared for varying room temperatures. You may find the testing room colder or warmer than you expected—plan accordingly.

If you need to remove an item of clothing during the exam (e.g., a sweater), you may place it on the back of your chair. Please note that outerwear, such as overcoats, windbreakers, rain jackets, hats or scarves (except for religious purposes), and down jackets, cannot be worn in the testing room.

What Will Happen When I Report to the Test Center?

The AAMC is deeply committed to ensuring the validity of test scores and to providing fair, equal, and secure testing conditions. These are primary concerns of all testing programs. Providing uniform testing procedures and maintaining test security serves the interest of examinees and test-score users.

To provide fair, equal, and secure testing conditions for all examinees, the staff at all test centers follow common policies and procedures. All examinees are required to comply with these policies and procedures.

Be Prepared for the Check-In Process

Arrive 30 minutes before the scheduled exam start time. (If you arrive much earlier, don't be alarmed if the test center is not yet open.) If you arrive after your exam start time, you may not be allowed to test.

> **MCAT INSIDER: Get to the test site early!**
>
> To make sure you are where you need to be on test day, plan to arrive early for your MCAT exam.

When you arrive at the test center, a test administrator will check you in. You will be asked to:

- Review the test center rules
- Provide a digital signature consenting to abide by the Candidate Rules Agreement
- Present a valid ID
- Have your palm scanned (a biometric authentication method based on the unique patterns of veins in the palms of people's hands)*
- Have a test-day photograph taken*
- Store your personal belongings in your locker or other storage solution and put your cell phone in a sealed bag, if provided

You may also be asked to:

- Turn your pockets inside-out to show they are empty
- Remove eye glasses for visual inspection
- Pull up your sleeves to display your wrists and forearms
- Be scanned with a metal detector wand

*Photographs and palm scans are used to verify the identity of MCAT examinees, prevent fraud, and protect the integrity of the exam and the medical school admissions process.

The test administrators will do their best to check in all examinees within 30 minutes. However, due to the individual nature of the check-in process, you may not begin testing precisely at your scheduled start time. This is not unusual, and many examinees may wait an additional half hour before starting the exam. This also means that examinees may be working on different parts of the exam or taking breaks at different times. Plan to be flexible, and plan your test-day schedule accordingly!

MCAT INSIDER: **Double-check your time zone.**

Know what time zone your test center adheres to, especially if you are crossing a state or county line. (It may differ from what you expect!) Don't let time zones trip you up—be sure you know the time zone for your test site, and plan accordingly.

Entering and Exiting the Testing Room

Examinees will be checked in and allowed into the testing room one at a time by the test administrator.

Every time you leave the testing room, you must raise your hand for assistance so the test administrator can escort you out. He or she will guide you through the check-out and check-in process, which may include some of the same steps as your initial check-in.

MCAT INSIDER: **Know where you are going.**

Make sure you have the current address of your test center—and know how to get there.

What Does the AAMC Do With My Identity Data?

The data the AAMC collects from you on test day may be used to identify you during the testing process, future MCAT administrations, and investigations and other responsive actions regarding MCAT-related or admissions-related fraud and other misconduct, or as required by law.

What Should I Expect Once I'm Inside the Testing Room?

Once you are inside the testing room, you will need to follow all the instructions of the test center staff. If you need assistance while taking the exam, raise your hand. The test administrator will either come to you or have you step outside the testing room for assistance.

Assigned Seats

As part of the testing room admissions process, you will be assigned a seat. This seat will be yours for the duration of the exam. You must return to your assigned seat every time after you leave it (e.g., after a break).

Testing Clock

You may not bring a timer or watch into the testing room. A clock will be visible on your testing monitor throughout the exam and will start counting down as soon as you begin your exam.

Time is counted down by section. If you finish a section early, you may continue on to the next section, but additional time will not be counted toward any subsequent sections or breaks. You cannot return to sections you've already completed.

No Eating, Drinking, or Smoking

You may not eat, drink, or smoke in the testing room.

You are permitted to bring your own snacks and/or lunch to the test center, which you must store with your personal items in the locker or other storage solution provided to you.

Using Your Noteboard

You may use the center-provided noteboard to take notes or write down calculations during any timed section of the exam, including the tutorial and breaks. If you need an additional noteboard during your exam, you may raise your hand, and a test administrator will replace your noteboard with a new noteboard. You cannot remove the noteboard from the testing room or erase any of the notes you write.

Other Security Rules and Procedures

Here are a few other good things to know:

- Access to the test center is restricted to test center personnel, examinees, and authorized observers.
- You may not wear hats or scarves (except for religious purposes) or outdoor clothing such as a jacket during the test. If your clothing has a hood, it must not cover your head at any time.
- You may not remove your shoes or sandals during the test.
- Your photo ID must be visible on your desk at all times.
- You will be under audio and video surveillance.

This may be obvious, but it is worth stating: While in the test center, you will be expected to conduct yourself in a civil manner. Aggressive, disruptive, or uncooperative examinees will be asked to leave and will not receive a refund.

What Happens Once the Exam Has Started?

Once the MCAT Exam Has Started, You Are Considered to Have Tested

You are considered to have tested even if you void or do not complete the test. While there is a way to void your score on test day (see the Canceling Your Results on Test Day [Voiding Your Exam] section), there is no way to stop your MCAT exam once it has started.

Responding to the Test-Day Certification Statement

The Test-Day Certification Statement asks you to certify that you have not engaged in and will not engage in any conduct that compromises the integrity, validity, or security of the MCAT exam. The Test-Day Certification Statement reminds you of the obligations under the Examinee Agreement and the *MCAT Essentials* you agreed to when you registered for the exam. You will have four minutes to read and agree to the Test-Day Certification Statement, and you must respond to this screen within the time limit. If you reject the Test-Day Certification, you will not be able to test that day or receive a refund.

Breaks and What You Can Access During Breaks

Two optional 10-minute breaks are provided between the first two and the last two test sections, and there's an optional 30-minute midexam break between the second and third sections.

Please factor in the time it will take to check out of and back into the testing room when planning your breaks.

Taking excessively long breaks will result in lost exam time or loss of the ability to void the exam.

During your scheduled breaks on the MCAT exam, you may access only food, water, and medication. These items must be stored in your locker or other storage solution when you are not on break. To access your food, a drink, or medication, remove the item from any bag, purse, or backpack you may have brought to the test center. The bag MUST remain in your locker or other storage solution at all times. You cannot access cell phones, books, study guides, or any other personal items.

Please be especially mindful of these additional policies, which apply from the beginning to the end of your exam:

- You may NOT access your cell phone or any other electronic device.
- You may NOT access any notes or other study materials.
- You may NOT leave the floor of the test center at any time during the exam or break unless the nearest available restroom is located elsewhere in the building.

Policies concerning breaks are detailed in the following AAMC publications, **which you are required to read:**

- *MCAT Essentials*. This publication is updated every year (available at students-residents.aamc.org/mcatessentials) and includes test-day policies, scoring details, suggestions to help you prepare for the MCAT exam, a list of contacts and online services, and other helpful information.
- *Test Center Regulations and Procedures*. This website includes a list of details about testing procedures (students-residents.aamc.org/applying-medical-school/article/mcat-testing-center-regulations-and-procedures).

Canceling Your Results on Test Day (Voiding Your Exam)

All examinees have the option at the end of their test to cancel (or "void") their test scores.

At the end of the exam, these two options will appear on the screen:

- I wish to have my MCAT exam SCORED.

OR

- I wish to VOID my MCAT exam.

Note that you will have only ONE opportunity to void your exam. Once you have made your choice, this selection cannot be reversed.

You will have three minutes to respond. If you fail to respond in the allotted time, the Void screen will default to "I wish to have my MCAT exam SCORED." The default selection to score your exam cannot be changed. If you select one of the options but do not select NEXT, your selection will be submitted automatically when the three minutes expire.

Satisfaction Survey

Immediately after completing the MCAT exam, you will be provided with an optional survey about your test-day experience. We encourage you to provide feedback about your day before you leave the test center.

What Happens After Test Day?

Once you complete the MCAT exam, you should consider submitting any concerns you might have about the test center and review your responsibilities about discussing the exam.

Submitting Test Center Concerns

If you have a concern regarding test-day procedures or the testing room environment, you should inform the test administrator at the time of the concern or on the day of testing and follow up by submitting your concern in writing to the AAMC. For details on reporting and submitting test center concerns, see students-residents.aamc.org/mcatessentials.

Your Responsibilities About (Not) Discussing the MCAT Exam

It's only natural to want to talk about the MCAT exam after you take the test. But everyone who takes the MCAT exam is expected to follow rules about that.

For example, the Examinee Agreement says that when you discuss the MCAT exam:

You **may**:

- Comment on your general exam experience, such as test center conditions, or how you generally felt about a particular section, such as the Biological and Biochemical Foundations of Living Systems section

You **may NOT**:

- Share or post the text (full or partial) of a test question and/or a test answer
- Reconstruct a list of topics tested in a particular section
- Mention a specific topic that was or was not tested on an exam
- Outline the steps or process to answer a question
- Speculate about which passages are field-test or experimental questions

Have concerns about your test center?

We strive to provide comfortable testing environments and fair, equal, and secure testing conditions. If you believe that test center circumstances interfered with your exam, you should contact the test administrator and the AAMC. Details about how to do this can be found in the MCAT Registration System.

The Examinee Agreement contains the guidelines the AAMC developed to help you understand the terms under which you sit for the MCAT exam and how to appropriately share your exam experience. It is the nondisclosure and terms-of-use agreement for the exam.

When you register for the exam, you must read and accept the terms of the MCAT Examinee Agreement. The Examinee Agreement is reproduced in the *MCAT Essentials* and is required reading for all examinees.

The Examinee Agreement is a binding contract and will be enforced as such. Just as a physician has a professional obligation to review a list of potential drug interactions carefully before ordering a prescription for a patient, aspiring doctors have an obligation to take the time to read the full MCAT Examinee Agreement.

One final tip: Rushing through this important information could lead to adverse consequences.

Violations of the MCAT Examinee Agreement are treated very seriously and may result in a warning, an investigation, a report to legitimately interested parties, or criminal or civil legal action.

Violations and Investigations

If the AAMC receives information that any individual has engaged in irregular behavior or conduct that may compromise the integrity of the MCAT exam (including copyright infringement or violation of the terms of the Examinee Agreement), MCAT exam officials will investigate the claim and may issue a report of the factual findings of the investigation.

Penalties for compromising the integrity of the MCAT exam, including cheating, can be severe. The AAMC may elect to send a report documenting the incident to legitimately interested parties, including places where the examinee has instructed that scores be sent. The AAMC may elect to cancel an examinee's test scores or elect to suspend an individual's eligibility to test. Finally, if it has reason to believe an examinee has violated the law, the AAMC may file a civil lawsuit against the examinee for material breaches of the Examinee Agreement and may refer an examinee to federal, state, or local prosecuting attorneys for criminal investigation and prosecution.

Any examinee who is the subject of an investigation by the AAMC is required by the Examinee Agreement to cooperate fully with the AAMC's investigation, produce all documents and materials requested by the AAMC, and submit to an in-person interview conducted by or on behalf of the AAMC at the AAMC's request. Examinees are required to answer all questions posed during investigative interviews truthfully and completely.

Look for more details about the procedures and policies for investigations online (see aamc.org/ students/applying/mcat/taking).

MCAT Security Tip Line

The MCAT program considers the integrity and security of the exam process to be very important. If you observe any irregular behavior or exam security violations before, during, or after an exam, please call the MCAT Security tip line at **202-903-0840** or send an email to MCATSecurity@aamc.org. The AAMC will maintain the confidentiality of any person who reports irregular behavior unless disclosure is required by law.

CHECKLIST: Keys to a Successful MCAT Exam Experience

Before You Test

☐ If applicable, apply for the Fee Assistance Program	The AAMC Fee Assistance Program assists MCAT examinees who, without financial assistance, would be unable to take the MCAT exam or apply to medical schools. Go to aamc.org/fap for more information. The Fee Assistance Program approval must be received before you schedule the exam.
☐ If applicable, apply for MCAT accommodations	If you have an impairment or condition that you believe requires an adjustment to the standard testing conditions, we encourage you to apply for accommodated testing. For time frames and types of accommodations, visit aamc.org/mcat/accommodations.
☐ Read the *MCAT Essentials*	This document is updated for each testing year and is online at students-residents.aamc.org/mcatessentials. Reading the *MCAT Essentials* is crucial to a successful experience during your MCAT exam. It provides critical information about MCAT policies and procedures and is required reading at the time you register for the MCAT exam.
☐ Register for the MCAT exam	Register for the MCAT exam **using the ID you'll bring with you on test day** so you enter your name correctly and are able to test. Refer to the *MCAT Essentials* for details about registration deadlines and fees associated.
☐ If you need to *reschedule* your test center or test date	You may reschedule by logging into the MCAT Registration System at aapps.aamc.org/mrs to view your current registration information and your current options.
☐ If you need to *cancel* your appointment	The cancellation policy grants a partial refund when a cancellation is filed before the Gold Zone scheduling deadline. To view your current cancellation options, log in to the MCAT Registration System at apps.aamc.org/mrs.
☐ Research your test center location	• Check to see where your test center is located. • Check to see how long it will take to get to your test center. • Verify the time zone of your test center because it may be different from your home or school time zone. • Log in to the MCAT Registration System 24 hours before your exam to ensure the location has not unexpectedly changed.
☐ Contact us with any questions	If you are experiencing problems while attempting to schedule, reschedule, or make necessary changes to your account, please contact AAMC Services via aamc.org/contactmcat.

(continued on next page)

CHECKLIST: Keys to a Successful MCAT Exam Experience *(continued from previous page)*	
On Test Day	
☐ Dress comfortably	Dress comfortably, possibly in layers, and be prepared for varying room temperatures since you may find the testing room colder or warmer than you expected.
☐ Know where you are going and arrive EARLY	Plan to arrive at your test location AT LEAST 30 minutes before the start of the exam, and double-check your route so you know where you are going.
☐ Double-check that your ID meets the necessary criteria	For registration and on test day, make sure that your personal identification meets MCAT exam requirements. Ensure that your ID: • Is current (it must have an expiration date that has not passed) • Has been issued by a government agency (e.g., a driver's license or passport) • Includes a photo that can be used to positively identify you • Includes your signature, which you will be asked to duplicate on test day • Matches the name you used to register for the exam For important additional details, see the *MCAT Essentials* at students-residents.aamc.org/mcatessentials.
☐ Verify what you can bring to the test center and testing room	Remember, no personal belongings will be allowed in the testing room. You must store personal belongings, including cell phones and other electronic devices, books, study materials, handbags, and food, in your locker or other storage solution provided for you. You are encouraged to leave personal items at home on test day. Neither the AAMC nor the test administrator is responsible for loss or damage to personal belongings. During your scheduled breaks, you will only have access to food, water, and medication. You will not be able to access your cell phone, electronic devices, or any notes or study materials during the break. Check the *MCAT Essentials* at students-residents.aamc.org/mcatessentials for specifics on what you may access during breaks.
☐ Confirm your identification on the name confirmation test screen	Once seated at your workstation, the first screen you will see on the test will display your first and last name, as well as a test-day photo. If your first and last names are correct, you must immediately acknowledge that by selecting "NEXT" at the bottom. If your name and/or photograph are NOT correct, you will need to raise your hand to contact the test administrator, and follow the instructions on the screen/prompt. Note that the middle name is not required to confirm your identification.
☐ Void or score your test	At the end of the test, you will be presented with an option to cancel, or "void," your test. You will need to indicate whether you wish to have your MCAT exam SCORED or if you wish to VOID your MCAT exam. You will have only one opportunity to void your exam, and once you have made your choice, the selection cannot be reversed. For important additional details, see the *MCAT Essentials* at students-residents.aamc.org/mcatessentials).
☐ Report test concerns	Each test center has test administrators on staff. In the event that you have a technical problem, please raise your hand to get their attention. If you believe that the test center conditions interfered with your exam, you should report that to the test center administrators on test day, and report a test center concern to the AAMC after test day. See aamc.org/mcattcc for details.

(continued on next page)

CHECKLIST: Keys to a Successful MCAT Exam Experience *(continued from previous page)*	
After You Test	
☐ Do not discuss MCAT questions	Remember that after the exam, you cannot discuss or disclose MCAT exam content orally, in writing, on the Internet, or through any other medium. Examples of prohibited acts include, but are not limited to, describing questions, passages, or graphics from the exam; discussing exam questions on chat rooms or through other means; identifying terms or concepts contained in exam questions; sharing answers to questions; referring others to information you saw on the exam; or reconstructing a list of topics tested.
☐ Check your scores	Check your scores in the MCAT Score Reporting System about 30–35 days after your exam. The Score Reporting System is accessible from the AAMC MCAT website, aamc.org/students/applying/mcat/. To check your scores, log on to the system. If your scores are available, you will be prompted to click through to view them.

Chapter 5

Everything You Always Wanted to Know About Your MCAT Scores

Broadly speaking, there are three major questions to consider about MCAT® scores:

- What is the MCAT score scale?
- How is the MCAT exam scored?
- What role do MCAT scores play in the medical school admissions process?

This chapter explores the first two of those questions in depth. Chapter 6 looks at the third question in detail.

What Is the MCAT Score Scale?

You will receive five results from your MCAT exam: one for each of the four sections and one combined, total score.

Section scores. Each of the four sections—Biological and Biochemical Foundations of Living Systems; Chemical and Physical Foundations of Biological Systems; Psychological, Social, and Biological Foundations of Behavior; and Critical Analysis and Reasoning Skills—is scored from a low of 118 to a high of 132, with a midpoint of 125. You will receive a score for each of the four sections.

Total score. Your scores for the four sections are combined to create your *total* score. The total score ranges from 472 to 528. The midpoint is 500.

For example, if you scored 128 on the Biological and Biochemical Foundations of Living Systems section, 125 on the Chemical and Physical Foundations of Biological Systems section, 129 on the Psychological, Social, and Biological Foundations of Behavior section, and 127 on the Critical Analysis and Reasoning Skills section, your total score would be 509.

MCAT® is a program of the
Association of American Medical Colleges

MCAT Score Scales

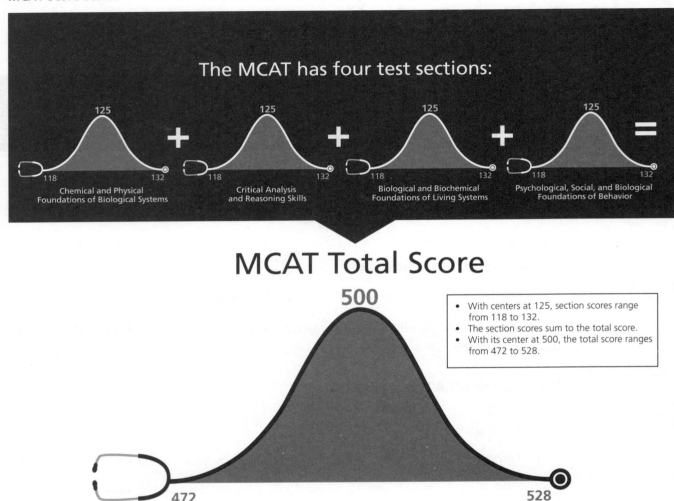

The MCAT has four test sections:

| 125 | + | 125 | + | 125 | + | 125 | = |

118 — 132
Chemical and Physical Foundations of Biological Systems

118 — 132
Critical Analysis and Reasoning Skills

118 — 132
Biological and Biochemical Foundations of Living Systems

118 — 132
Psychological, Social, and Biological Foundations of Behavior

MCAT Total Score

500

- With centers at 125, section scores range from 118 to 132.
- The section scores sum to the total score.
- With its center at 500, the total score ranges from 472 to 528.

472   **528**

How Is the MCAT Exam Scored?

The MCAT exam is scaled and equated so that scores have the same meaning, no matter when you test. This section of the guide provides more detail on the scoring process.

Your number-correct scores on the four sections of the MCAT exam are based on the number of multiple-choice questions you answer correctly. Wrong answers are scored exactly the same as unanswered questions and do not affect your score. There is no additional penalty for wrong answers, so even if you are unsure of the correct answer to a question, you should make your best guess.

The number-correct score for each section is converted to a scaled score ranging from 118 to 132. For example, if your number-correct score on one of the sections is between 35 and 37, your converted score might be 123. Number-correct scores ranging from 46 to 48 might have a converted score of 128, and so forth.

Why Are Raw Scores Converted to Scaled Scores?

In a given testing year, many different test forms are administered, any one of which you could see on your exam day. The different forms of the exam are designed to measure the same basic concepts and skills, but each form contains different sets of questions. Although care is taken to make sure each form is about equivalent in difficulty, one form may be slightly more or less difficult than another. The conversion of number-correct scores to scaled scores, through a process called equating, compensates for small variations in difficulty between sets of questions. The exact conversion of number-correct to scaled scores is not constant because each conversion is tailored to the specific set of questions on a test form.

The scaled score, reported on the 118 to 132 scale, tends to provide a more stable and accurate assessment of a student's performance than the number-correct score. Two students with equal preparation who answer different sets of questions would be expected to get the same scaled score, even though there might be a slight difference between the number-correct scores each student obtained on their test form.

Is the Exam Graded on a Curve?

Test takers often ask if obtaining a high score is easier or harder at different times of the testing year or, in other words, if the exam is scored on a curve. For exams graded on a curve, a final score depends on how an individual performs compared with other test takers from the same test day or the same time of year.

The MCAT exam is not graded on a curve. Instead, the exam is scaled and equated so that scores have the same meaning no matter when you test or who tests at the same time you did.

Although there may be small differences in the form of the MCAT exam you took compared with another examinee (because you answered different sets of questions), the scoring process accounts for these differences. For example, a 124 earned on the Critical Analysis and Reasoning section of one test form means the same thing as a 124 earned on that section on another form. How you score on the MCAT exam is not reflective of the particular form you took, the group of examinees you tested with, the test date, or the time of year since any difference in difficulty level is accounted for when your scaled scores are calculated (see above for information about score conversion).

Understanding the MCAT Score Report

Your MCAT score report provides a great deal of information designed to highlight your strengths and weaknesses.

Understanding the components of your MCAT score report—percentile ranks, confidence bands, and score profiles—is important for you personally and for admissions committees, which use the components to evaluate your readiness for success in medical school curricula.

Percentile Ranks

The percentile ranks provided on your score report show the percentages of test takers whose scores were the same as or lower than yours. They show how your scores compare with the scores of other examinees.

Every year on May 1, the percentile ranks are updated using data from recent testing years. These annual updates will ensure that the percentile ranks reflect current and stable information about your scores. This means changes in percentile ranks from one year to another reflect meaningful changes in the scores of examinees, rather than year-to-year fluctuations. Updating percentile ranks is consistent with industry practice.

If you look at your scores in the Score Reporting System after May 1, you will see these percentile ranks. Please note that updated percentile ranks will not change much from one year to the next.

Example MCAT Score Report

AAMC

Name: Tom Jones
Exam Date: 04/18/2015

AAMC ID: 20001856
Date of Birth: 01/07/1970

Section	Score	Confidence Band [1]	Percentile Rank of Score [2]	Score Profile [3]
Chemical and Physical Foundations of Biological Systems	124	123 ◆ 125	44%	118 — 125 — 132
Critical Analysis and Reasoning Skills	123	122 ◆ 124	36%	118 — 125 — 132
Biological and Biochemical Foundations of Living Systems	127	126 ◆ 128	75%	118 — 125 — 132
Psychological, Social, and Biological Foundations of Behavior	127	126 ◆ 128	75%	118 — 125 — 132
MCAT Total	501	499 ◆ 503	54%	

Notes

[1] Test scores, like other measurements, are not perfectly precise. The confidence bands around test scores mark the ranges in which the test taker's true scores probably lie. The diamond shapes and shading show that the test taker's true scores are more likely to be their reported scores (in the second column) than the other scores in the confidence bands.

[2] The percentile ranks of scores are the percentages of test takers who received the same scores or lower scores. The percentile ranks are updated on May 1 every year to reflect the results from previous calendar year(s).

[3] For the four sections, non-overlapping confidence bands show a test taker's likely strengths and weaknesses. Overlapping confidence bands suggest that there are not meaningful differences in performance between sections.

Confidence Bands

Confidence bands show the accuracy of your section and total scores. Similar to other standardized tests, scores from the MCAT exam will not be perfectly precise. Scores can be influenced by many factors, such as fatigue, test anxiety, and less-than-optimal test-room conditions. Conversely, they can be boosted by recent exposure to some of the tested topics. Confidence bands mark the ranges in which your "true scores" likely lie. They help signal the inaccuracy of test scores and are intended to discourage distinctions between applicants with similar scores.

Score Profiles

Score profiles are included to show you your strengths and weaknesses across all four sections of the exam. This section of the score report can be used to help you determine areas to focus on, should you decide to retake the exam.

How Do I Check My Scores?

The MCAT score-release process is handled through the MCAT program's computerized Score Reporting System (apps.aamc.org/score-reporting-web). You will log into it with the same username and password you used to register and schedule your exam.

To check your scores, log into the system. If your scores are available, you will be prompted to click through to view them. Please note that if your scores are not yet available, you will not see your recent MCAT test date within the Score Reporting System. You will see that date and score details once scores have been released.

How Are My Scores Released?

You have already released your scores just by sitting for the MCAT exam. This section details information about how to get your scores where you want them to go.

Primary Release

When you register, you automatically authorize release of your scores to the AAMC and its affiliated institutions for research purposes. This release allows the AAMC to report summary statistics for MCAT examinees by gender, undergraduate major, and other academic and demographic characteristics. Please understand that these summaries maintain the confidentiality of your scores and we will not report them in any way that identifies you.

Secondary Release

Here's where the scores tie back to you personally. Unless you void your scores (see page 36 for information on this option), the American Medical College Application Service® (AMCAS®) will receive your scores automatically. The AMCAS program is a centralized application-processing service, operated by the AMCAS program, for applicants to first-year entering classes at participating U.S. medical schools. Most U.S. medical schools participate in the AMCAS program. You can learn more about the AMCAS program and see whether the schools you plan to apply to are on the list by visiting aamc.org/amcas. For details, see the section titled "How Do I Send My Scores?"

There are three different score-release options that may help you as you pursue admission to medical school. (Note that you must select these options when you register for the MCAT exam.)

Release to the Prehealth Advisor

This release gives the AAMC permission to include your scores and demographic information (including contact information) in a web-based report to your undergraduate prehealth advisor, who may find such data useful when counseling you. In addition, advisors may share your scores with members of their premedical committees or others involved in preparing letters of recommendation; however, they will not share your information with other students or medical schools without your express permission.

The only time to opt in to this release is during the registration process. You will specify your undergraduate institution within the "Use of Personal Info" screen in the MCAT Registration System. If you do not opt in by the Bronze Zone deadline of your exam and you wish your prehealth advisor to have your scores, you will be required to send a print version of your scores (with verification code) to your undergraduate prehealth advisor (see "How Do I Send My Scores?").

Release to Med-MAR

The Medical Minority Applicant Registry (Med-MAR) is a service created to enhance admission opportunities for U.S. citizens from groups currently underrepresented in medicine (aamc.org/students/minorities/med-mar). If you select this option within the registration process, you give the AAMC permission to include your scores and basic biographical (including contact) information in Med-MAR.

Release to the MCAT Recruiting Service

This release gives the AAMC permission to include your contact and MCAT score information in reports produced by the MCAT Recruiting Service. Accredited U.S. and Canadian medical, DO-granting, podiatry, and veterinary medicine schools and other health-related programs, along with scholarship programs of the U.S. government (including those of the U.S. military), may request information about examinees and use that information as part of their recruiting efforts.

You indicate whether you wish to be a part of the MCAT Recruiting Service during the registration process.

Which programs use MCAT scores?

- American Medical College Application Service (AMCAS)

- American Association of Colleges of Osteopathic Medicine Application Service (AACOMAS)

- Texas Medical and Dental Schools Application Service (TMDSAS)

- Ontario Medical School Application Service (OMSAS)

- Other Canadian medical schools requiring MCAT scores

- American Association of Colleges of Podiatric Medicine Application Service (AACPM)

- Schools of Public Health Application Service (SOPHAS)

A number of individual schools and graduate programs use MCAT scores. Many of these schools and programs are listed separately within the MCAT Score Reporting System.

How Do I Send My Scores?

You have several options for sending your MCAT scores to medical schools.

Getting My Scores Into the AMCAS System

Your scores are automatically released to the AMCAS system. This means you do not need to take any additional steps to insert your scores into your application, but this also means you cannot withhold any scores from the AMCAS system.

MCAT INSIDER: Releasing Pre-2003 Scores

If you need to release scores from a test taken before 2003, please use the MCAT Score Reporting System, apps.aamc.org/score-reporting-web.

To learn more about applying to medical school, visit aamc.org/amcas.

Sending My Scores to Non-AMCAS Institutions

Scores can be sent to other centralized application services (such as the American Association of Colleges of Osteopathic Medicine Application Service [AACOMAS], the Centralized Application Service for Physician Assistants [CASPA], and the School of Public Health Application Service [SOPHAS]) or individual institutions in two ways: electronically through the MCAT Score Reporting System or by printing a copy of your official score report from the Score Reporting System and mailing it. If you wish to send a print version of your scores, the receiving institution will get a unique verification code to confirm that your scores have not been altered in any way.

For details and instructions about reporting scores, please refer to the Frequently Asked Questions within the Score Reporting System website.

How Do I Review the Status of My MCAT Score Reporting System Request(s)

You can check what you have sent to which programs and when and the status of any pending requests through the MCAT Score Reporting System. Please note that although the AAMC may have successfully sent your scores as requested, it may take the receiving institution some time to match your scores to your application.

I Have My Scores—Now What?

Once you receive your test scores, you may have further questions. Suppose, for example, your scores are not what you were expecting—what then? This section provides some guidance.

Can I Get My MCAT Exam Rescored—and if So, How?

The AAMC and the MCAT Program Office maintain a variety of quality-control procedures to ensure the accuracy of scores. If, however, you think a scoring error has occurred, you may request that your answers be rescored by hand. You will receive the results of this rescoring in writing, and the response letter will either confirm that your original scores are correct as reported or inform you of the corrected scores for each test section.

The fastest, most reliable secure way to submit a rescore request is through the MCAT Registration System. Once you have submitted such a request, our team will send you an invoice for the rescoring cost. Once the payment has been processed, you will receive the official communication about your request via email within three weeks.

How Long Are MCAT Scores Valid?

Medical schools generally accept scores dating back two or three years. If you have taken the exam before, we recommend that you consult the Medical School Admission Requirements™ (aamc.org/msar) to check the application policies of each school to which you intend to apply.

The AAMC will continue to report scores from the previous version of the exam (administered from 1991 through January 2015) through the 2019 AMCAS application cycle. However, individual medical schools may or may not continue to accept these scores through the 2019 AMCAS application cycle.

The AAMC conducted a survey about medical schools' policies for accepting scores from the previous version of the MCAT exam. The results of that survey can be found in the MCAT Score Policies (students-residents.aamc.org/mcatscorepolicies).

> **MCAT INSIDER: The Shelf Life of MCAT Scores**
>
> Individual medical schools set their own policies for how long scores are valid.

I Think I Can Do Better: Should I Retake the MCAT Exam?

If you are not happy with your performance on the MCAT exam, you have the option to take it again. But it's a tough decision.

There are times when a retake is well worth considering. Perhaps you discovered your coursework or study didn't cover the topics thoroughly. Or there's a large discrepancy between your grade in a subject and your score on a particular section. Or maybe you simply didn't feel well the day of the exam. Sometimes . . . you just know.

To What Degree Do Retakers Improve or Impair Their Scores?

Oftentimes, you don't "just know," and you need cold, hard data to help you judge how likely your scores are to increase, stay the same, or—and, of course, this is a risk—actually decrease.

As you might expect, the data show that increases in retest scores are more likely for those examinees who initially score at the lower end of the scale. They have more "room for improvement." Conversely, the higher your score, the more likely you are to do worse on the second attempt. You'll be better able to judge the cost-benefit ratio of a retest if you know where the "break-even point" lies.

The table below shows the break-even point. Although it is fairly self-explanatory, we'll draw out a few data points to illustrate the findings. The data came from 2015 and 2016 test takers who tested multiple times, and they show changes in scores from the first to the second attempt.

Let's consider, for example, examinees who scored from 498 to 501 initially. Looking at the row for 498–501, we see that of the 4,197 retakers who fell into this range, 7% stayed the same on the second attempt, 8% increased by one point, 8% increased by two points, and so on. Looking at it from the other side, we see that 6% decreased by one point, 4% by two points, and so on. Looking further across, we can see that in this particular range, more people's scores went up than down from the first to second attempts. (To help you quickly discern where the greatest score changes occurred, be they increases or decreases, we've highlighted those entries with percentages of 8% or more).

Changes in MCAT Total scores between first and second attempts, as a function of scores on the first attempt (results reported as percentages)*

Initial Total Score Range	N	Percent of examinees	-5 or less	-4	-3	-2	-1	0	1	2	3	4	5	6	7	8	9	10 or more
472-473	26	<1	0	0	0	0	4	12	8	15	15	12	12	12	8	0	0	4
474-477	208	1	<1	1	1	6	11	14	12	11	9	10	6	8	3	4	1	2
478-481	790	3	3	2	4	5	8	10	11	13	10	9	8	5	4	3	1	4
482-485	1,468	6	3	2	4	6	9	8	10	12	9	10	7	6	4	3	2	5
486-489	2,622	11	3	2	5	5	7	9	9	10	10	9	8	7	5	4	2	6
490-493	3,681	16	4	3	4	5	6	8	9	9	10	9	8	7	6	4	3	7
494-497	4,298	19	4	3	3	5	6	9	9	9	9	9	8	6	6	4	3	7
498-501	4,197	18	5	3	4	4	6	7	8	8	9	9	8	6	6	5	4	7
502-505	3,199	14	4	3	4	5	7	7	8	10	8	9	8	7	6	4	4	6
506-509	1,769	8	6	3	4	5	6	8	9	10	9	8	8	6	7	5	3	6
510-513	652	3	5	3	4	6	8	8	10	8	9	10	9	7	4	2	2	3
514-517	121	1	10	2	8	6	7	9	11	4	7	7	10	8	5	4	0	1
518-528	26	<1	19	8	0	15	4	8	12	8	4	15	4	4	0	0	0	0

*Based on the combined sample of 2015 and 2016 examinees who tested at least twice. Their first two scores were used to create the table.

As you review the Changes in MCAT Total scores table to gauge how likely you are to improve your total score, you're also apt to wonder to what degree examinees increase or decrease their scores in any one exam section. Therefore, we have broken the data down in the following tables to show the changes in scores for each of the four sections (again, based on initial scores).

You'll notice quickly that the shaded entries—those with percentages of a least 8%—skew to the right in the lower-scoring rows and to the left in the rows with the higher initial scores. That illustrates the point we made earlier: first-time examinees with lower initial scores tend to gain more when they retest, and test takers with higher initial scores tend to gain less (or decrease more) the second time around.

The table of changes in scores for each section of the exam—Biological and Biochemical Foundations of Living Systems Section (BBLS), Chemical and Physical Foundations of Biological Systems (CPBS), Psychological, Social, and Biological Foundations of Behavior (PSBB), and Critical Analysis and Reasoning Skills (CARS)—broken down by initial scores are shown on pages 52 and 53.

Changes in MCAT Biological and Biochemical Foundations of Living Systems (BBLS) scores between first and second attempts, as a function of scores on the first attempt (results reported as percentages)*

Initial BBLS Score	N	Percent of examinees	-4 or less	-3	-2	-1	0	1	2	3	4	5	6	7 or more
118	204	1	0	0	0	0	24	19	29	11	8	4	<1	4
119	467	2	0	0	0	12	17	27	22	13	6	2	<1	<1
120	996	4	0	0	4	10	23	23	20	13	4	2	<1	<1
121	1,943	8	0	1	4	11	20	25	19	10	5	2	1	<1
122	2,764	12	<1	1	5	12	21	23	18	11	5	3	1	<1
123	3,546	15	<1	1	5	13	19	22	19	11	6	3	1	<1
124	3,640	16	<1	2	6	13	23	21	16	11	5	2	1	<1
125	3,162	14	1	2	7	15	19	20	18	11	4	2	1	<1
126	2,515	11	2	4	10	16	18	20	18	8	4	1	<1	0
127	1,765	8	2	5	12	15	21	21	10	9	3	1	0	0
128	1,103	5	5	6	11	20	23	16	14	4	2	0	0	0
129	551	2	5	7	16	26	18	19	6	4	0	0	0	0
130	290	1	8	10	27	18	20	10	7	0	0	0	0	0
131	88	<1	13	16	11	25	18	17	0	0	0	0	0	0
132	23	<1	13	17	17	26	26	0	0	0	0	0	0	0

*Based on the combined sample of 2015 and 2016 examinees who tested at least twice. Their first two scores were used to create the table.

Changes in MCAT Chemical and Physical Foundations of Biological Systems (CPBS) scores between first and second attempts, as a function of scores on the first attempt (results reported as percentages)*

Initial CPBS Score	N	Percent of examinees	-4 or less	-3	-2	-1	0	1	2	3	4	5	6	7 or more
118	290	1	0	0	0	0	24	18	21	19	10	2	2	3
119	392	2	0	0	0	10	14	21	26	15	8	4	1	1
120	1,039	5	0	0	6	8	21	24	20	13	6	2	1	<1
121	1,854	8	0	2	5	13	19	22	21	10	5	3	1	<1
122	2,767	12	1	2	6	13	20	24	17	11	5	2	<1	<1
123	3,501	15	1	2	6	14	22	21	17	10	5	2	<1	<1
124	3,718	16	1	2	9	16	20	21	16	10	4	1	<1	<1
125	2,942	13	1	4	9	17	21	18	16	8	3	1	<1	<1
126	2,435	11	2	5	10	16	20	23	14	7	3	1	<1	0
127	2,018	9	2	5	11	18	23	19	12	7	2	<1	0	0
128	1,168	5	4	7	13	18	24	17	13	4	1	0	0	0
129	534	2	5	7	16	22	20	19	8	2	0	0	0	0
130	296	1	4	12	20	23	24	13	5	0	0	0	0	0
131	78	<1	8	17	18	33	10	14	0	0	0	0	0	0
132	25	<1	16	8	44	24	8	0	0	0	0	0	0	0

*Based on the combined sample of 2015 and 2016 examinees who tested at least twice. Their first two scores were used to create the table.

Changes in MCAT Psychological, Social, and Biological Foundations of Behavior (PSBB) scores between first and second attempts, as a function of scores on the first attempt (results reported as percentages)*

Initial PSBB Score	N	Percent of examinees	-4 or less	-3	-2	-1	0	1	2	3	4	5	6	7 or more
118	226	1	0	0	0	0	28	18	23	14	7	4	1	4
119	407	2	0	0	0	10	20	22	23	14	5	3	2	1
120	1,089	5	0	0	5	9	21	25	17	11	7	4	1	1
121	1,924	8	0	1	4	10	17	22	19	13	7	5	2	1
122	2,834	12	<1	1	5	10	19	18	18	13	9	4	2	1
123	3,164	14	<1	2	6	12	15	20	16	13	8	4	2	1
124	3,446	15	1	2	7	12	18	18	17	12	7	3	1	1
125	3,262	14	1	4	7	13	19	17	15	12	7	3	1	<1
126	2,773	12	2	5	10	15	18	17	16	8	5	2	1	0
127	1,854	8	4	6	12	19	20	16	12	8	3	1	0	0
128	1,170	5	6	9	15	18	21	15	10	5	2	0	0	0
129	502	2	8	12	18	23	17	12	7	3	0	0	0	0
130	287	1	15	15	22	17	17	9	4	0	0	0	0	0
131	83	<1	24	12	19	20	11	13	0	0	0	0	0	0
132	36	<1	31	25	25	11	8	0	0	0	0	0	0	0

*Based on the combined sample of 2015 and 2016 examinees who tested at least twice. Their first two scores were used to create the table.

Changes in MCAT Critical Analysis and Reasoning Skills (CARS) scores between first and second attempts, as a function of scores on the first attempt (results reported as percentages)*

Initial CARS Score	N	Percent of examinees	-4 or less	-3	-2	-1	0	1	2	3	4	5	6	7 or more
118	250	1	0	0	0	0	22	22	30	19	6	2	<1	0
119	505	2	0	0	0	11	18	30	23	12	4	1	<1	<1
120	1,389	6	0	0	4	8	24	28	21	11	3	<1	<1	<1
121	2,182	9	0	1	4	13	22	28	17	11	4	1	<1	<1
122	3,313	14	<1	1	4	14	24	23	18	10	4	2	<1	<1
123	3,788	16	<1	2	6	15	22	23	16	9	4	2	1	<1
124	3,687	16	<1	3	8	17	23	19	15	10	3	2	<1	<1
125	3,074	13	1	4	11	17	22	19	15	8	3	1	<1	<1
126	2,158	9	2	5	13	19	22	19	11	6	2	1	<1	0
127	1,432	6	4	8	14	20	20	17	11	5	1	<1	0	0
128	714	3	5	10	16	22	20	15	8	3	1	0	0	0
129	362	2	9	11	20	25	15	12	5	2	0	0	0	0
130	135	1	16	15	21	25	13	6	4	0	0	0	0	0
131	51	<1	20	22	27	24	6	2	0	0	0	0	0	0
132	17	<1	29	35	0	24	12	0	0	0	0	0	0	0

*Based on the combined sample of 2015 and 2016 examinees who tested at least twice. Their first two scores were used to create the table.

As mentioned in Chapter 2, certain rules pertain to the retaking of the MCAT exam, including how many times you can retake the test within a certain period of time. Go to aamc.org/mcat and the *MCAT Essentials* for the latest updates.

How Are Multiple MCAT Scores Used in the Admissions Process?

Each medical school has its own method of dealing with multiple MCAT exam scores. A recent survey of medical school admissions officers suggests that multiple sets of scores are considered in the following ways:

- All sets of scores are weighed equally and improvements noted.
- Consideration is given only to the most recent set of scores.
- An average is taken of all sets of scores.
- Only the highest set of scores is considered.
- A combination of the highest individual section scores is considered.

To understand how a particular medical school considers multiple scores, check that school's policies and the Medical School Admission Requirements website at aamc.org/msar.

Should I Consider Delaying My Application for Medical School?

If circumstances are not aligning for you to get into medical school now but you don't want to stop trying to gain admittance, there are alternatives. Are you willing to delay your entry into medical school by one year? If so, you could spend more time studying for the exam on your own or take additional courses at your home institution or a community college. Or, you may wish to enroll in a postbaccalaureate program that can help you strengthen your performance in academic areas where you might be weak and thus better position yourself for another attempt at the MCAT exam in a year or so. If you'd like to learn more about the various postbaccalaureate programs, visit a searchable database of them at services.aamc.org/postbacc.

Chapter 6

The Role That MCAT Scores Play in the Medical School Admissions Process

Keep in mind that medical schools' admissions offices use an evaluation process directly linked to the mission, goals, and diversity interests of their institution. They decide which applicants will best serve the needs of the school, patients, community, and medical profession at large; contribute to the diversity that will drive excellence in the school's learning environment; and benefit most from the school's educational program.

Admissions committees intentionally select individual applicants who make up a broadly diverse medical school class or cohort that will help the schools achieve their mission. When a school reviews your application, it will be looking for evidence of knowledge, skills, attitudes, and behaviors that might fit well with the school's particular mission and goals. For example, depending on its mission, one school might be looking for applicants who demonstrate service to communities underserved by the current health care system, while another may seek applicants who have shown creativity and independent productivity in scholarly activities.

MCAT Scores Are a Standardized Measure—But They Are Just *One* Measure

As we've mentioned, MCAT scores provide admissions officers with a standardized measure by which to compare applicants. It is important to remember, though, that applicants accepted to medical school have a wide range of MCAT scores and GPAs. Those measures are used in conjunction with many other factors.

The Holistic Approach to Evaluation of Applications

Another very important thing to keep in mind is that medical schools often take a holistic approach to evaluating individual applicants. One way to think about this is that many admissions committee members and other evaluators use a flexible, individualized, balanced approach as they assess your experiences, attributes, and academic metrics. They also consider how you might contribute to both the learning environment at that school and the practice of medicine. This means that admissions officers and committees carefully review a wide range of factors in order to fully assess your application. They do not base their decisions on just one or two factors.

While academic metrics, such as your grades and test scores, are important components in the decision making, they are only part of the overall package. They do not tell the full story of who you are.

How and what you have learned from your life experiences, as well as your personal attributes, are essential in rounding out your story and setting the context for your academic record. For example, when considered together, your experiences, attributes, and academic metrics can highlight your ability to balance multiple priorities and demonstrate a strong sense of responsibility and resilience. That balanced consideration helps explain why applicants with a broad range of MCAT scores and GPAs are accepted into medical school, rather than just applicants with high scores. Taken together, these factors also assist medical schools in assessing whether you can help a school fulfill its institutional mission.

During the application process, you provide a great deal of information about your experiences, attributes, and academic record through your primary and secondary applications, statements of purpose, experience descriptions, and interviews. Each of these tools provides valuable opportunities for you to reflect on and describe what you have learned and how that might shape your approach to practicing medicine. Letters of evaluation also provide rich information about your experiential, personal, and academic attributes.

The AAMC Experiences-Attributes-Metrics Model graphic on the next page depicts the relatively wide lens through which admissions committees might view applicants. By considering a range of experiences, attributes, and academic metrics, medical schools identify criteria that are grounded in their institutional mission and goals; explore a broader, mission-driven understanding of diversity; and consider what each applicant might contribute as a medical student and future physician.

AAMC Experiences-Attributes-Metrics Model

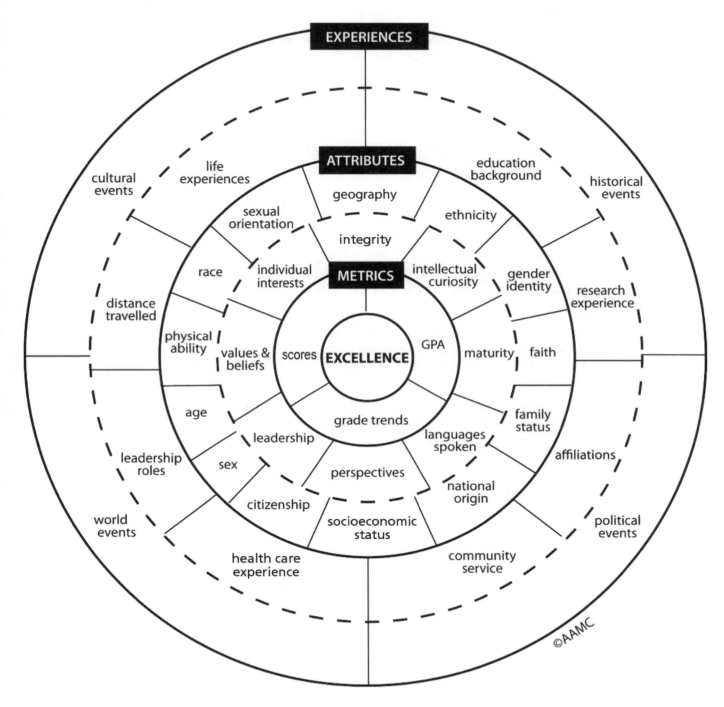

Source: Adapted from *Workforce America: Managing Employee Diversity as a Vital Resource*, McGraw Hill Publishing, 1990.

MCAT Scores and Other Application Information— Insights from an AAMC Survey

To learn more about the holistic review of applicants' qualifications, AAMC staff asked admissions officers from U.S. medical schools—both public and private—to rate the importance of various application information to their admissions decisions.

The table on the next page lists some of the key variables that medical schools consider, organized into four categories: academic metrics, experiences, demographics, and other data. They are grouped by overall mean value of the importance ratings medical school admissions officers said they give in deciding which applicants to interview and which to admit. How did different academic metrics and experiences rate?

The factors ranked as being of *highest* importance included applicants' undergraduate cumulative science/math GPAs, MCAT total scores, upward or downward grade trends, cumulative total GPAs, grade data for students who completed postbaccalaureate programs, and whether or not applicants were on track to meet premedical course requirements. In addition, applicants' community service or volunteer experience, physician shadowing or clinical observations, and leadership experience also ranked highly, as did coming from underserved rural or urban areas. For applicants invited to interview, interview ratings got high importance ratings.

The factors that were rated as being of *medium* importance included completion of challenging upper-level science courses and cumulative "all other" (not science/math) undergraduate GPAs, along with such factors as paid employment, research or lab experience, other extracurricular activities, and military service. Applicants' race/ethnicity and socioeconomic status also got medium importance ratings.

Citizenship and residency requirements got high importance ratings at public medical schools and medium importance ratings at private medical schools that had citizenship or residency requirements.

Mean Importance Ratings of Academic, Experiential, Demographic, and Interview Data (N = 127)[1]

Mean Importance Ratings[2]	Academic Metrics	Experiences	Demographics	Other Data
Highest Importance Ratings (≥3.0)	• GPA: cumulative biology, chemistry, physics, and math • MCAT total score • GPA: grade trend • GPA: cumulative total • GPA: cumulative total from postbaccalaureate premedical program • MCAT total score trend • Completion of premedical course requirements	• Community service/volunteer: medical/clinical • Community service/volunteer: not medical/clinical • Physician shadowing/clinical observation • Leadership	• U.S. citizenship/permanent residency (Public)[3] • State residency (Public)[3] • Rural/urban underserved background	• Interview results[4]
Medium Importance Ratings (≥2.5 and <3.0)	• Completion of challenging upper-level science courses • GPA: cumulative "all other" (not biology, chemistry, physics, and math)	• Paid employment: medical/clinical • Research/lab • Other extracurricular activities • Military service	• Race/ethnicity • U.S. citizenship/permanent residency (Private)[3] • Parental education/occupation/socioeconomic status (SES)	
Lowest Importance Ratings (<2.5)	• Degree from graduate or professional program • Completion of challenging nonscience courses • Selectivity of undergraduate institution(s) • Undergraduate major	• Teaching/tutoring/teaching assistant • Paid employment: not medical/clinical • Intercollegiate athletics • Honors, awards, recognition • Conferences attended, presentations, posters, publications	• First-generation immigrant status • Fluency in multiple languages • Gender • English language learners • State residency (Private)[3] • Legacy status • Community college attendance • Age	

1. The 2015 survey asked, "How important were the following data about academic preparation, experiences, attributes/personal competencies, biographic/demographic characteristics, and interview results in identifying the applicants to [interview, offer an acceptance]?"
2. Importance was rated on a four-point scale ranging from 1 to 4 ("Not Important," "Somewhat Important," "Important," and "Very Important," respectively). For each variable, we computed an overall mean importance rating based on admissions officers' ratings of importance for making decisions about whom to interview and whom to accept (the mean importance rating for the interview variable is the exception to this rule because interview data were not available until applicants were invited to interview). We chose to classify variables using overall mean importance ratings because their mean importance ratings were similar for the interview and the acceptance phases. Variables are ordered by overall mean importance rating.
3. Overall mean importance ratings for public and private institutions were significantly different from one another.
4. Only available at the admissions stage where admissions committees make a decision to offer an acceptance.

AN IMPORTANT CAVEAT!

The table summarizes importance ratings across medical schools and may not describe individual schools well. Each medical school has its own policies and approaches to using MCAT score information. Check with individual schools for details about their admissions policies and practices or read about them on the Medical School Admission Requirements™ website at aamc.org/msar.

How Medical Schools Use MCAT Scores

Geoffrey H. Young, PhD
Senior Director, Student Affairs and Programs
Association of American Medical Colleges (AAMC)

Research has shown that MCAT scores and undergraduate GPAs are strong predictors of success in medical school. Consequently, almost every medical school uses them at some point in assessing applicants. At the same time, though, applicants accepted for medical school have a wide range of MCAT scores and undergraduate GPAs.

In practice, medical schools invest considerable time and energy in identifying candidates for admissions who not only have performed competitively in their premedical studies and mastered relevant concepts, but also have personal experiences, characteristics, and attributes necessary for the future practice of medicine. I have found this last statement to be true at the three schools where I served on the admissions committee, most recently as the associate dean for admissions at the Medical College of Georgia at Augusta University.

The Assessment Process: A Holistic Approach

While all three schools where I served used MCAT scores in their decision making, each school also used additional criteria. The criteria included science and overall GPA, academic history, extracurricular activities related to medicine (for example, "shadowing" experience, volunteer experiences in the medical field, and clinical work experience), "distance traveled" (that is, life challenges one has faced and conquered), leadership and research experiences, community service and other extracurricular activities, personal statements, and letters of recommendation. I would caution you, however, not to approach your extracurricular activities with the idea of "checking off" a wide range and number of pursuits in order to impress an admissions committee. In fact, three or four in-depth experiences from which you gained valuable lessons are far more significant—and telling—to admissions officers than dozens of short-term involvements.

Medical schools use these criteria to take a holistic approach to assessing applicants. That is, admissions committees seek to appreciate the applicant as a "whole" person. It is true that committees clearly assess and highly value applicants' academic accomplishments, such as MCAT scores. However, committees also assess attributes and experiences that indicate the ability to develop and maintain effective relationships with patients, work collaboratively with other team members, act ethically and compassionately, and in many other ways master the "art" of medicine. Remember, the ultimate goal of medical school is to develop caring, knowledgeable, and medically and culturally competent physicians who will care for a range of patient populations.

The Interview Is Key

Perhaps the most critical component of the admissions process is the interview. Medical schools usually interview three, four, or even five times as many applicants as their class size. The interview is likely to be the chief determining factor at this phase in the assessment of whether or not you are accepted. The very fact that interviews are given at all is a significant distinction of medical schools, since some professional schools do not require them. This alone attests to the degree to which admissions officers seek—and medical schools value—qualities and characteristics such as empathy, self-awareness, communication ability, and interpersonal skills that can best be judged in a direct interview situation.

Medical Schools Are Different

Medical schools are not alike. Those of us who work in medical education often say, "If you've seen one medical school . . . you've seen one medical school." Some of these differences are rather obvious. Some schools are located in the East; some in the West. Some are private; others, public. Some have a large entering class; others, small. Medical schools also vary in the content of their courses, in the way they teach, and even in the way they grade students. A school's mission typically determines the emphasis placed on the applicants' characteristics. For example, one school may actively seek students from specific geographic or rural areas. Others may look for students with a high potential for a research career. Still others may seek to increase the number of doctors who plan to practice in their state. The differing missions among schools will be reflected in their admissions policies and standards.

In conclusion, medical schools use various approaches in their application and admissions activities. Each approach includes an assessment of academic predictors of success in medical school coupled with an assessment of other indicators of success in the practice of medicine. Clearly, the MCAT exam is one of those predictors of academic success. While the emphasis placed on each predictor and each indicator differs from school to school, please be assured that medical school admissions committees take seriously their responsibility to select knowledgeable, altruistic, skillful, and dutiful candidates who will become our future physicians.

Similarly, you, as the applicant, should be looking for the best possible "fit" between you and the medical school. Does the school's mission fit with your career goals? Does the curriculum match your learning style? Does the school offer social and academic support resources that will maximize your success? And will the school's diversity enhance your overall educational learning experience?

I encourage you to work hard, perform academically at your highest level, keep informed about trends in medicine and health care more generally, and seek experiences that will expand and challenge your thinking and enhance and facilitate your personal, social, and professional growth.

How Likely (or Not) Am I to Gain Admission Based on My MCAT Scores and GPA Combined?

As we have emphasized, admissions officers do not view MCAT scores in isolation, but rather in concert with your undergraduate GPA and a host of other factors. Historically, data show the better your grades and the higher your MCAT scores, the more likely you are to be accepted. However, past history also shows that applicants with a wide range of MCAT scores and undergraduate GPAs have been successful in gaining acceptance into one or more medical schools.

Admissions committees consider the other selection factors we mentioned previously. Do you have exceptionally striking letters of recommendation, perhaps, or a remarkable tale of overcoming hardship? What about a year's stint volunteering in a medical clinic in an underserved community? Factors such as these may help tilt the scales in your favor.

To see current data on MCAT scores and undergraduate GPAs and admission to medical school, see aamc.org/data/facts.

Using the Medical School Admission Requirements Publications for a Closer Look at Selection Factors

The AAMC resource guidebook *The Official Guide to Medical School Admissions* and the Medical School Admission Requirements™ (MSAR®) website (aamc.org/msar) are key resources for you. *The Official Guide to Medical School Admissions* has information to guide you in applying to medical school and in the medical education process, including chapters on selecting the right schools for you, the American Medical College Application Service® (AMCAS® service), financing your education, and dual-degree programs. The website includes comprehensive profiles of U.S. and Canadian medical schools and baccalaureate-MD programs.

You can also use the MSAR website to view specifics about how a particular school uses selection factors in admissions decisions. Take a close look at the Selection Factors section to find schools for which admissions requirements are a good fit for your interests. For example, if you have a strong interest in research, you can look at each school's profile to see what research opportunities are available as well as the amount of funding the school receives from the National Institutes of Health and whether the school has an MD-PhD program.

MCAT INSIDER: Researching medical schools

Medical schools are all different. You should research them and visit, if possible. You can use the Medical School Admission Requirements website to help you find schools that match your strengths and interests.

Chapter 7

Ready, Set . . . Test!

As the preceding chapters suggest, there's a lot to know about taking the MCAT® exam. But if you have read those chapters carefully and followed our advice, you should be well prepared to tackle the mechanics of the test. That's an important stepping stone for success on the MCAT exam.

The other important stepping stone for success on the exam is knowing what's on the exam itself. The MCAT exam tests for the academic competencies that lay the foundation for success in medical school. These include a solid grounding in 10 foundational concepts and your ability to apply your scientific inquiry and reasoning skills to solving interdisciplinary, real-world problems, as well as to use your critical analysis and reasoning skills. We'll discuss more about that in the next section of this book (Part II).

But before we dive into the material on the test, remember that the MCAT exam is one component in a comprehensive, holistic admissions process that medical schools have designed to find the students who can best fit with their programs and succeed as physicians. It is important to remember that while the MCAT exam is a crucial step for getting into medical school, it is only one part of the medical school admissions process. So, step back for a moment to think about the MCAT exam and put it into perspective. It's not a final destination, but part of the journey.

If you have decided to pursue a career in medicine, you have chosen a path that can be deeply rewarding personally and highly valuable to society. You are likely to encounter many challenges along the way, but if you are inspired by a career in medicine, we applaud you and encourage you to work hard in pursuit of your goals. As you take the MCAT exam and embark on your career, we wish you all the very best, wherever your career path and life's journey ultimately take you.

Not Sure Where to Begin?

The MCAT exam may be your first interaction with the AAMC, but it surely won't be your last. The AAMC is committed to supporting you in your journey to becoming a doctor. We are here to help you from when you first begin to think about becoming a doctor to when you are an experienced, practicing physician.

The AAMC has the resources you need. The Aspiring Docs website shares real-life inspirational stories and resources to help you figure out all the basics (aamc.org/aspiringdocs). Our short fact sheets cover how to shadow a doctor, how to make the most of your gap year, what it's like to take the MCAT exam, and much more. Aspiring Docs is the place to start in your premed journey.

How Will I Afford Medical School?

The AAMC has tools to help you figure out how to pay for medical school on the Financial Information, Resources, Services, and Tools (FIRST) website (aamc.org/first). FIRST is the AAMC's financial aid and debt management program. On the website, you will find a customizable financial aid toolkit that helps you search for resources by topic, education level, or information format. The site also provides a library of financial aid fact sheets about a variety of financial topics, such as budgeting, understanding credit cards, and debt management. The site has videos and podcasts that provide answers to many questions related to financial aid, as well as the Medloans® Organizer and Calculator, where you can store all your loan information in one secure, centralized place and run your own repayment scenarios. FIRST can help you make educated borrowing decisions and develop sound debt management skills.

How Do I Choose a Medical School?

The AAMC developed the Medical School Admission Requirements™ website to assist you in deciding which medical schools are right for you (aamc.org/msar). It's the only comprehensive source of accurate, unbiased data on U.S. and Canadian MD-granting programs and that includes selection factors, such as MCAT and GPA data, medical school class profiles, and research opportunities. The Medical School Admissions Requirements website is accurate because the AAMC has access to the American Medical College Application Service® (AMCAS®) application and MCAT data and verifies the data with schools, rather than relying on self-reported data. You'll be able to compare schools "apples to apples" because the data from each school are configured identically, with very few noted exceptions.

You can use the Medical School Admissions Requirements website to perform advanced searches, sort data, browse schools at a glance, save favorites, compare schools, save notes, and access more information and data than you can anywhere else.

Do I Have to Submit an Application to Each Medical School I Want to Apply To?

You will need to submit just one application to the American Medical College Application Service (AMCAS). The AMCAS program is the AAMC's centralized application service, available to applicants in the first-year entering class at participating U.S. medical schools. (For a list of participating schools, go to students-residents.aamc.org/applying-medical-school/article/participating-medical-schools-deadlines.)

Fifth Edition
The Official Guide to the MCAT® Exam
64
MCAT® is a program of the
Association of American Medical Colleges

You can think of it as the Common Application, but for medical school. While medical schools also require supplemental applications, the AMCAS application forms the basis of the information the schools review.

The AMCAS program collects, verifies, and delivers application information, letters of evaluation, and MCAT scores to the schools you choose. Each participating school is then responsible for making its own individual admissions decision.

Visit the AMCAS website to download the Applicant Guide, read application tips, watch tutorials, and take advantage of other useful tools (aamc.org/amcas).

How Can I Get Medical Experience Before Medical School?

The description of any medical experiences you've had is an important part of your medical school application. There are many different ways to gain experience, such as volunteering, shadowing a physician, working in a lab, and becoming a medical scribe.

One experience to consider is the Summer Health Professions Education Program (SHPEP), a FREE six-week academic enrichment program for college freshmen and sophomores interested in health professions such as medicine, dentistry, and public health. It's a transformative experience for students who are underrepresented in the health professions and/or who have demonstrated an interest in issues affecting underserved populations. SHPEP presents a variety of career opportunities to students and improves their chances for admission to health professional schools. Students participate in rigorous classes that cover basic sciences and quantitative topics, career development activities, learning and study skills workshops, and clinical experiences. The SHPEP application opens in the fall each year. Visit shpep.org for more information.

What About Getting Support During and After Medical School?

The AAMC is here to support you as a medical student and beyond. We'll help you choose a medical specialty through Careers in Medicine® (CiM), apply for residency through the Electronic Residency Application Service® (ERAS®), find clinical rotations in the United States and abroad to gain new educational experiences and explore residency opportunities, and find medical positions through our job board (CareerConnect).

We wish you the best in your journey to becoming a doctor.

For more information about helpful AAMC resources, go to aamc.org/students.

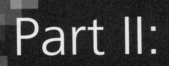

Part II:

Preparing for the MCAT® Exam

Chapter 8

Introduction to MCAT Content and Part II

Among other resources, the AAMC offers these two free tools to help you navigate the MCAT exam:

- The **Course-Mapping Tool for the MCAT Exam** is designed to help you choose what undergraduate courses can best help you prepare for the content on the exam. This tool is an Excel spreadsheet summarizing MCAT exam content and skills. With it, you and your prehealth advisor can identify the course levels from which MCAT exam content is drawn, filter content by course level, and map course content to MCAT exam content. See students-residents.aamc.org/ mcatcoursemappingtool.

- **What's on the MCAT Exam?** is an interactive, student-friendly resource that will help you learn about the new exam. It offers an overview of the exam sections, as well as details about foundational concepts and skills you will be asked to demonstrate on the exam, in both video and text format. See students-residents.aamc.org/ mcatexam.

In Part I, we showed you how to take the MCAT® exam. Now it's time to take a look at what's on the exam.

Part II of this book takes an in-depth look at the MCAT exam's content and format. After first exploring the conceptual framework behind the exam, Part II takes a deep dive into the concepts and content tested by each of the MCAT's four test sections. For each section, we'll provide numerous Sample Test questions along with detailed analysis to help you better understand the questions and what they are asking you to do.

Plan to invest adequate time in studying Part II. If you study it, especially the questions, very carefully, you will be better prepared to take the MCAT exam.

Conceptual Framework

What competencies does the MCAT exam test for? In Chapter 9, we'll look at the conceptual framework behind the exam.

Starting with the "big ideas" in the sciences that provide the foundation for learning in medical school, Chapter 9 explores the exam's foundational concepts and content categories, as well as the scientific inquiry and reasoning skills on which the exam's questions are based.

Read Chapter 9 carefully to understand how the MCAT exam is organized and why it asks the questions it does.

The Four Exam Sections

In the chapters that follow, we will take a close look at the MCAT exam's four test sections:

Chapter 10: Biological and Biochemical Foundations of Living Systems

Chapter 11: Chemical and Physical Foundations of Biological Systems

Chapter 12: Psychological, Social, and Biological Foundations of Behavior

Chapter 13: Critical Analysis and Reasoning Skills

See the Summary of the MCAT Exam table on the next page for more detail.

Each of these chapters goes into detail about specific content categories, linking that content directly to the key foundational concepts that the MCAT exam tests. Each chapter also includes extensive sample test questions with answers.

At the beginning of each chapter, you will find a brief summary of the approximate percentages of questions you'll see on the exam for each discipline, foundational concept, and scientific inquiry and reasoning skill.

The more you know about the MCAT exam, the better you are likely to do on it. So, use the information in the chapters that follow to strengthen your understanding of the exam and your test-taking skills. Good luck!

Part II introduces the four sections of the MCAT exam in the order of the 10 foundational concepts that are the conceptual framework of the exam content. (See Chapter 9 for a list of the foundational concepts.) On test day, the sections are presented in the following order:

- Chemical and Physical Foundations of Biological Systems
- Critical Analysis and Reasoning Skills
- Biological and Biochemical Foundations of Living Systems
- Psychological, Social, and Biological Foundations of Behavior

See the chart on page 5 for details about MCAT test day.

Summary of the MCAT Exam

Section of the MCAT Exam	Number of questions	Number of minutes
Biological and Biochemical Foundations of Living Systems This section asks you to combine your knowledge of foundational concepts in the biological and biochemical sciences with your scientific inquiry, reasoning, and research and statistics skills to solve problems that demonstrate readiness for medical school. Understanding the processes unique to living organisms, such as growing and reproducing, maintaining a constant internal environment, acquiring materials and energy, sensing and responding to environmental changes, and adapting, is important to the study of medicine. You will be tested on your knowledge of how cells and organ systems within an organism act both independently and together to accomplish these processes, as well as on your ability to reason about these processes at various levels of biological organization within a living system.	59	95
Chemical and Physical Foundations of Biological Systems This section asks you to combine your knowledge of foundational concepts in the chemical and physical sciences with your scientific inquiry, reasoning, and research and statistics skills to solve problems that demonstrate readiness for medical school. Understanding the mechanical, physical, and biochemical functions of tissues, organs, and organ systems is important to the study of medicine. You will be tested on your knowledge of the basic chemical and physical principles that underlie the mechanisms operating in the human body and on your ability to apply an understanding of these general principles to living systems.	59	95
Psychological, Social, and Biological Foundations of Behavior This section tests your knowledge and use of the concepts in psychology, sociology, biology, research methods, and statistics that provide a solid foundation for learning in medical school about the behavioral and sociocultural determinants of health and health outcomes. Understanding the behavioral and sociocultural determinants of health is important to the study of medicine. You will be tested on your knowledge of the ways that psychological, social, and biological factors influence perceptions and reactions to the world; behavior and behavior change; what people think about themselves and others; the cultural and social differences that influence well-being; and the relationships among social stratification, access to resources, and well-being.	59	95
Critical Analysis and Reasoning Skills This section asks you to critically analyze information from a wide range of social sciences and humanities disciplines. Specific knowledge of these disciplines is *not* required for this section; all the information you will need appears in the passages provided. Content is drawn from several areas, including (but not limited to) ethics and philosophy, studies of diverse cultures, and population health.	53	90

MCAT® is a program of the
Association of American Medical Colleges

Chapter 9

The MCAT exam has four test sections:

1) Biological and Biochemical Foundations of Living Systems,

2) Chemical and Physical Foundations of Biological Systems,

3) Psychological, Social, and Biological Foundations of Behavior, and

4) Critical Analysis and Reasoning Skills.

The two natural sciences sections and the behavioral and social sciences section each test foundational concepts and content categories. They test your scientific inquiry and reasoning skills, such as knowing how to "do" science and bring together concepts from different disciplines to solve complex problems.

This chapter describes the conceptual framework for the natural, behavioral, and social sciences sections of the MCAT® exam. The fourth section, Critical Analysis and Reasoning Skills, is the focus of Chapter 13. It tests the analysis and reasoning skills you will need to be successful in medical school.

How the Sections Are Organized

The two natural sciences sections and the Psychological, Social, and Biological Foundations of Behavior section of the exam are organized around foundational concepts, or "big ideas," in the sciences. They reflect current research about the most effective ways for students to learn and use science, emphasizing deep knowledge of the most important scientific concepts over shallow knowledge of many discrete scientific facts. The blueprints for the MCAT exam are based on the recommendations from this research. Leaders in science education say that some of the most important foundational concepts in the sciences ask students to bring together information from different disciplines and to combine their scientific knowledge with their inquiry and reasoning skills.

The natural, behavioral, and social sciences sections of the test are organized around three dimensions:

1) **Foundational Concepts**—the "big ideas" in the sciences that provide the foundation for learning in medical school,

2) **Content Categories**—the topics and subtopics needed to understand foundational concepts, and

3) **Scientific Inquiry and Reasoning Skills**—the inquiry and reasoning skills required to solve scientific problems.

Next, we'll take a closer look at each of these dimensions.

Foundational Concepts and Content Categories

Altogether, the two natural sciences sections of the MCAT exam and the Psychological, Social, and Biological Foundations of Behavior section test 10 foundational concepts. Each section focuses on different foundations:

- The Biological and Biochemical Foundations of Living Systems section is organized around Foundational Concepts 1–3,

- The Chemical and Physical Foundations of Biological Systems section is organized around Foundational Concepts 4–5, and

- The Psychological, Social, and Biological Foundations of Behavior section is organized around Foundational Concepts 6–10.

This section describes the foundational concepts and the content categories that support them. Further details about the foundational concepts, content categories, and skills, along with Sample Test questions, are provided in the chapter for each test section.

Biological and Biochemical Foundations of Living Systems (see Chapter 10)

Foundational Concept 1: *Biomolecules have unique properties that determine how they contribute to the structure and function of cells and how they participate in the processes necessary to maintain life.*

The content categories for this foundational concept include

1A. Structure and function of proteins and their constituent amino acids

1B. Transmission of genetic information from the gene to the protein

1C. Transmission of heritable information from generation to generation and the processes that increase genetic diversity

1D. Principles of bioenergetics and fuel molecule metabolism

Chapter 9

Conceptual Framework: How Does the MCAT Exam Test Competencies in the Natural, Behavioral, and Social Sciences?

Foundational Concept 2: *Highly-organized assemblies of molecules, cells, and organs interact to carry out the functions of living organisms.*

The content categories for this foundational concept include

2A. Assemblies of molecules, cells, and groups of cells within single cellular and multicellular organisms

2B. The structure, growth, physiology, and genetics of prokaryotes and viruses

2C. Processes of cell division, differentiation, and specialization

Foundational Concept 3: *Complex systems of tissues and organs sense the internal and external environments of multicellular organisms, and through integrated functioning, maintain a stable internal environment within an ever-changing external environment.*

The content categories for this foundational concept include

3A. Structure and functions of the nervous and endocrine systems and ways in which these systems coordinate the organ systems

3B. Structure and integrative functions of the main organ systems

Chemical and Physical Foundations of Biological Systems (see Chapter 11)

Foundational Concept 4: *Complex living organisms transport materials, sense their environment, process signals, and respond to changes using processes understood in terms of physical principles.*

The content categories for this foundational concept include

4A. Translational motion, forces, work, energy, and equilibrium in living systems

4B. Importance of fluids for the circulation of blood, gas movement, and gas exchange

4C. Electrochemistry and electrical circuits and their elements

4D. How light and sound interact with matter

4E. Atoms, nuclear decay, electronic structure, and atomic chemical behavior

Foundational Concept 5: *The principles that govern chemical interactions and reactions form the basis for a broader understanding of the molecular dynamics of living systems.*

The content categories for this foundational concept include

5A. Unique nature of water and its solutions

5B. Nature of molecules and intermolecular interactions

5C. Separation and purification methods

5D. Structure, function, and reactivity of biologically-relevant molecules

5E. Principles of chemical thermodynamics and kinetics

General Mathematical Concepts and Techniques

Before you look at the sample passages and questions in the following chapters (10–12), it's important for you to know that questions on the natural, behavioral, and social sciences sections will ask you to use certain mathematical concepts and techniques. As the descriptions of the scientific inquiry and reasoning skills suggest, some questions will ask you to analyze and manipulate scientific data to show that you can

- Recognize and interpret linear, semilog, and log-log scales and calculate slopes from data found in figures, graphs, and tables

- Demonstrate a general understanding of significant digits and the use of reasonable numerical estimates in performing measurements and calculations

- Use metric units, including converting units within the metric system and between metric and English units (conversion factors will be provided when needed), and dimensional analysis (using units to balance equations)

- Perform arithmetic calculations involving the following: probability, proportion, ratio, percentage, and square-root estimations

- Demonstrate a general understanding (Algebra II–level) of exponentials and logarithms (natural and base 10), scientific notation, and solving simultaneous equations

- Demonstrate a general understanding of the following trigonometric concepts: definitions of basic (sine, cosine, tangent) and inverse ($\sin^{-1}$, $\cos^{-1}$, $\tan^{-1}$) functions; sin and cos values of 0°, 90°, and 180°; relationships between the lengths of sides of right triangles containing angles of 30°, 45°, and 60°

- Demonstrate a general understanding of vector addition and subtraction and the right-hand rule (knowledge of dot and cross products is not required)

Note also that an understanding of calculus is *not* required, and a periodic table will be provided during the exam.

Chapter 9

Conceptual Framework: How Does the MCAT Exam Test Competencies in the Natural, Behavioral, and Social Sciences?

Psychological, Social, and Biological Foundations of Behavior (see Chapter 12)

Foundational Concept 6: *Biological, psychological, and sociocultural factors influence the ways that individuals perceive, think about, and react to the world.*

The content categories for this foundational concept include

6A. Sensing the environment

6B. Making sense of the environment

6C. Responding to the world

Foundational Concept 7: *Biological, psychological, and sociocultural factors influence behavior and behavior change.*

The content categories for this foundational concept include

7A. Individual influences on behavior

7B. Social processes that influence human behavior

7C. Attitude and behavior change

Foundational Concept 8: *Psychological, sociocultural, and biological factors influence the way we think about ourselves and others, as well as how we interact with others.*

The content categories for this foundational concept include

8A. Self-identity

8B. Social thinking

8C. Social interactions

Foundational Concept 9: *Cultural and social differences influence well-being.*

The content categories for this foundational concept include

9A. Understanding social structure

9B. Demographic characteristics and processes

Foundational Concept 10: *Social stratification and access to resources influence well-being.*

The content category for this foundational concept is

10A. Social inequality

Scientific Inquiry and Reasoning Skills

Leaders in medical education believe that tomorrow's physicians need to be able to combine scientific knowledge with skills in scientific inquiry and reasoning. With that in mind, the MCAT exam will ask you to demonstrate four scientific inquiry and reasoning skills that natural, behavioral, and social scientists rely on to advance their work:

Knowledge of Scientific Concepts and Principles

- Demonstrating understanding of scientific concepts and principles
- Identifying the relationships between closely-related concepts

Scientific Reasoning and Problem Solving

- Reasoning about scientific principles, theories, and models
- Analyzing and evaluating scientific explanations and predictions

Reasoning about the Design and Execution of Research

- Demonstrating understanding of important components of scientific research
- Reasoning about ethical issues in research

Data-Based and Statistical Reasoning

- Interpreting patterns in data presented in tables, figures, and graphs
- Reasoning about data and drawing conclusions from them

The discussion that follows describes each of the skills and how you may be asked to demonstrate them. Three Sample Test questions are provided to illustrate each skill: one from the Psychological, Social, and Biological Foundations of Behavior section; one from the Biological and Biochemical Foundations of Living Systems section; and one from the Chemical and Physical Foundations of Biological Systems section. Also included are explanations of how each question tests a specific scientific inquiry and reasoning skill.

SKILL 1: KNOWLEDGE OF SCIENTIFIC CONCEPTS AND PRINCIPLES

The questions in this skill category will ask you to demonstrate your knowledge of the 10 foundational concepts described earlier in this chapter. These questions will ask you to recognize, recall, or define basic concepts in the natural, behavioral, and social sciences, as well as their relationships with one another. The concepts and scientific principles may be represented by words, graphs, tables, diagrams, or formulas.

As you work on these questions, you may be asked to recognize a scientific fact or define a concept. Or you may be asked to apply a scientific principle to a problem. Questions may ask you to identify the relationships between closely-related concepts or relate verbal to graphic representations of science content. They may ask you to identify examples of observations that illustrate scientific principles. Questions may ask you to recognize a scientific concept shown in a diagram or represented in a graph. Or they may give you a mathematical equation and ask you to use it to solve a problem.

Chapter 9

Conceptual Framework: How Does the MCAT Exam Test Competencies in the Natural, Behavioral, and Social Sciences?

Questions that test this skill will ask you to show that you understand scientific concepts and principles by, for example,

- Recognizing correct scientific principles
- Identifying the relationships among closely-related concepts
- Identifying the relationships between different representations of concepts (e.g., verbal, symbolic, graphic)
- Identifying examples of observations that illustrate scientific principles
- Using mathematical equations to solve problems

By way of example, questions from the Psychological, Social, and Biological Foundations of Behavior section may ask you to demonstrate your knowledge of scientific concepts and principles by

- Recognizing the principle of retroactive interference
- Using Weber's Law to identify physical differences that are detectable
- Identifying the behavioral change (extinction) that will occur when a learned response is no longer followed by a reinforcer
- Identifying the relationship between operant conditioning and classical conditioning
- Identifying a graph that illustrates the relationship between educational attainment and life expectancy
- Recognizing conditions that result in learned helplessness
- Recognizing a demographic trend that is represented in a population pyramid

The three sample questions that follow illustrate Skill 1 questions from, respectively, the Psychological, Social, and Biological Foundations of Behavior section; the Biological and Biochemical Foundations of Living Systems section; and the Chemical and Physical Foundations of Biological System section of the MCAT exam.

SKILL 1 EXAMPLE FROM THE PSYCHOLOGICAL, SOCIAL, AND BIOLOGICAL FOUNDATIONS OF BEHAVIOR SECTION:

Which series correctly sequences the types of cells involved in the transmission of information from sound detection to the moment when an individual turns his or her head in response to the sound?

- A. Sensory neurons, interneurons, afferent neurons, skeletal muscle cells
- B. Sensory neurons, efferent neurons, interneurons, skeletal muscle cells
- C. Mechanoreceptors, sensory neurons, interneurons, motor neurons, skeletal muscle cells
- D. Mechanoreceptors, sensory neurons, interneurons, afferent neurons, skeletal muscle cells

The correct answer is C. This Skill 1 question tests your knowledge of the scientific concepts and principles described by Content Category 6A, *Sensing the environment*, and is a Skill 1 question because it requires you to relate scientific concepts. This question asks you to recognize and sequence the correct order of receptors and neurons involved in sensory processing and to conclude that C is the correct answer.

SKILL 1 EXAMPLE FROM THE BIOLOGICAL AND BIOCHEMICAL FOUNDATIONS OF LIVING SYSTEMS SECTION:

How are the basal layer of the epidermis and the innermost lining of the small intestine similar?

    A. Both are nondividing tissues.
    B. Both are derived from ectoderm.
    C. Both are composed of squamous cells.
    D. The cells of both are connected by tight junctions.

The correct answer is D. It is a Skill 1 question and assesses knowledge of Content Category 2A, *Assemblies of molecules, cells, and groups of cells within singular cellular and multicellular organisms.* It is a Skill 1 question because it requires you to recall the structural and embryological characteristics of two tissues and relate them to one another. To answer this question correctly, you must identify a similarity between the basal layer of the epidermis and the innermost lining of the small intestine.

SKILL 1 EXAMPLE FROM THE CHEMICAL AND PHYSICAL FOUNDATIONS OF BIOLOGICAL SYSTEMS SECTION:

In Michaelis-Menten enzyme kinetics, what is the velocity of the reaction when the substrate concentration is equal to K_M?

    A. $\frac{1}{4}V_{max}$
    B. $\frac{1}{2}V_{max}$
    C. V_{max}
    D. $2V_{max}$

The correct answer is B. This is a Skill 1 question and relates to Content Category 5E, *Principles of chemical thermodynamics and kinetics.* It is a Skill 1 question because you must recognize the relationship between two variables in the context of an experiment. To answer the question, you must recognize K_M, recall its significance in Michaelis-Menten enzyme kinetics, and relate it to another fundamental variable, V_{max}.

SKILL 2: SCIENTIFIC REASONING AND PROBLEM SOLVING

Questions that test scientific reasoning and problem-solving skills differ from questions in the previous category by asking you to use your scientific knowledge to solve problems in the natural, behavioral, and social sciences.

As you work on questions that test this skill, you may be asked to use scientific theories to explain observations or make predictions about natural or social phenomena. Questions may ask you to judge the credibility of scientific explanations or to evaluate arguments about cause and effect. Or they may ask you to use scientific models and observations to draw conclusions. They may ask you to recognize scientific findings that call a theory or model into question. Questions in this category may ask you to look at pictures or diagrams and draw conclusions from them. Or they may ask you to determine and then use scientific formulas to solve problems.

Chapter 9

Conceptual Framework: How Does the MCAT Exam Test Competencies in the Natural, Behavioral, and Social Sciences?

You will be asked to show that you can use scientific principles to solve problems by, for example,

- Reasoning about scientific principles, theories, and models
- Analyzing and evaluating scientific explanations and predictions
- Evaluating arguments about causes and consequences
- Bringing together theory, observations, and evidence to draw conclusions
- Recognizing scientific findings that challenge or invalidate a scientific theory or model
- Determining and using scientific formulas to solve problems

By way of illustration, questions from the Psychological, Social, and Biological Foundations of Behavior section may ask you demonstrate this skill by

- Using the main premises of symbolic interactionism to reason about an observational study of physician-patient interactions
- Predicting how an individual will react to cognitive dissonance
- Reasoning about whether a causal explanation is possible when given an example of how somebody's gender or personality predicts his or her behavior
- Concluding which stage of cognitive development a child is in, according to Piaget's theory, when presented with a description of how a child responds to a conservation problem
- Determining whether an example, such as when an anorexic teenager restricts eating to satisfy esteem needs, is compatible with the premises of Maslow's hierarchy of needs
- Drawing a conclusion about which sociological theory would be most consistent with a conceptual diagram that explains how social and environmental factors influence health
- Identifying the relationship between social institutions that is suggested by an illustration used in a public health campaign

For more context, let's consider three Skill 2 questions linked to different foundational concepts in the Psychological, Social, and Biological Foundations of Behavior section; the Biological and Biochemical Foundations of Living Systems section; and the Chemical and Physical Foundations of Biological Systems section.

SKILL 2 EXAMPLE FROM THE PSYCHOLOGICAL, SOCIAL, AND BIOLOGICAL FOUNDATIONS OF BEHAVIOR SECTION:

The concept of cultural capital predicts that:

    A. cultural distinctions associated with the young will be more valued within a society.
    B. with improved communication, there will eventually be a convergence of cultural practices of all classes.
    C. cultural distinctions by class will become less important during a recession because people will have less money to spend.
    D. cultural distinctions associated with elite classes will be more valued within a society.

The correct answer is D. It is a Skill 2 question and assesses knowledge of Content Category 10A, *Social inequality*. It is a Skill 2 question because it requires you to make a prediction based on a particular concept. This question requires you to understand the concept of cultural capital in order to evaluate which prediction about social stratification would be most consistent with the concept.

SKILL 2 EXAMPLE FROM THE BIOLOGICAL AND BIOCHEMICAL FOUNDATIONS OF LIVING SYSTEMS SECTION:

Starting with the translation initiation codon, the following sequence encodes a polypeptide of how many amino acids?

5'-CUGCCAAUGUGCUAAUCGCGGGGG-3'

   A. 2
   B. 3
   C. 6
   D. 8

The correct answer is A. This is a Skill 2 question, and you must use knowledge from Content Category 1B, *Transmission of genetic information from the gene to the protein*, to solve this problem. In addition to recalling the sequence for the start codon, this is a Skill 2 question because it requires you to apply the scientific principle of the genetic code to the provided RNA sequence. As a Skill 2 question, reasoning about the role of the stop codon in translation will allow you to arrive at the conclusion that this polypeptide has two amino acids.

SKILL 2 EXAMPLE FROM THE CHEMICAL AND PHYSICAL FOUNDATIONS OF BIOLOGICAL SYSTEMS SECTION:

The radius of the aorta is about 1.0 cm and blood passes through it at a velocity of 30 cm/s. A typical capillary has a radius of about 4×10^{-4} cm with blood passing through at a velocity of 5×10^{-2} cm/s. Using this data, what is the approximate number of capillaries in a human body?

   A. 1×10^4
   B. 2×10^7
   C. 4×10^9
   D. 7×10^{12}

The correct answer is C. This Skill 2 question relates to Content Category 4B, *Importance of fluids for the circulation of blood, gas movement, and gas exchange.* This question asks you to use a mathematical model to make predictions about natural phenomena. To answer this question, you must be able to recognize the principles of flow characteristics of blood in the human body and apply the appropriate mathematical model to an unfamiliar scenario. Answering this question first requires recognition that the volume of blood flowing through the aorta is the same volume of blood flowing through the capillaries. It is a Skill 2 question because you then need to use reasoning skills to find the difference in the volumes that the aorta and capillaries can each carry in order to calculate the total number of capillaries.

SKILL 3: REASONING ABOUT THE DESIGN AND EXECUTION OF RESEARCH

Questions that test reasoning about the design and execution of research will ask you to demonstrate your scientific inquiry skills by showing that you can "do" science. They will ask you to demonstrate your understanding of important components of scientific methodology. These questions will ask you to demonstrate your knowledge of the ways in which natural, behavioral, and social scientists conduct research to test and extend scientific knowledge.

As you work on these questions, you may be asked to show how scientists use theory, past research findings, and observations to ask testable questions and pose hypotheses. Questions that test this skill may ask you to reason about the ways in which scientists gather data from samples of members of the population about which they would like to draw inferences. They may ask you to identify how scientists manipulate and control variables to test their hypotheses. Questions may ask you to reason about the ways scientists take measurements and record results. These questions may ask you to recognize faulty research logic or point out the limitations of the research studies that are described. Or they may ask you to identify factors that might confuse the inferences you can draw from the results.

These questions may also ask you to demonstrate and use your understanding of the ways scientists adhere to ethical guidelines to protect the rights of research participants, the integrity of their work, and the interests of research consumers.

Questions that test this skill will ask you to use your knowledge of important components of scientific methodology by, for example,

- Identifying the role of theory, past findings, and observations in scientific questioning
- Identifying testable research questions and hypotheses
- Distinguishing between samples and populations and between results that do and do not support generalizations about populations
- Identifying the relationships among the variables in a study (e.g., independent versus dependent variables; control and confounding variables)
- Reasoning about the appropriateness, precision, and accuracy of tools used to conduct research in the natural sciences
- Reasoning about the appropriateness, reliability, and validity of tools used to conduct research in the behavioral and social sciences
- Reasoning about the features of research studies that suggest associations between variables or causal relationships between them (e.g., temporality, random assignment)
- Reasoning about ethical issues in scientific research

Questions from the Psychological, Social, and Biological Foundations of Behavior section may ask you to reason about the design and execution of research by, for example,

- Identifying the basic components of survey methods, ethnographic methods, experimental methods, or other types of research designs in psychology and sociology
- Selecting a hypothesis about semantic activation
- Identifying the extent to which a finding can be generalized to the population when given details about how participants were recruited for an experiment in language development
- Identifying the experimental setup in which researchers manipulate self-confidence
- Identifying the most appropriate way of assessing prejudice in a study on implicit bias
- Reasoning about the implications of relying on self-report measures for a specific study
- Identifying the third variable that may be confounding the findings from a correlational study
- Making judgments about the reliability and validity of specific measures when given information about the response patterns of participants
- Identifying whether researchers violated any ethical codes when given information about a study

The three sample questions that follow illustrate Skill 3 questions from, respectively, the Psychological, Social, and Biological Foundations of Behavior section; the Biological and Biochemical Foundations of Living Systems section; and the Chemical and Physical Foundations of Biological Systems section of the MCAT exam.

SKILL 3 EXAMPLE FROM THE PSYCHOLOGICAL, SOCIAL, AND BIOLOGICAL FOUNDATIONS OF BEHAVIOR SECTION:

Researchers conducted an experiment to test social loafing. They asked participants to prepare an annual report or a tax return. Some participants performed the task individually and others performed it as a group. What are the independent and dependent variables?

A. The independent variable is the overall productivity of the group, and the dependent variable is each participant's contribution to the task.
B. The independent variable is the type of task, and the dependent variable is whether the participants worked alone or in a group.
C. The independent variable is whether the participant worked alone or in a group, and the dependent variable is each participant's contribution to the task.
D. The independent variable is whether the participant worked alone or in a group, and the dependent variable is the type of the task.

The correct answer is C. This Skill 3 question assesses knowledge of Content Category 7B, *Social processes that influence human behavior*. This question is a Skill 3 question because it requires you to reason about research design. This question requires you to understand social loafing and draw inferences about the dependent and independent variables based on this concept and the description of the experimental design.

SKILL 3 EXAMPLE FROM THE BIOLOGICAL AND BIOCHEMICAL FOUNDATIONS OF LIVING SYSTEMS SECTION:

Sodium dodecyl sulfate (SDS) contains a 12-carbon tail attached to a sulfate group and is used in denaturing gel electrophoresis of proteins. Numerous SDS molecules will bind to the exposed hydrophobic regions of denatured proteins. The use of SDS in this experiment allows for the separation of proteins by:

A. charge.
B. molecular weight.
C. shape.
D. solubility.

The correct answer is B. This is a Skill 3 question and requires knowledge from Content Category 1A, *Structure and function of proteins and their constituent amino acids*. It is a Skill 3 question because it requires you to understand the design of a denaturing gel electrophoresis experiment and the role that SDS plays in this technique. Based on this understanding, you will be able to determine that proteins will be separated only by molecular weight.

SKILL 3 EXAMPLE FROM THE CHEMICAL AND PHYSICAL FOUNDATIONS OF BIOLOGICAL SYSTEMS SECTION:

A test for proteins in urine involves precipitation but is often complicated by precipitation of calcium phosphate. Which procedure prevents precipitation of the salt?

  A. Addition of buffer to maintain high pH
  B. Addition of buffer to maintain neutral pH
  C. Addition of calcium hydroxide
  D. Addition of sodium phosphate

The correct answer is B. This is a Skill 3 question and relates to Content Category 5B, *Nature of molecules and intermolecular interactions.* In this Skill 3 question, you must identify a change in an experimental approach that would eliminate a frequently encountered complication. The complication in this case is related to the test for protein-involving precipitation. The test will give a false positive if calcium phosphate precipitates. To answer this Skill 3 question, you need to reason about how changing experimental parameters will eliminate the complication.

SKILL 4: DATA-BASED AND STATISTICAL REASONING

Like questions about the third skill, questions that test the fourth skill will ask you to show that you can "do" science, this time by demonstrating your data-based and statistical reasoning skills. Questions that test this skill will ask you to reason with data. They will ask you to read and interpret results using tables, graphs, and charts. These questions will ask you to demonstrate that you can identify patterns in data and draw conclusions from evidence.

Questions that test this skill may ask you to demonstrate your knowledge of the ways natural, behavioral and social scientists use measures of central tendency and dispersion to describe their data. These questions may ask you to demonstrate your understanding of the ways scientists think about random and systematic errors in their experiments and datasets. They may also ask you to demonstrate your understanding of how scientists think about uncertainty and the implications of uncertainty for statistical testing and the inferences they can draw from their data. These questions may ask you to show how scientists use data to make comparisons between variables or explain relationships between them or make predictions. They may ask you to use data to answer research questions or draw conclusions.

These questions may ask you to demonstrate your knowledge of the ways scientists draw inferences from their results about associations between variables or causal relationships between them. Questions that test this skill may ask you to examine evidence from a scientific study and point out statements that go beyond the evidence. Or they may ask you to suggest alternative explanations for the same data.

Questions that test this skill will ask you to use your knowledge of data-based and statistical reasoning by, for example,

- Using, analyzing, and interpreting data in figures, graphs, and tables
- Evaluating whether representations make sense for particular scientific observations and data
- Using measures of central tendency (mean, median, and mode) and measures of dispersion (range, inter-quartile range, and standard deviation) to describe data
- Reasoning about random and systematic error
- Reasoning about statistical significance and uncertainty (e.g., interpreting statistical significance levels, interpreting a confidence interval)
- Using data to explain relationships between variables or make predictions
- Using data to answer research questions and draw conclusions
- Identifying conclusions that are supported by research results
- Determining the implications of results for real-world situations

Questions from the Psychological, Social, and Biological Foundations of Behavior section may ask you to demonstrate your use of data-based and statistical reasoning by, for example,

- Identifying the correlation between a demographic variable, such as race/ethnicity, gender, or age, with life expectancy or another health outcome
- Identifying the relationship between demographic variables and health variables reported in a table or figure
- Explaining why income data are usually reported using the median rather than the mean
- Reasoning about what inference is supported by a table of correlations between different socioeconomic variables and level of participation in different physical activities
- Reasoning about the type of comparisons made in an experimental study of cognitive dissonance and what the findings imply for attitude and behavior change
- Drawing conclusions about the type of memory affected by an experimental manipulation when you are shown a graph of findings from a memory experiment
- Distinguishing the kinds of claims that can be made when using longitudinal data, cross-sectional data, or experimental data in studies of social interaction
- Identifying which conclusion about mathematical understanding in young children is supported by time data reported in a developmental study
- Evaluating data collected from different types of research studies, such as comparing results from a qualitative study of mechanisms for coping with stress with results from a quantitative study of social support networks
- Using data, such as interviews with cancer patients or a national survey of health behaviors, to determine a practical application based on a study's results

The three questions that follow illustrate Skill 4 questions from, respectively, the Psychological, Social, and Biological Foundations of Behavior section; the Biological and Biochemical Foundations of Living Systems section; and the Chemical and Physical Foundations of Biological Systems section of the MCAT exam.

Chapter 9

Conceptual Framework: How Does the MCAT Exam Test Competencies in the Natural, Behavioral, and Social Sciences?

SKILL 4 EXAMPLE FROM THE PSYCHOLOGICAL, SOCIAL, AND BIOLOGICAL FOUNDATIONS OF BEHAVIOR SECTION:

Which correlation supports the bystander effect?

- A. The number of bystanders is positively correlated with the time it takes for someone to offer help in the case of an emergency.
- B. The number of bystanders is negatively correlated with the time it takes for someone to offer help in the case of an emergency.
- C. The number of bystanders is positively correlated with whether people judge a situation to be an emergency.
- D. The number of bystanders is negatively correlated with whether people judge a situation to be an emergency.

The correct answer is A. This Skill 4 question assesses knowledge of Content Category 7B, *Social processes that influence human behavior*. It is a Skill 4 question because it requires you to engage in statistical reasoning. This question requires you to understand the distinction between negative and positive correlations and make a prediction about data based on your knowledge of the bystander effect.

SKILL 4 EXAMPLE FROM THE BIOLOGICAL AND BIOCHEMICAL FOUNDATIONS OF LIVING SYSTEMS SECTION:

In the figure, the three curves represent hemoglobin oxygen binding at three different pH values, pH 7.2, pH 7.4, and pH 7.6.

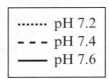

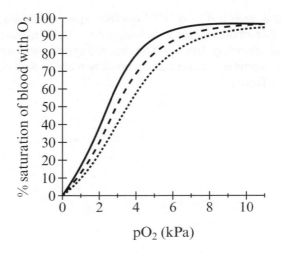

What conclusion can be drawn from these data about the oxygen binding of hemoglobin at different pH values?

    A. Low pH favors the high affinity oxygen binding state.
    B. Low pH favors the low affinity oxygen binding state.
    C. Oxygen affinity is independent of pH.
    D. Oxygen binding is non-cooperative at low pH.

The correct answer is B. This Skill 4 question draws on knowledge from Content Category 1A, *Structure and function of proteins and their constituent amino acids*. This is a Skill 4 question because it asks you to use data to explain a property of hemoglobin. You must evaluate the hemoglobin oxygen binding data for each pH value and compare them to determine the relationship between pH and hemoglobin oxygen affinity in order to conclude that low pH favors the low affinity oxygen binding state.

Fifth Edition
The Official Guide to the MCAT® Exam
88
MCAT® is a program of the
Association of American Medical Colleges

SKILL 4 EXAMPLE FROM THE CHEMICAL AND PHYSICAL FOUNDATIONS OF BIOLOGICAL SYSTEMS SECTION:

Four different solutions of a single amino acid were titrated, and the pK values of the solute were determined.

Solution	pK₁	pK₂	pK₃
1	2.10	3.86	9.82
2	2.10	4.07	9.47
3	2.32	9.76	Not Applicable
4	2.18	9.04	12.48

Which solution contains an amino acid that would be most likely to stabilize an anionic substrate in an enzyme pocket at physiological pH?

  A. Solution 1
  B. Solution 2
  C. Solution 3
  D. Solution 4

The correct answer is D. This Skill 4 question includes a table and assesses knowledge of Content Category 5D, *Structure, function, and reactivity of biologically-relevant molecules*. Here you see that four different solutions of a single amino acid were titrated, and the pK values were determined. These values are found in the table. This is a Skill 4 question because you must recognize a data pattern in the table, make comparisons, and use those comparisons to make a prediction. Using knowledge of amino acids and peptide bonds and the patterns you see in the data, you can determine that the *N*- and *C*-terminus pK values, roughly 2 and 9 for all solutions, can be ignored since these groups will be involved in peptide bond formation. With further analyses, you can determine that only Solution 4 will be cationic at physiological pH.

How the Content Categories and Skills Fit Together

The MCAT exam asks you to solve problems by combining your knowledge of concepts with your scientific inquiry and reasoning skills. Figure 1 illustrates how foundational concepts, content categories, and scientific inquiry and reasoning skills intersect to create test questions.

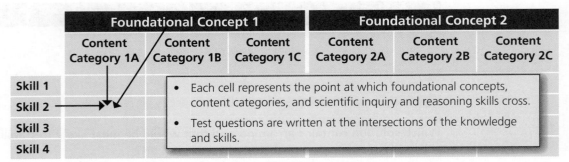

	Foundational Concept 1			Foundational Concept 2		
	Content Category 1A	Content Category 1B	Content Category 1C	Content Category 2A	Content Category 2B	Content Category 2C
Skill 1						
Skill 2						
Skill 3						
Skill 4						

- Each cell represents the point at which foundational concepts, content categories, and scientific inquiry and reasoning skills cross.
- Test questions are written at the intersections of the knowledge and skills.

Figure 1 How MCAT Questions Intersect Foundational Concepts, Content, and Skills

We're going to use an example from the Biological and Biochemical Foundations of Living Systems section to illustrate how this works. In the following example, you are asked to solve a scientific problem by combining your knowledge of the digestive system with your data-based and statistical reasoning skills. It combines

- **Foundational Concept 3:** Complex systems of tissues and organs sense the internal and external environments of multicellular organisms, and through integrated functioning, maintain a stable internal environment within an ever-changing external environment.

- **Content Category 3B:** Structure and integrative functions of the main organ systems (See Chapter 10 for a complete list of topics and subtopics.)

- **Scientific Inquiry and Reasoning Skill 4:** Data-based and statistical reasoning skills

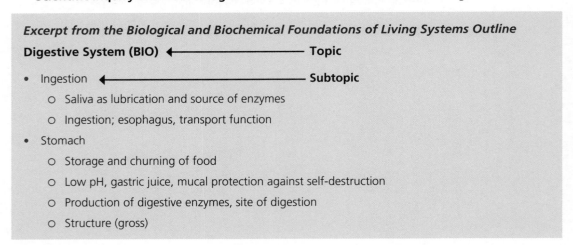

Excerpt from the Biological and Biochemical Foundations of Living Systems Outline

Digestive System (BIO) ◄——————————— **Topic**

- Ingestion ◄——————————— **Subtopic**
  - ○ Saliva as lubrication and source of enzymes
  - ○ Ingestion; esophagus, transport function
- Stomach
  - ○ Storage and churning of food
  - ○ Low pH, gastric juice, mucal protection against self-destruction
  - ○ Production of digestive enzymes, site of digestion
  - ○ Structure (gross)

The abbreviation in parentheses indicates the course in which undergraduate students at many colleges and universities learn about the topics and associated subtopics. The course abbreviation in this example is BIO, for two-semester sequence of introductory biology.

Chapter 9

Conceptual Framework: How Does the MCAT Exam Test Competencies in the Natural, Behavioral, and Social Sciences?

Sample Passage

In many animals, including mice and humans, the liver quickly regenerates to its original size after a partial hepatectomy in which two-thirds of the organ is removed. Hepatocyte proliferation in response to this surgery is significantly reduced in mice with inadequate platelet activity or number.

Platelets carry 95 percent of blood serotonin, which is synthesized from tryptophan and secreted by endocrine cells in the lining of the gastrointestinal tract. Researchers experimentally tested the hypothesis that platelet serotonin is responsible for the platelets' positive effect on hepatocyte proliferation. The number of hepatocytes expressing the Ki67 protein, which is detected exclusively in the nuclei of proliferating cells, was used as a measure of liver regeneration.

Experiment 1

Wild-type mice were treated with an anti-platelet antibody that destroys 90 percent of their circulating platelets; a subset of these mice was also injected with a serotonin agonist, which mimics serotonin's actions on its receptors (Figure 1).

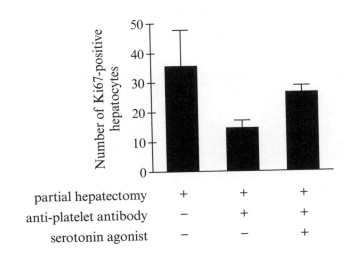

partial hepatectomy	+	+	+
anti-platelet antibody	−	+	+
serotonin agonist	−	−	+

Figure 1 Effects of platelet depletion and serotonin agonist on hepatocyte proliferation

Experiment 2

Wild-type mice were treated with antagonists of the serotonin receptors 5-HT2A and 5-HT2B, receptors that are expressed on hepatocytes and other cell types (Figure 2).

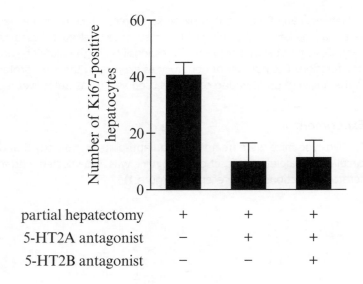

partial hepatectomy	+	+	+
5-HT2A antagonist	−	+	+
5-HT2B antagonist	−	−	+

Figure 2 Effects of serotonin receptor antagonists on hepatocyte proliferation

Experiment 3

This experiment used *TPH1*⁻/⁻ mice, which lack the gastrointestinal cell enzyme TPH1 necessary to make circulating serotonin; some of the *TPH1*⁻/⁻ mice were injected with a serotonin biosynthetic precursor that could be converted into serotonin and then imported into platelets (Figure 3).

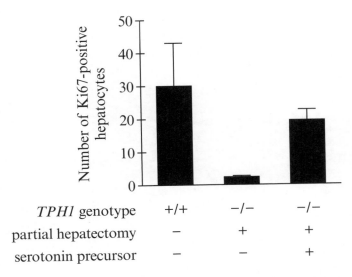

TPH1 genotype	+/+	−/−	−/−
partial hepatectomy	−	+	+
serotonin precursor	−	−	+

Figure 3 Effects of *TPH1*⁻/⁻ genotype and serotonin precursor on hepatocyte proliferation

Source: Adapted from a paper by M. Lesurtel et al. Copyright 2006 by the American Association for the Advancement of Science.

Sample Question

Which finding, when combined with the data in the passage, is most likely to lead researchers to conclude that the 5-HT2A and 5-HT2B receptor subtypes mediate serotonin-dependent liver regeneration?

   A. Administration of 5-HT2A receptor agonist resulted in reduced Ki67 staining.
   B. RNA for seven different receptor subtypes was detectible in naïve liver tissue.
   C. Up-regulation of 5-HT2A and 5-HT2B was observed during periods of peak hepatocyte proliferation.
   D. Administration of 5-HT2C and 5-HT3 receptor antagonists reduced the number of Ki67-positive cells.

The answer to this question is C. On the actual exam, a passage of text plus questions (i.e., a *passage set*) includes at least four questions. Refer to Chapter 10 for additional sample questions for this passage. You will also find in Chapter 10 additional passages and questions for the Biological and Biochemical Foundations of Living Systems section.

Chapter 10

What Will the Biological and Biochemical Foundations of Living Systems Section Test?

The Biological and Biochemical Foundations of Living Systems section asks you to solve problems by combining your knowledge of biological and biochemical concepts with your scientific inquiry and reasoning skills. This section tests processes that are unique to living organisms, such as growing and reproducing, maintaining a constant internal environment, acquiring materials and energy, sensing and responding to environmental changes, and adapting. It also tests how cells and organ systems within an organism act independently and in concert to accomplish these processes, and it asks you to reason about these processes at various levels of biological organization within a living system.

To recap from Part I, this section is designed to

- test introductory-level biology, organic chemistry, and inorganic chemistry concepts;

- test biochemistry concepts at the level taught in many colleges and universities in first-semester biochemistry courses;

- test cellular and molecular biology topics at the level taught in many colleges and universities in introductory biology sequences and first-semester biochemistry courses;

- test basic research methods and statistics concepts described by many baccalaureate faculty as important to success in introductory science courses; and

- require you to demonstrate your scientific inquiry and reasoning, research methods, and statistics skills as applied to the natural sciences.

Test Section	Number of Questions	Time
Biological and Biochemical Foundations of Living Systems	59 *(note that questions are a combination of passage-based and discrete questions)*	95 minutes

MCAT® is a program of the
Association of American Medical Colleges

Biological and Biochemical Foundations of Living Systems Distribution of Questions

Distribution of Questions by Discipline, Foundational Concept, and Scientific Inquiry and Reasoning Skill

You may wonder how much biochemistry you'll see on this section of the MCAT exam, how many questions you'll get about a particular foundational concept, or how the scientific inquiry and reasoning skills will be distributed on your exam. The questions that you see are likely to be distributed in the ways described below. These are the approximate percentages of questions you'll see on a test for each discipline, foundational concept, and scientific inquiry and reasoning skill.*

Discipline:
- First-semester biochemistry, 25%
- Introductory biology, 65%
- General chemistry, 5%
- Organic chemistry, 5%

Foundational Concept:
- Foundational Concept 1, 55%
- Foundational Concept 2, 20%
- Foundational Concept 3, 25%

Scientific Inquiry and Reasoning Skill:
- Skill 1, 35%
- Skill 2, 45%
- Skill 3, 10%
- Skill 4, 10%

---

*These percentages have been approximated to the nearest 5% and will vary from one test to another for a variety of reasons. These reasons include, but are not limited to, controlling for question difficulty, using groups of questions that depend on a single passage, and using unscored field-test questions on each test form.

Understanding the Foundational Concepts and Content Categories

The following are detailed explanations of each foundational concept and related content categories tested in the Biological and Biochemical Foundations of Living Systems section. To help you prepare for the MCAT exam, we provide content lists that describe specific topics and subtopics that define each content category for this section. The same content lists are provided to the writers who develop the content of the exam. An excerpt from the content list is at the top of the next page.

Excerpt from Biological and Biochemical Foundations of Living Systems Outline

Metabolism of Fatty Acids and Proteins (BIO, BC) ◀——— Topic

- Description of fatty acids (BC) ◀——————— **Subtopic**
- Digestion, mobilization, and transport of fats
- Oxidation of fatty acids
  - ○ Saturated fats
  - ○ Unsaturated fats
- Ketone bodies (BC)
- Anabolism of fats (BIO)
- Non-template synthesis: biosynthesis of lipids and polysaccharides (BIO)
- Metabolism of proteins (BIO)

The abbreviations in parentheses indicate the courses in which undergraduate students at many colleges and universities learn about the topics and associated subtopics. The course abbreviations are

- BC: first-semester biochemistry
- BIO: two-semester sequence of introductory biology
- GC: two-semester sequence of general chemistry
- OC: two-semester sequence of organic chemistry

In preparing for the MCAT exam, you will be responsible for learning the topics and associated subtopics at the levels at which they are taught at many colleges and universities in the courses listed in parentheses. A small number of subtopics have course abbreviations indicated in parentheses. In those cases, you are responsible *only* for learning the subtopics as they are taught in the course(s) indicated.

Using the excerpt above as an example,

- You are responsible for learning about the topic Metabolism of Fatty Acids and Proteins at the level at which it is taught in a typical two-semester introductory biology sequence *and* in a typical first-semester biochemistry course.

- You are responsible for learning about the subtopics Anabolism of fats, Non-template synthesis: biosynthesis of lipids and polysaccharides, and Metabolism of proteins *only* at the levels at which they are taught in a typical two-semester sequence of introductory biology.

- You are responsible for learning about the subtopics Description of fatty acids and Ketone bodies *only* at the levels at which they are taught in a typical first-semester biochemistry course.

Remember that course content at your school may differ from course content at other colleges and universities. The topics and subtopics described in this and the next two chapters may be covered in courses with titles that are different from those listed here. Your prehealth advisor and faculty are important resources for your questions about course content.

Biological and Biochemical Foundations of Living Systems

Foundational Concept 1

Biomolecules have unique properties that determine how they contribute to the structure and function of cells, and how they participate in the processes necessary to maintain life.

The unique chemical and structural properties of biomolecules determine the roles they play in cells. The proper functioning of a living system depends on the many components acting harmoniously in response to a constantly changing environment. Biomolecules are constantly formed or degraded in response to the perceived needs of the organism.

Content Categories

- *Category 1A* focuses on the structural and functional complexity of proteins, which is derived from their component amino acids, the sequence in which the amino acids are covalently bonded, and the three-dimensional structures the proteins adopt in an aqueous environment.

- *Category 1B* focuses on the molecular mechanisms responsible for the transfer of sequence-specific biological information between biopolymers which ultimately results in the synthesis of proteins.

- *Category 1C* focuses on the mechanisms that function to transmit the heritable information stored in DNA from generation to generation.

- *Category 1D* focuses on the biomolecules and regulated pathways involved in harvesting chemical energy stored in fuel molecules, which serves as the driving force for all the processes that take place within a living system.

With these building blocks, medical students will be able to learn how the major biochemical, genetic, and molecular functions of the cell support health and lead to disease.

Content Category 1A: **Structure and function of proteins and their constituent amino acids**

Macromolecules formed from amino acids adopt well-defined, three-dimensional structures with chemical properties that are responsible for their participation in virtually every process occurring within and between cells. The three-dimensional structure of proteins is a direct consequence of the nature of the covalently-bonded sequence of amino acids, their chemical and physical properties, and the way in which the whole assembly interacts with water.

Enzymes are proteins that interact in highly regio- and stereo-specific ways with dissolved solutes. They either facilitate the chemical transformation of these solutes, or allow for their transport innocuously. Dissolved solutes compete for protein-binding sites, and protein conformational dynamics give rise to mechanisms capable of controlling enzymatic activity.

The infinite variability of potential amino acid sequences allows for adaptable responses to pathogenic organisms and materials. The rigidity of some amino acid sequences makes them suitable for structural roles in complex living systems.

Content in this category covers a range of protein behaviors which originate from the unique chemistry of amino acids themselves. Amino acid classifications and protein structural elements are covered. Special emphasis is placed on enzyme catalysis, including mechanistic considerations, kinetics, models of enzyme-substrate interaction, and regulation. The topics and subtopics in this category are the following:

Please Note

Topics that appear on multiple content lists will be treated differently. Questions will focus on the topics as they are described in the narrative for the content category.

Amino Acids (BC, OC)
- Description
  - Absolute configuration at the α position
  - Amino acids as dipolar ions
  - Classifications
    - Acidic or basic
    - Hydrophobic or hydrophilic
- Reactions
  - Sulfur linkage between a pair of cysteines
  - Peptide linkage: polypeptides and proteins
  - Hydrolysis

Protein Structure (BIO, BC, OC)
- Structure
  - 1° structure of proteins
  - 2° structure of proteins
  - 3° structure of proteins; role of proline, cystine, hydrophobic bonding
  - 4° structure of proteins (BIO, BC)

MCAT® is a program of the
Association of American Medical Colleges

- Conformational stability
  - ○ Denaturing and folding
  - ○ Hydrophobic interactions
  - ○ Solvation layer (entropy) (BC)
- Separation techniques
  - ○ Isoelectric point
  - ○ Electrophoresis

Non-Enzymatic Protein Function (BIO, BC)

- Binding (BC)
- Immune system
- Motors

Enzyme Structure and Function (BIO, BC)

- Function of enzymes in catalyzing biological reactions
- Enzyme classification by reaction type
- Reduction of activation energy
- Substrates and enzyme specificity
- Active Site Model
- Induced-fit Model
- Mechanism of catalysis
  - ○ Cofactors
  - ○ Coenzymes
  - ○ Water-soluble vitamins
- Effects of local conditions on enzyme activity

Control of Enzyme Activity (BIO, BC)

- Kinetics
  - ○ General (catalysis)
  - ○ Michaelis–Menten
  - ○ Cooperativity
- Feedback regulation
- Inhibition—types
  - ○ Competitive
  - ○ Non-competitive
  - ○ Mixed (BC)
  - ○ Uncompetitive (BC)
- Regulatory enzymes
  - ○ Allosteric enzymes
  - ○ Covalently-modified enzymes
  - ○ Zymogen

Fifth Edition
The Official Guide to the MCAT® Exam
100
MCAT® is a program of the
Association of American Medical Colleges

Content Category 1B: Transmission of genetic information from the gene to the protein

Biomolecules and biomolecular assemblies interact in specific, highly-regulated ways to transfer sequence information between biopolymers in living organisms. By storing and transferring biological information, DNA and RNA enable living organisms to reproduce their complex components from one generation to the next. The nucleotide monomers of these biopolymers, being joined by phosphodiester linkages, form a polynucleotide molecule with a "backbone" composed of repeating sugar-phosphate units and "appendages" of nitrogenous bases. The unique sequence of bases in each gene provides specific information to the cell.

DNA molecules are composed of two polynucleotides that spiral around an imaginary axis, forming a double helix. The two polynucleotides are held together by hydrogen bonds between the paired bases and van der Waals interactions between the stacked bases. The pairing between the bases of two polynucleotides is very specific, and its complementarity allows for a precise replication of the DNA molecule.

The DNA inherited by an organism leads to specific traits by dictating the synthesis of the biomolecules (RNA molecules and proteins) involved in protein synthesis. While every cell in a multicellular organism inherits the same DNA, its expression is precisely regulated such that different genes are expressed by cells at different stages of development, by cells in different tissues, and by cells exposed to different stimuli.

The topics included in this category concern not only the molecular mechanisms of the transmission of genetic information from the gene to the protein (*transcription* and *translation*), but also the biosynthesis of the important molecules and molecular assemblies that are involved in these mechanisms. The control of gene expression in prokaryotes and eukaryotes is also included.

Broadly speaking, the field of biotechnology uses biological systems, living organisms, or derivatives thereof, to make or modify products or processes for specific use. The biotechnological techniques emphasized in this category, however, are those that take advantage of the complementary structure of double-stranded DNA molecules to synthesize, sequence, and amplify them, and to analyze and identify unknown polynucleotide sequences. Included within this treatment of biotechnology are those practical applications which directly impact humans, such as medical applications, human gene therapy, and pharmaceuticals.

Content in this category covers the biopolymers, including ribonucleic acid (RNA), deoxyribonucleic acid (DNA), proteins, and the biochemical processes involved in carrying out the transfer of biological information from DNA. The topics and subtopics in this category are the following:

Nucleic Acid Structure and Function (BIO, BC)
- Description
- Nucleotides and nucleosides
    - Sugar phosphate backbone
    - Pyrimidine, purine residues
- Deoxyribonucleic acid (DNA): double helix, Watson–Crick model of DNA structure
- Base pairing specificity: A with T, G with C
- Function in transmission of genetic information (BIO)
- DNA denaturation, reannealing, hybridization

DNA Replication (BIO)
- Mechanism of replication: separation of strands, specific coupling of free nucleic acids
- Semi-conservative nature of replication
- Specific enzymes involved in replication
- Origins of replication, multiple origins in eukaryotes
- Replicating the ends of DNA molecules

Repair of DNA (BIO)
- Repair during replication
- Repair of mutations

Genetic Code (BIO)
- Central Dogma: DNA → RNA → protein
- The triplet code
- Codon–anticodon relationship
- Degenerate code, wobble pairing
- Missense, nonsense codons
- Initiation, termination codons
- Messenger RNA (mRNA)

Transcription (BIO)
- Transfer RNA (tRNA); ribosomal RNA (rRNA)
- Mechanism of transcription
- mRNA processing in eukaryotes, introns, exons
- Ribozymes, spliceosomes, small nuclear ribonucleoproteins (snRNPs), small nuclear RNAs (snRNAs)
- Functional and evolutionary importance of introns

Translation (BIO)
- Roles of mRNA, tRNA, rRNA
- Role and structure of ribosomes
- Initiation, termination co-factors
- Post-translational modification of proteins

Eukaryotic Chromosome Organization (BIO)
- Chromosomal proteins
- Single copy vs. repetitive DNA
- Supercoiling
- Heterochromatin vs. euchromatin
- Telomeres, centromeres

Control of Gene Expression in Prokaryotes (BIO)
- Operon Concept, Jacob–Monod Model
- Gene repression in bacteria
- Positive control in bacteria

Control of Gene Expression in Eukaryotes (BIO)

- Transcriptional regulation
- DNA binding proteins, transcription factors
- Gene amplification and duplication
- Post-transcriptional control, basic concept of splicing (introns, exons)
- Cancer as a failure of normal cellular controls, oncogenes, tumor suppressor genes
- Regulation of chromatin structure
- DNA methylation
- Role of non-coding RNAs

Recombinant DNA and Biotechnology (BIO)

- Gene cloning
- Restriction enzymes
- DNA libraries
- Generation of cDNA
- Hybridization
- Expressing cloned genes
- Polymerase chain reaction
- Gel electrophoresis and Southern blotting
- DNA sequencing
- Analyzing gene expression
- Determining gene function
- Stem cells
- Practical applications of DNA technology: medical applications, human gene therapy, pharmaceuticals, forensic evidence, environmental cleanup, agriculture
- Safety and ethics of DNA technology

Content Category 1C: *Transmission of heritable information from generation to generation and the processes that increase genetic diversity*

The information necessary to direct life functions is contained within discrete nucleotide sequences transmitted from generation to generation by mechanisms that, by nature of their various processes, provide the raw materials for evolution by increasing genetic diversity. Specific sequences of deoxyribonucleic acids store and transfer the heritable information necessary for the continuation of life from one generation to the next. These sequences, called *genes*—being part of longer DNA molecules—are organized, along with various proteins, into biomolecular assemblies called *chromosomes*.

Chromosomes pass from parents to offspring in sexually-reproducing organisms. The processes of *meiosis* and *fertilization* maintain a species' chromosome count during the sexual life cycle. Because parents pass on discrete heritable units that retain their separate identities in offspring, the laws of probability can be used to predict the outcome of some, but not all, genetic crosses.

The behavior of chromosomes during meiosis and fertilization is responsible for most of the genetic variation that arises each generation. Mechanisms that contribute to this genetic variation include independent assortment of chromosomes, crossing over, and random fertilization. Other mechanisms, such as mutation, random genetic drift, bottlenecks, and immigration, exist with the potential to affect the genetic diversity of individuals and populations. Collectively, the genetic diversity that results from these processes provides the raw material for evolution by natural selection.

The content in this category covers the mechanisms by which heritable information is transmitted from generation to generation, and the evolutionary processes that generate and act upon genetic variation.

The topics and subtopics in this category are the following:

Evidence That DNA Is Genetic Material (BIO)

Mendelian Concepts (BIO)
- Phenotype and genotype
- Gene
- Locus
- Allele: single and multiple
- Homozygosity and heterozygosity
- Wild-type
- Recessiveness
- Complete dominance
- Co-dominance
- Incomplete dominance, leakage, penetrance, expressivity
- Hybridization: viability
- Gene pool

Meiosis and Other Factors Affecting Genetic Variability (BIO)
- Significance of meiosis
- Important differences between meiosis and mitosis
- Segregation of genes
  - Independent assortment
  - Linkage
  - Recombination
    - Single crossovers
    - Double crossovers
    - Synaptonemal complex
    - Tetrad
  - Sex-linked characteristics
  - Very few genes on Y chromosome
  - Sex determination
  - Cytoplasmic/extranuclear inheritance
- Mutation
  - General concept of mutation—error in DNA sequence
  - Types of mutations: random, translation error, transcription error, base substitution, inversion, addition, deletion, translocation, mispairing
  - Advantageous vs. deleterious mutation
  - Inborn errors of metabolism
  - Relationship of mutagens to carcinogens
- Genetic drift
- Synapsis or crossing-over mechanism for increasing genetic diversity

Analytic Methods (BIO)
- Hardy–Weinberg Principle
- Testcross (Backcross; concepts of parental, F1, and F2 generations)
- Gene mapping: crossover frequencies
- Biometry: statistical methods

Evolution (BIO)
- Natural selection
  - Fitness concept
  - Selection by differential reproduction
  - Concepts of natural and group selection
  - Evolutionary success as increase in percent representation in the gene pool of the next generation
- Speciation
  - Polymorphism
  - Adaptation and specialization
  - Inbreeding
  - Outbreeding
  - Bottlenecks
- Evolutionary time as measured by gradual random changes in genome

Fifth Edition
The Official Guide to the MCAT® Exam
105
MCAT® is a program of the
Association of American Medical Colleges

Content Category 1D: Principles of bioenergetics and fuel molecule metabolism

Living things harness energy from fuel molecules in a controlled manner in order to sustain all the processes responsible for maintaining life. Cell maintenance and growth is energetically costly. Cells harness the energy stored in fuel molecules, such as carbohydrates and fatty acids, and convert it into smaller units of chemical potential known as *adenosine triphosphate* (ATP).

The hydrolysis of ATP provides a ready source of energy for cells that can be coupled to other chemical processes in order to make them thermodynamically favorable. Fuel molecule mobilization, transport, and storage are regulated according to the needs of the organism.

The content in this category covers the principles of bioenergetics and fuel molecule catabolism. Details of oxidative phosphorylation including the role of chemiosmotic coupling and biological electron transfer reactions are covered, as are the general features of fatty acid and glucose metabolism. Additionally, regulation of these metabolic pathways, fuel molecule mobilization, transport, and storage are covered. The topics and subtopics in this category are the following:

Principles of Bioenergetics (BC, GC)
- Bioenergetics/thermodynamics
  - Free energy/K_{eq}
    - Equilibrium constant
    - Relationship of the equilibrium constant and $\Delta G°$
  - Concentration
    - Le Châtelier's Principle
  - Endothermic/exothermic reactions
  - Free energy: G
  - Spontaneous reactions and $\Delta G°$
- Phosphoryl group transfers and ATP
  - ATP hydrolysis $\Delta G << 0$
  - ATP group transfers
- Biological oxidation-reduction
  - Half-reactions
  - Soluble electron carriers
  - Flavoproteins

Carbohydrates (BC, OC)
- Description
  - Nomenclature and classification, common names
  - Absolute configuration
  - Cyclic structure and conformations of hexoses
  - Epimers and anomers
- Hydrolysis of the glycoside linkage
- Monosaccharides
- Disaccharides
- Polysaccharides

Glycolysis, Gluconeogenesis, and the Pentose Phosphate Pathway (BIO, BC)

- Glycolysis (aerobic), substrates and products
    - Feeder pathways: glycogen, starch metabolism
- Fermentation (anaerobic glycolysis)
- Gluconeogenesis (BC)
- Pentose phosphate pathway (BC)
- Net (maximum) molecular and energetic results of respiration processes

Principles of Metabolic Regulation (BC)

- Regulation of metabolic pathways (BIO, BC)
    - Maintenance of a dynamic steady state
- Regulation of glycolysis and gluconeogenesis
- Metabolism of glycogen
- Regulation of glycogen synthesis and breakdown
    - Allosteric and hormonal control
- Analysis of metabolic control

Citric Acid Cycle (BIO, BC)

- Acetyl-CoA production (BC)
- Reactions of the cycle, substrates and products
- Regulation of the cycle
- Net (maximum) molecular and energetic results of respiration processes

Metabolism of Fatty Acids and Proteins (BIO, BC)

- Description of fatty acids (BC)
- Digestion, mobilization, and transport of fats
- Oxidation of fatty acids
    - Saturated fats
    - Unsaturated fats
- Ketone bodies (BC)
- Anabolism of fats (BIO)
- Non-template synthesis: biosynthesis of lipids and polysaccharides (BIO)
- Metabolism of proteins (BIO)

Oxidative Phosphorylation (BIO, BC)

- Electron transport chain and oxidative phosphorylation, substrates and products, general features of the pathway
- Electron transfer in mitochondria
    - NADH, NADPH
    - Flavoproteins
    - Cytochromes
- ATP synthase, chemiosmotic coupling
    - Proton motive force
- Net (maximum) molecular and energetic results of respiration processes
- Regulation of oxidative phosphorylation
- Mitochondria, apoptosis, oxidative stress (BC)

Hormonal Regulation and Integration of Metabolism (BC)

- Higher level integration of hormone structure and function
- Tissue specific metabolism
- Hormonal regulation of fuel metabolism
- Obesity and regulation of body mass

Fifth Edition
The Official Guide to the MCAT® Exam
107
MCAT® is a program of the
Association of American Medical Colleges

Biological and Biochemical Foundations of Living Systems

Foundational Concept 2

Highly-organized assemblies of molecules, cells, and organs interact
to carry out the functions of living organisms.

Cells are the basic unit of structure in all living things. Mechanisms of cell division provide not only for the growth and maintenance of organisms, but also for the continuation of the species through asexual and sexual reproduction. The unique micro-environment to which a cell is exposed during development and division determines the fate of the cell by impacting gene expression and ultimately the cell's collection and distribution of macromolecules, and its arrangement of subcellular organelles.

In multicellular organisms, the processes necessary to maintain life are executed by groups of cells that are organized into specialized structures with specialized functions—both of which result from the unique properties of the cells' component molecules.

Content Categories

- *Category 2A* focuses on the assemblies of molecules, cells, and groups of cells within single cellular and multicellular organisms that function to execute the processes necessary to maintain life.

- *Category 2B* focuses on the structure, growth, physiology, and genetics of prokaryotes, and the structure and life cycles of viruses.

- *Category 2C* focuses on the processes of cell and nuclear division, and the mechanisms governing cell differentiation and specialization.

With these building blocks, medical students will be able to learn how cells grow and integrate to form tissues and organs that carry out essential biochemical and physiological functions.

Category 2A: *Assemblies of molecules, cells, and groups of cells within single cellular and multicellular organisms*

The processes necessary to maintain life are executed by assemblies of molecules, cells, and groups of cells, all of which are organized into highly-specific structures as determined by the unique properties of their component molecules. The processes necessary to maintain life require that cells create and maintain internal environments within the cytoplasm and within certain organelles that are different from their external environments.

Cell membranes separate the internal environment of the cell from the external environment. The specialized structure of the membrane, as described in the fluid mosaic model, allows the cell to be selectively permeable and dynamic, with homeostasis maintained by the constant movement of molecules across the membranes through a combination of active and passive processes driven by several forces, including electrochemical gradients.

Eukaryotic cells also maintain internal membranes that partition the cell into specialized regions. These internal membranes facilitate cellular processes by minimizing conflicting interactions and increasing surface area where chemical reactions can occur. Membrane-bound organelles localize different processes or enzymatic reactions in time and space.

Through interactions between proteins bound to the membranes of adjacent cells, or between membrane-bound proteins and elements of the extracellular matrix, cells of multicellular organisms organize into tissues, organs, and organ systems. Certain membrane-associated proteins also play key roles in providing identification of tissues or recent events in the cell's history for purposes of recognition of "self" versus foreign molecules.

The content in this category covers the composition, structure, and function of cell membranes; the structure and function of the membrane-bound organelles of eukaryotic cells; and the structure and function of the major cytoskeletal elements. It covers the energetics of and mechanisms by which molecules, or groups of molecules, move across cell membranes. It also covers how cell–cell junctions and the extracellular matrix interact to form tissues with specialized functions. Epithelial tissue and connective tissue are covered in this category. The topics and subtopics in this category are the following:

Plasma Membrane (BIO, BC)
- General function in cell containment
- Composition of membranes
  - Lipid components (BIO, BC, OC)
    - Phospholipids (and phosphatids)
    - Steroids
    - Waxes
  - Protein components
  - Fluid mosaic model
- Membrane dynamics

- Solute transport across membranes
  - Thermodynamic considerations
  - Osmosis
    - Colligative properties; osmotic pressure (GC)
  - Passive transport
  - Active transport
    - Sodium/potassium pump
- Membrane channels
- Membrane potential
- Membrane receptors
- Exocytosis and endocytosis
- Intercellular junctions (BIO)
  - Gap junctions
  - Tight junctions
  - Desmosomes

Membrane-Bound Organelles and Defining Characteristics of Eukaryotic Cells (BIO)

- Defining characteristics of eukaryotic cells: membrane bound nucleus, presence of organelles, mitotic division
- Nucleus
  - Compartmentalization, storage of genetic information
  - Nucleolus: location and function
  - Nuclear envelope, nuclear pores
- Mitochondria
  - Site of ATP production
  - Inner and outer membrane structure (BIO, BC)
  - Self-replication
- Lysosomes: membrane-bound vesicles containing hydrolytic enzymes
- Endoplasmic reticulum
  - Rough and smooth components
  - Rough endoplasmic reticulum site of ribosomes
  - Double membrane structure
  - Role in membrane biosynthesis
  - Role in biosynthesis of secreted proteins
- Golgi apparatus: general structure and role in packaging and secretion
- Peroxisomes: organelles that collect peroxides

Cytoskeleton (BIO)

- General function in cell support and movement
- Microfilaments: composition and role in cleavage and contractility
- Microtubules: composition and role in support and transport
- Intermediate filaments, role in support
- Composition and function of cilia and flagella
- Centrioles, microtubule organizing centers

Tissues Formed From Eukaryotic Cells (BIO)

- Epithelial cells
- Connective tissue cells

Content Category 2B: *The structure, growth, physiology, and genetics of prokaryotes and viruses*

The highly-organized assembly of molecules that is the cell represents the fundamental unit of structure, function, and organization in all living organisms. In the hierarchy of biological organization, the cell is the simplest collection of matter capable of carrying out the processes that distinguish living organisms. As such, cells have the ability to undergo metabolism; maintain homeostasis, including ionic gradients; the capacity to grow; move in response to their local environments; respond to stimuli; reproduce; and adapt to their environment in successive generations.

Life at cellular levels arises from structural order and its dynamic modulation. It does so in response to signals, thereby reflecting properties that result from individual and interactive features of molecular assemblies, their compartmentalization, and their interaction with environmental signals at many spatial and temporal scales.

The content in this category covers the classification, structure, growth, physiology, and genetics of prokaryotes, and the characteristics that distinguish them from eukaryotes. Viruses are also covered here. The topics and subtopics in this category are the following:

Cell Theory (BIO)
- History and development
- Impact on biology

Classification and Structure of Prokaryotic Cells (BIO)
- Prokaryotic domains
  - Archaea
  - Bacteria
- Major classifications of bacteria by shape
  - Bacilli (rod-shaped)
  - Spirilli (spiral-shaped)
  - Cocci (spherical)
- Lack of nuclear membrane and mitotic apparatus
- Lack of typical eukaryotic organelles
- Presence of cell wall in bacteria
- Flagellar propulsion, mechanism

Growth and Physiology of Prokaryotic Cells (BIO)
- Reproduction by fission
- High degree of genetic adaptability, acquisition of antibiotic resistance
- Exponential growth
- Existence of anaerobic and aerobic variants
- Parasitic and symbiotic
- Chemotaxis

Genetics of Prokaryotic Cells (BIO)
- Existence of plasmids, extragenomic DNA
- Transformation: incorporation into bacterial genome of DNA fragments from external medium
- Conjugation
- Transposons (also present in eukaryotic cells)

Virus Structure (BIO)

- General structural characteristics (nucleic acid and protein, enveloped and nonenveloped)
- Lack organelles and nucleus
- Structural aspects of typical bacteriophage
- Genomic content—RNA or DNA
- Size relative to bacteria and eukaryotic cells

Viral Life Cycle (BIO)

- Self-replicating biological units that must reproduce within specific host cell
- Generalized phage and animal virus life cycles
  - Attachment to host, penetration of cell membrane or cell wall, and entry of viral genetic material
  - Use of host synthetic mechanism to replicate viral components
  - Self-assembly and release of new viral particles
- Transduction: transfer of genetic material by viruses
- Retrovirus life cycle: integration into host DNA, reverse transcriptase, HIV
- Prions and viroids: subviral particles

Content Category 2C: *Processes of cell division, differentiation, and specialization*

The ability of organisms to reproduce their own kind is the characteristic that best distinguishes living things. In sexually reproducing organisms, the continuity of life is based on the processes of cell division and meiosis.

The process of cell division is an integral part of the cell cycle. The progress of eukaryotic cells through the cell cycle is regulated by a complex molecular control system. Malfunctions in this system can result in unabated cellular division, and ultimately the development of cancer.

In the embryonic development of multicellular organisms, a fertilized egg gives rise to cells that differentiate into many different types of cells, each with a different structure, corresponding function, and location within the organism. During development, spatial–temporal gradients in the interactions between gene expression and various stimuli result in the structural and functional divergence of cells into specialized structure, organs, and tissues. The interaction of stimuli and genes is also explained by the progression of stem cells to terminal cells.

The content in this category covers the cell cycle; the causes, genetics, and basic properties of cancer; the processes of meiosis and gametogenesis; and the mechanisms governing cell specialization and differentiation. The topics and subtopics in this category are the following:

Mitosis (BIO)
- Mitotic process: prophase, metaphase, anaphase, telophase, interphase
- Mitotic structures
    - Centrioles, asters, spindles
    - Chromatids, centromeres, kinetochores
    - Nuclear membrane breakdown and reorganization
    - Mechanisms of chromosome movement
- Phases of cell cycle: G0, G1, S, G2, M
- Growth arrest
- Control of cell cycle
- Loss of cell cycle controls in cancer cells

Biosignalling (BC)
- Oncogenes, apoptosis

Reproductive System (BIO)
- Gametogenesis by meiosis
- Ovum and sperm
    - Differences in formation
    - Differences in morphology
    - Relative contribution to next generation
- Reproductive sequence: fertilization; implantation; development; birth

Embryogenesis (BIO)
- Stages of early development (order and general features of each)
  - Fertilization
  - Cleavage
  - Blastula formation
  - Gastrulation
    - First cell movements
    - Formation of primary germ layers (endoderm, mesoderm, ectoderm)
  - Neurulation
- Major structures arising out of primary germ layers
- Neural crest
- Environment–gene interaction in development

Mechanisms of Development (BIO)
- Cell specialization
  - Determination
  - Differentiation
  - Tissue types
- Cell–cell communication in development
- Cell migration
- Pluripotency: stem cells
- Gene regulation in development
- Programmed cell death
- Existence of regenerative capacity in various species
- Senescence and aging

Biological and Biochemical Foundations of Living Systems

Foundational Concept 3

Complex systems of tissues and organs sense the internal and external environments of multicellular organisms, and through integrated functioning, maintain a stable internal environment within an ever-changing external environment.

As a result of the integration of a number of highly specialized organ systems, complex living things are able to maintain homeostasis while adapting to a constantly changing environment and participating in growth and reproduction. The interactions of these organ systems involves complex regulatory mechanisms that help maintain a dynamic and healthy equilibrium, regardless of their current state and environment.

Content Categories

- *Category 3A* focuses on the structure and functions of the nervous and endocrine systems, and the ways in which the systems work together to coordinate the responses of other body systems to both external and internal stimuli.

- *Category 3B* focuses on the structure and functions of the organ systems—circulatory, respiratory, digestive, immune, lymphatic, muscular, skeletal, and reproductive—and the ways these systems interact to fulfill their concerted roles in the maintenance and continuance of the living organism.

With these building blocks, medical students will be able to learn how the body responds to internal and external stimuli to support homeostasis and the ability to reproduce.

Content Category 3A: *Structure and functions of the nervous and endocrine systems and ways in which these systems coordinate the organ systems*

The nervous and endocrine systems work together to detect external and internal signals, transmit and integrate information, and maintain homeostasis. They do all this by producing appropriate responses to internal and external cues and stressors. The integration of these systems both with one another, and with the other organ systems, ultimately results in the successful and adaptive behaviors that allow for the propagation of the species.

Animals have evolved a nervous system that senses and processes internal and external information that is used to facilitate and enhance survival, growth, and reproduction. The nervous system interfaces with sensory and internal body systems to coordinate physiological and behavioral responses ranging from simple movements and small metabolic changes to long-distance migrations and social interactions. The physiological processes for nerve signal generation and propagation involve specialized membranes with associated proteins that respond to ligands and/or electrical field changes, signaling molecules and, by extension, the establishment and replenishment of ionic electrochemical gradients requiring ATP.

The endocrine system of animals has evolved to produce chemical signals that function internally to regulate stress responses, reproduction, development, energy metabolism, growth, and various individual and interactive behaviors. The integrated contributions of the nervous and endocrine systems to bodily functions are exemplified by the process whereby the signaling of neurons regulates hormone release, and by the targeting of membrane or nuclear receptors on neurons by circulating hormones.

The content in this category covers the structure, function, and basic aspects of nervous and endocrine systems, and their integration. The structure and function of nerve cells is also included in this category. The topics and subtopics in this category are the following:

Nervous System: Structure and Function (BIO)
- Major Functions
  - High level control and integration of body systems
  - Adaptive capability to external influences
- Organization of vertebrate nervous system
- Sensor and effector neurons
- Sympathetic and parasympathetic nervous systems: antagonistic control
- Reflexes
  - Feedback loop, reflex arc
  - Role of spinal cord and supraspinal circuits
- Integration with endocrine system: feedback control

Nerve Cell (BIO)

- Cell body: site of nucleus, organelles
- Dendrites: branched extensions of cell body
- Axon: structure and function
- Myelin sheath, Schwann cells, insulation of axon
- Nodes of Ranvier: propagation of nerve impulse along axon
- Synapse: site of impulse propagation between cells
- Synaptic activity: transmitter molecules
- Resting potential: electrochemical gradient
- Action potential
  - Threshold, all-or-none
  - Sodium/potassium pump
- Excitatory and inhibitory nerve fibers: summation, frequency of firing
- Glial cells, neuroglia

Electrochemistry (GC)

- Concentration cell: direction of electron flow, Nernst equation

Biosignalling (BC)

- Gated ion channels
  - Voltage gated
  - Ligand gated
- Receptor enzymes
- G protein-coupled receptors

Lipids (BC, OC)

- Description; structure
  - Steroids
  - Terpenes and terpenoids

Endocrine System: Hormones and Their Sources (BIO)

- Function of endocrine system: specific chemical control at cell, tissue, and organ level
- Definitions of endocrine gland, hormone
- Major endocrine glands: names, locations, products
- Major types of hormones
- Neuroendocrinology—relation between neurons and hormonal systems

Endocrine System: Mechanisms of Hormone Action (BIO)

- Cellular mechanisms of hormone action
- Transport of hormones: blood supply
- Specificity of hormones: target tissue
- Integration with nervous system: feedback control
- Regulation by second messengers

Category 3B: *Structure and integrative functions of the main organ systems*

Animals use a number of highly-organized and integrated organ systems to carry out the necessary functions associated with maintaining life processes. Within the body, no organ system is an island. Interactions and coordination between organ systems allow organisms to engage in the processes necessary to sustain life. For example, the organs and structures of the circulatory system carry out a number of functions, such as transporting:

- nutrients absorbed in the digestive system;

- gases absorbed from the respiratory system and muscle tissue;

- hormones secreted from the endocrine system; and

- blood cells produced in bone marrow to and from cells in the body to help fight disease.

The content in this category covers the structure and function of the major organ systems of the body including the respiratory, circulatory, lymphatic, immune, digestive, excretory, reproductive, muscle, skeletal, and skin systems. Also covered in this category is the integration of these systems and their control and coordination by the endocrine and nervous systems. The topics and subtopics in this category are the following:

Respiratory System (BIO)
- General function
    - Gas exchange, thermoregulation
    - Protection against disease: particulate matter
- Structure of lungs and alveoli
- Breathing mechanisms
    - Diaphragm, rib cage, differential pressure
    - Resiliency and surface tension effects
- Thermoregulation: nasal and tracheal capillary beds; evaporation, panting
- Particulate filtration: nasal hairs, mucus/cilia system in lungs
- Alveolar gas exchange
    - Diffusion, differential partial pressure
    - Henry's Law (GC)
- pH control
- Regulation by nervous control
    - CO_2 sensitivity

Circulatory System (BIO)
- Functions: circulation of oxygen, nutrients, hormones, ions and fluids, removal of metabolic waste
- Role in thermoregulation
- Four-chambered heart: structure and function
- Endothelial cells
- Systolic and diastolic pressure
- Pulmonary and systemic circulation
- Arterial and venous systems (arteries, arterioles, venules, veins)
    - Structural and functional differences
    - Pressure and flow characteristics

- Capillary beds
  - Mechanisms of gas and solute exchange
  - Mechanism of heat exchange
  - Source of peripheral resistance
- Composition of blood
  - Plasma, chemicals, blood cells
  - Erythrocyte production and destruction; spleen, bone marrow
  - Regulation of plasma volume
- Coagulation, clotting mechanisms
- Oxygen transport by blood
  - Hemoglobin, hematocrit
  - Oxygen content
  - Oxygen affinity
- Carbon dioxide transport and level in blood
- Nervous and endocrine control

Lymphatic System (BIO)
- Structure of lymphatic system
- Major functions
  - Equalization of fluid distribution
  - Transport of proteins and large glycerides
  - Production of lymphocytes involved in immune reactions
  - Return of materials to the blood

Immune System (BIO)
- Innate (non-specific) vs. adaptive (specific) immunity
- Adaptive immune system cells
  - T-lymphocytes
  - B-lymphocytes
- Innate immune system cells
  - Macrophages
  - Phagocytes
- Tissues
  - Bone marrow
  - Spleen
  - Thymus
  - Lymph nodes
- Concept of antigen and antibody
- Antigen presentation
- Clonal selection
- Antigen-antibody recognition
- Structure of antibody molecule
- Recognition of self vs. non-self, autoimmune diseases
- Major histocompatibility complex

Digestive System (BIO)

- Ingestion
    - Saliva as lubrication and source of enzymes
    - Ingestion; esophagus, transport function
- Stomach
    - Storage and churning of food
    - Low pH, gastric juice, mucal protection against self-destruction
    - Production of digestive enzymes, site of digestion
    - Structure (gross)
- Liver
    - Structural relationship of liver within gastrointestinal system
    - Production of bile
    - Role in blood glucose regulation, detoxification
- Bile
    - Storage in gall bladder
    - Function
- Pancreas
    - Production of enzymes
    - Transport of enzymes to small intestine
- Small Intestine
    - Absorption of food molecules and water
    - Function and structure of villi
    - Production of enzymes, site of digestion
    - Neutralization of stomach acid
    - Structure (anatomic subdivisions)
- Large Intestine
    - Absorption of water
    - Bacterial flora
    - Structure (gross)
- Rectum: storage and elimination of waste, feces
- Muscular control
    - Peristalsis
- Endocrine control
    - Hormones
    - Target tissues
- Nervous control: the enteric nervous system

Excretory System (BIO)

- Roles in homeostasis
    - Blood pressure
    - Osmoregulation
    - Acid–base balance
    - Removal of soluble nitrogenous waste
- Kidney structure
    - Cortex
    - Medulla

- Nephron structure
  - Glomerulus
  - Bowman's capsule
  - Proximal tubule
  - Loop of Henle
  - Distal tubule
  - Collecting duct
- Formation of urine
  - Glomerular filtration
  - Secretion and reabsorption of solutes
  - Concentration of urine
  - Counter-current multiplier mechanism
- Storage and elimination: ureter, bladder, urethra
- Osmoregulation: capillary reabsorption of H_2O, amino acids, glucose, ions
- Muscular control: sphincter muscle

Reproductive System (BIO)
- Male and female reproductive structures and their functions
  - Gonads
  - Genitalia
  - Differences between male and female structures
- Hormonal control of reproduction
  - Male and female sexual development
  - Female reproductive cycle
  - Pregnancy, parturition, lactation
  - Integration with nervous control

Muscle System (BIO)
- Important functions
  - Support: mobility
  - Peripheral circulatory assistance
  - Thermoregulation (shivering reflex)
- Structure of three basic muscle types: striated, smooth, cardiac
- Muscle structure and control of contraction
  - T-tubule system
  - Contractile apparatus
  - Sarcoplasmic reticulum
  - Fiber type
  - Contractile velocity of different muscle types
- Regulation of cardiac muscle contraction
- Oxygen debt: fatigue
- Nervous control
  - Motor neurons
  - Neuromuscular junction, motor end plates
  - Sympathetic and parasympathetic innervation
  - Voluntary and involuntary muscles

Specialized Cell - Muscle Cell (BIO)

- Structural characteristics of striated, smooth, and cardiac muscle
- Abundant mitochondria in red muscle cells: ATP source
- Organization of contractile elements: actin and myosin filaments, crossbridges, sliding filament model
- Sarcomeres: "I" and "A" bands, "M" and "Z" lines, "H" zone
- Presence of troponin and tropomyosin
- Calcium regulation of contraction

Skeletal System (BIO)

- Functions
    - Structural rigidity and support
    - Calcium storage
    - Physical protection
- Skeletal structure
    - Specialization of bone types, structures
    - Joint structures
    - Endoskeleton vs. exoskeleton
- Bone structure
    - Calcium/protein matrix
    - Cellular composition of bone
- Cartilage: structure and function
- Ligaments, tendons
- Endocrine control

Skin System (BIO)

- Structure
    - Layer differentiation, cell types
    - Relative impermeability to water
- Functions in homeostasis and osmoregulation
- Functions in thermoregulation
    - Hair, erectile musculature
    - Fat layer for insulation
    - Sweat glands, location in dermis
    - Vasoconstriction and vasodilation in surface capillaries
- Physical protection
    - Nails, calluses, hair
    - Protection against abrasion, disease organisms
- Hormonal control: sweating, vasodilation, and vasoconstriction

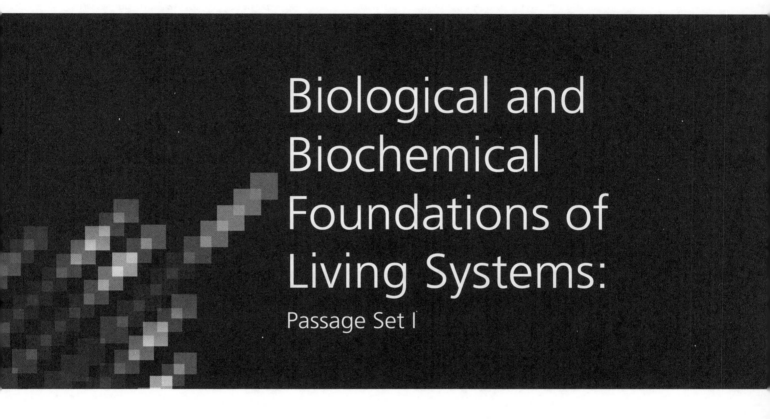

Biological and Biochemical Foundations of Living Systems:

Passage Set I

Sample Test Questions: Biological and Biochemical Foundations of Living Systems

To give you an idea of what to expect from this section of the exam, sample test questions for the Biological and Biochemical Foundations of Living Systems section are provided below. The answer key appears below each question, along with the foundational concept, the content category, and the skill it targets.

Biological and Biochemical Foundations of Living Systems

Passage I: Questions 1–4

A researcher obtained three cultures (A, B, and C) of human skeletal muscle cells. Each culture was known to represent one of the skeletal muscle fiber subtypes. The researcher made observations on two of the three cultures (Culture A and Culture B) and was able to infer the identity of Culture C from these observations.

Culture A appeared white when visualized with a microscope. When an electrical current was applied to the culture medium, the concentrations of lactate and H^+ ions in that medium increased. The pH of the medium changed from 7 to 5 after 2 minutes of continuous, electrically-stimulated contractions.

Microscopic visualization showed that Culture B was red in appearance and had a high mitochondrial density, numerous intact capillaries, and abundant intracellular triglyceride deposits. Upon electrical stimulation, these cells exhibited a slow contraction phase of approximately 10 contractions per second and a very slow rate of ATP utilization.

In both cultures, the addition of acetylcholine to the culture media altered the intracellular electrical charge of the cells. However, only cells from Culture B were able to maintain contractile activity after 30 minutes of continuous acetylcholine infusion.

The researcher combined the results of the observations with the information in Table 1 to identify the muscle subtype represented by each cell culture.

Table 1 Biochemical and Contractile Properties of the Skeletal Muscle Fiber Subtypes

Property	Muscle fiber subtype		
	I	IIa	IIx
Twitch duration	long	moderately fast	fast
Size of motor neuron	small	medium	large
Activity used for	aerobic	long-term anaerobic	short-term anaerobic
Maximum duration of use	hours	<30 minutes	<5 minutes
Power produced	low	medium	high
Oxidative capacity	high	high	intermediate
Glycolytic capacity	low	high	high

Source: Adapted from A.C. Guyton and J.E. Hall, Textbook of Medical Physiology, 9 ed. Copyright 1996 W.B. Saunders Company.

1. The muscle subtype represented by Culture C is LEAST likely to be characterized by:

   A. a fast rate of muscle contraction.
   B. the ability to engage in oxidative and anaerobic respiration.
   C. the presence of medium-sized motor units.
   D. low densities of mitochondria and capillaries.

2. Which steps involved in the contraction of a skeletal muscle require binding and/or hydrolysis of ATP?

   I. Dissociation of myosin head from actin filament
   II. Attachment of myosin head to actin filament
   III. Conformational change that moves actin and myosin filaments relative to one another
   IV. Binding of troponin to actin filament
   V. Release of calcium from the sarcoplasmic reticulum
   VI. Reuptake of calcium into the sarcoplasm

   A. I, II, and III only
   B. II, III, and IV only
   C. I, III, and VI only
   D. III, IV, and VI only

3. The addition of acetylcholine to the medium most likely induced:

   A. depolarization of the cell membrane that resulted in contraction.
   B. repolarization of the cell membrane that resulted in relaxation.
   C. hyperpolarization of the cell membrane that resulted in contraction.
   D. depolarization of the cell membrane that resulted in relaxation.

4. The terminal electron acceptor in the metabolic pathway responsible for the chemical changes observed when Culture A was electrically stimulated is:

   A. pyruvate.
   B. oxygen.
   C. NAD^+.
   D. water.

Solutions for this passage begin on next page.

1. The muscle subtype represented by Culture C is LEAST likely to be characterized by:

    A. a fast rate of muscle contraction.
    B. the ability to engage in oxidative and anaerobic respiration.
    C. the presence of medium-sized motor units.
    D. low densities of mitochondria and capillaries.

Foundational Concept: 3
Complex systems of tissues and organs sense the internal and external environments of multicellular organisms and, through integrated functioning, maintain a stable internal environment within an ever-changing external environment.

Content Category: 3B
Structure and integrative functions of the main organ systems

Scientific Inquiry and Reasoning Skill: 2
Scientific Reasoning and Problem Solving

Key: D
The data in the passage and table allow the student to conclude that Culture A represents skeletal muscle subtype IIx, and Culture B represents skeletal muscle subtype I. Culture C, then, must represent skeletal muscle subtype IIa. Based on the information in Table 1, subtype IIa is characterized as having a fast rate of muscle contraction, the ability to engage in oxidative and anaerobic respiration, and medium-sized motor units. Given that this muscle subtype engages in oxidative respiration, it is not likely that the subtype would be characterized by low numbers of mitochondria and few capillaries. Thus, D is the correct response.

Distractors

A   This is incorrect. The table shows that skeletal muscle subtype IIa has a fast rate of muscle contraction.

B   This is incorrect. The table shows that skeletal muscle subtype IIa can engage in oxidative and anaerobic respiration.

C   This is incorrect. The table shows that skeletal muscle subtype IIa has medium-sized motor units.

 TIP: When presented with a large table, look at the legend and row/column headings to see what data are shown. Knowing how to navigate the table more efficiently will save time.

2. Which steps involved in the contraction of a skeletal muscle require binding and/or hydrolysis of ATP?

    I.   Dissociation of myosin head from actin filament
    II.   Attachment of myosin head to actin filament
    III.   Conformational change that moves actin and myosin filaments relative to one another
    IV.   Binding of troponin to actin filament
    V.   Release of calcium from the sarcoplasmic reticulum
    VI.   Reuptake of calcium into the sarcoplasm

A. I, II, and III only
B. II, III, and IV only
C. I, III, and VI only
D. III, IV, and VI only

Foundational Concept: 1
Biomolecules have unique properties that determine how they contribute to the structure and function of cells and how they participate in the processes necessary to maintain life.

Content Category: 1A
Structure and function of proteins and their constituent amino acids

Scientific Inquiry and Reasoning Skill: 1
Knowledge of Scientific Concepts and Principles

Key: C
Dissociation of the myosin head from the actin filament requires the binding of ATP (I). Attachment of the myosin head to the actin filament requires calcium and a troponin/tropomyosin shift (II). The conformational changes that move actin and myosin relative to one another require that ATP be hydrolyzed, for these changes occur upon release of the products of hydrolysis (ADP and Pi) by the myosin head (III). Binding of troponin to actin does not require the hydrolysis of ATP (IV). Release of calcium from the sarcoplasmic reticulum also does not require ATP hydrolysis. This release occurs when calcium ions move via voltage-gated ion channels down their concentration gradient (V). The reuptake of calcium into the sarcoplasmic reticulum occurs via an ATP-hydrolyzing pump that moves calcium against its concentration gradient (VI). Thus, C is the correct response.

Distractors
A   This is incorrect. Step II does not require binding and/or hydrolysis of ATP.

B   This is incorrect. Steps II and IV do not require binding and/or hydrolysis of ATP.

D   This is incorrect. Step IV does not require binding and/or hydrolysis of ATP.

TIP: Where ordered number series are presented as options, take advantage of the ascending order in the possible answers. In this example, where I, III, and VI is the correct answer, option B can be eliminated immediately just by looking at the first number in the series. Then, by looking at the next number, option A is also quickly eliminated.

Fifth Edition
The Official Guide to the MCAT® Exam
127
MCAT® is a program of the
Association of American Medical Colleges

3. The addition of acetylcholine to the medium most likely induced:

    A. depolarization of the cell membrane that resulted in contraction.
    B. repolarization of the cell membrane that resulted in relaxation.
    C. hyperpolarization of the cell membrane that resulted in contraction.
    D. depolarization of the cell membrane that resulted in relaxation.

Foundational Concept: 3

Complex systems of tissues and organs sense the internal and external environments of multicellular organisms and, through integrated functioning, maintain a stable internal environment within an ever-changing external environment.

Content Category: 3B

Structure and integrative functions of the main organ systems

Scientific Inquiry and Reasoning Skill: 2

Scientific Reasoning and Problem Solving

Key: A

Acetylcholine is released at the neuromuscular junction where it binds to receptors on the muscle cells and, depending on the type of muscle cell, causes depolarization or hyperpolarization of the cell membrane. In skeletal muscles, acetylcholine binds to its receptors, which leads to depolarization of the muscle cell membrane and muscle contraction.

Distractors

B   This is incorrect. Acetylcholine induces contraction, not relaxation, in skeletal muscles.

C   This is incorrect. The cell membrane of skeletal muscle depolarizes in response to acetylcholine.

D   This is incorrect. Depolarization of the cell membrane induces muscle contraction, not relaxation.

 TIP: Remember that unlike cardiac muscle, skeletal muscle does not have intrinsic spontaneous activity, and muscle contraction is stimulated by acetylcholine release at the neuromuscular junction. Also, skeletal muscle relation occurs as the cell membrane returns to its resting potential and calcium is taken back up into the sarcoplasmic reticulum.

4. The terminal electron acceptor in the metabolic pathway responsible for the chemical changes observed when Culture A was electrically stimulated is:

A. pyruvate.
B. oxygen.
C. NAD^+.
D. water.

Foundational Concept: 1
Biomolecules have unique properties that determine how they contribute to the structure and function of cells and how they participate in the processes necessary to maintain life.

Content Category: 1D
Principles of bioenergetics and fuel molecule metabolism

Scientific Inquiry and Reasoning Skill: 1
Knowledge of Scientific Concepts and Principles

Key: A
The muscle cells in Culture A use lactic acid fermentation to provide the energy for the contractions that result from electrical stimulation. In this process, NADH reduces pyruvate to produce lactate. Therefore, pyruvate serves as the electron acceptor in production of lactate.

Distractors

B   This is incorrect. Oxygen serves as the terminal electron acceptor in aerobic respiration. The generation of lactate when electric current is applied suggests that Culture A uses fermentation to metabolize pyruvate.

C   This is incorrect. NADH reduces pyruvate to produce lactate and regenerate NAD^+ so glycolysis can continue.

D   This is incorrect. In aerobic respiration, water forms when electrons are passed to oxygen through a chain of carriers in the mitochondria. The passage describes the production of lactate by Culture A, which is consistent with fermentation and not aerobic respiration.

Biological and Biochemical Foundations of Living Systems:

Passage Set II

MCAT® is a program of the
Association of American Medical Colleges

Biological and Biochemical Foundations of Living Systems

Passage II: Questions 5–9

In contrast to the conventional thought that prokaryotic transcription and translation are coupled, scientists have observed the intracellular localization of mRNA in *Escherichia coli*. The locations of *cat* and *lacY* transcripts were determined in living *E. coli* cells. The gene *cat* encodes the soluble protein chloramphenicol acetyltransferase, and *lacY* encodes the membrane-bound lactose permease. Six copies of the binding sequence (6xbs) for the phage MS2 coat protein were inserted upstream of these genes in *E. coli* cells. The locations of the transcripts were visualized using fluorescence microscopy of cells expressing the MS2 coat protein fused to green fluorescent protein (MS2–GFP). The cat_{6xbs} transcript formed a helix-like structure within the cytoplasm, and the $lacY_{6xbs}$ transcript was localized near the cell membrane.

Next, the cellular targeting of polycistronic mRNAs was examined. The *bgl* operon, which encodes the BglG transcription factor, the BglF membrane-bound sugar permease, and the soluble BglB phospho-β-glucosidase, was deleted from the cells. The cells were then transformed with plasmids encoding the individual genes and fractionated, and the transcripts were monitored by real-time PCR. Fluorescence microscopy revealed the transcripts' subcellular locations (Figure 1).

After transcription and translation were uncoupled by the application of chloramphenicol, a competitive inhibitor of the enzyme involved in translation elongation, targeting was determined to be a product of the mRNA transcript. To characterize the mRNA element that targets the transcripts to the membrane, scientists fused the 6xbs to either the portion of the transcript encoding the hydrophilic protein domain or to the portion of the transcript encoding the hydrophobic protein domain, and followed their subcellular localization. Transcript elements were found to localize in accordance with the localization of their encoded protein.

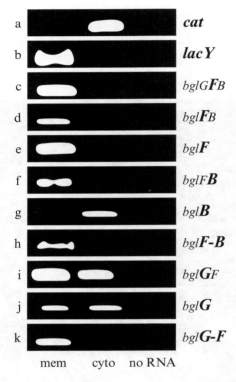

Figure 1 Real-time PCR amplification of the transcripts encoded by the *bgl* operon. Bold lettering indicates the gene(s) whose sequence(s) was(were) amplified. In (h) and (k), the junction region between the bolded genes was amplified. (Note: mem = membrane, cyto = cytosol.)

Source: Adapted from a paper by K. Nevo-Dinur, et al. Copyright 2011 by the American Association for the Advancement of Science.

5. What control experiment was necessary to ensure that the apparent subcellular locations of the cat_{6xbs} and $lacY_{6xbs}$ transcripts were NOT skewed by the location preference of the bound MS2–GFP?

   A. Determination of expression of MS2–GFP in cells that lacked the 6xbs insertion upstream of the cat and $lacY$ genes

   B. Use of E. coli cells that expressed only MS2 instead of the MS2–GFP fusion protein

   C. Insertion of the 6xbs region upstream of both the cat and $lacY$ genes in the same cells

   D. Determination of expression of both MS2 and GFP as separate proteins rather than as a fusion protein

6. Which other cellular components are likely to be located near the $lacY_{6xbs}$ transcript in the cell membrane?

   A. Proteins and glycolipids
   B. Glycolipids and sterols
   C. Sterols and phospholipids
   D. Phospholipids and proteins

7. Using knowledge of Michaelis–Menten kinetics, what effect would the addition of chloramphenicol have on the kinetics of its target enzyme?

   A. V_{max} decreases, and K_M increases.
   B. V_{max} decreases, and K_M remains unchanged.
   C. V_{max} remains unchanged, and K_M increases.
   D. V_{max} remains unchanged, and K_M decreases.

8. The bglF transcript is known to have a short half-life within the cytosol. What mechanism is most likely responsible for transport of this transcript to the cytoplasmic membrane once it is synthesized?

   A. Diffusion across the cytoplasm
   B. Transport via attachment to the mitotic spindle
   C. Active transport along cytoskeletal filaments
   D. Transport from the endoplasmic reticulum in vesicles

9. Chloramphenicol did NOT inhibit translation in E. coli cells containing the cat_{6xbs} expression plasmid. What experimental parameter could be changed in order to affect translation inhibition?

   A. Increase the chloramphenicol concentration.
   B. Increase the chloramphenicol incubation time.
   C. Alter the incubation temperature by a few degrees.
   D. Use an alternate antibiotic.

Solutions for this passage begin on next page.

5. What control experiment was necessary to ensure that the apparent subcellular locations of the cat_{6xbs} and $lacY_{6xbs}$ transcripts were NOT skewed by the location preference of the bound MS2–GFP?

    A.   Determination of expression of MS2–GFP in cells that lacked the 6xbs insertion upstream of the *cat* and *lacY* genes

    B.   Use of *E. coli* cells that expressed only MS2 instead of the MS2–GFP fusion protein

    C.   Insertion of the 6xbs region upstream of both the *cat* and *lacY* genes in the same cells

    D.   Determination of expression of both MS2 and GFP as separate proteins rather than as a fusion protein

---

Foundational Concept: 1
Biomolecules have unique properties that determine how they contribute to the structure and function of cells and how they participate in the processes necessary to maintain life.

Content Category: 1B
Transmission of genetic information from the gene to the protein

Scientific Inquiry and Reasoning Skill: 3
Reasoning about the Design and Execution of Research

Key: A
Lack of the 6xbs sequence would leave the MS2–GFP protein without a binding partner. It would then be located in either the cytoplasm or the membrane (in this case, the cytoplasm) based on the properties of the MS2–GFP protein itself rather than being restricted to the location of the cat_{6xbs} and $lacY_{6xbs}$ transcripts. Thus, A is the correct response.

Distractors

B   This is incorrect. The MS2 coat protein would still bind to the target 6xbs sequence, but nothing could be visualized in the fluorescence microscopy experiment because GFP is the chromophore.

C   This is incorrect. Inserting the 6xbs region upstream of both genes in the same cells would only complicate the experiment because signal from both soluble and membrane-bound transcripts would obscure each other.

D   This is incorrect. The MS2 protein would still bind to the requisite locations on the cat_{6xbs} and $lacY_{6xbs}$ transcripts, but it would not be visualized because it is not tethered to GFP. The fluorescence signal observed in the experiment would report solely on the location preference of GFP rather without informing on the location preference of the MS2–GFP fusion protein.

 TIP: Note that in this question, answers B and D either only look at MS2, or MS2 and GFP separately. These are not suitable controls in experiments using a MS2–GFP fusion protein.

6. Which other cellular components are likely to be located near the *lacY*$_{6xbs}$ transcript in the cell membrane?

    A. Proteins and glycolipids
    B. Glycolipids and sterols
    C. Sterols and phospholipids
    D. Phospholipids and proteins

Foundational Concept: 2
Highly-organized assemblies of molecules, cells, and organs interact to carry out the functions of living organisms.

Content Category: 2B
Structure, growth, physiology, and genetics of prokaryotes and viruses

Scientific Inquiry and Reasoning Skill: 1
Knowledge of Scientific Concepts and Principles

Key: D
E. coli membranes are roughly 75% protein and 25% phospholipid, by mass.

Distractors
A   This is incorrect. *E. coli* membranes do not contain glycolipids.

B   This is incorrect. *E. coli* membranes contain neither glycolipids nor sterols.

C   This is incorrect. *E. coli* membranes do not contain sterols.

7. Using knowledge of Michaelis–Menten kinetics, what effect would the addition of chloramphenicol have on the kinetics of its target enzyme?

A. V_{max} decreases, and K_M increases.
B. V_{max} decreases, and K_M remains unchanged.
C. V_{max} remains unchanged, and K_M increases.
D. V_{max} remains unchanged, and K_M decreases.

Foundational Concept: 1
Biomolecules have unique properties that determine how they contribute to the structure and function of cells and how they participate in the processes necessary to maintain life.

Content Category: 1A
Structure and function of proteins and their constituent amino acids

Scientific Inquiry and Reasoning Skill: 1
Knowledge of Scientific Concepts and Principles

Key: C
A competitive inhibitor binds to the same site as the substrate. It thereby increases K_M while leaving V_{max} unchanged.

Distractors
A   This is incorrect. A competitive inhibitor does not change the V_{max} because high substrate concentrations displace the inhibitor.

B   This is incorrect. A competitive inhibitor does not change the V_{max} because high substrate concentrations displace the inhibitor. However, at low substrate concentrations, a competitor inhibitor competes well for the binding site so the K_M increases.

D   This is incorrect. A competitive inhibitor does not change the V_{max} but the K_M will increase, not decrease.

 TIP: This question combines expected knowledge of enzyme kinetics with passage-based information on the specific function of chloramphenicol. Applying scientific knowledge to passage-based information is crucial for determining the correct answer.

8. The *bglF* transcript is known to have a short half-life within the cytosol. What mechanism is most likely responsible for transport of this transcript to the cytoplasmic membrane once it is synthesized?

    A. Diffusion across the cytoplasm
    B. Transport via attachment to the mitotic spindle
    C. Active transport along cytoskeletal filaments
    D. Transport from the endoplasmic reticulum in vesicles

Foundational Concept: 2

Highly-organized assemblies of molecules, cells, and organs interact to carry out the functions of living organisms.

Content Category: 2A

Assemblies of molecules, cells, and groups of cells within single cellular and multicellular organisms

Scientific Inquiry and Reasoning Skill: 2

Scientific Reasoning and Problem Solving

Key: C

This would allow for more rapid transport than diffusion.

Distractors

A   This is incorrect. This process would not be preferable because it would take too long.

B   This is incorrect. *E. coli* cells and, more generally, prokaryotes do not undergo mitosis.

D   This is incorrect. *E. coli* cells do not have endoplasmic reticulum or vesicles.

 TIP: Assuming this question just concerns modes of transport could lead to the incorrect answer. The passage is about prokaryotic cells. Therefore, answers that pertain only to eukaryotic cells can be easily eliminated.

9. Chloramphenicol did NOT inhibit translation in *E. coli* cells containing the cat_{6xbs} expression plasmid. What experimental parameter could be changed in order to affect translation inhibition?

A. Increase the chloramphenicol concentration.
B. Increase the chloramphenicol incubation time.
C. Alter the incubation temperature by a few degrees.
D. Use an alternate antibiotic.

Foundational Concept: 1
Biomolecules have unique properties that determine how they contribute to the structure and function of cells and how they participate in the processes necessary to maintain life.

Content Category: 1A
Structure and function of proteins and their constituent amino acids

Scientific Inquiry and Reasoning Skill: 3
Reasoning about the Design and Execution of Research

Key: D
As stated in the passage, the *cat* transcript encodes chloramphenicol acetyltransferase. Without even being familiar with this protein, the reader should be able to tell by looking at the name of the protein that it is an enzyme (-ase) that causes chloramphenicol to undergo a chemical change (acetyl transfer). This renders chloramphenicol ineffective and confers antibiotic resistance to the cell regardless of the chloramphenicol concentration or incubation time. A moderate increase in the temperature should increase the translation efficiency. Thus, use of an alternate antibiotic is the only reasonable choice of those presented. Thus, D is the correct response.

Distractors

A   This is incorrect. As chloramphenicol is rendered ineffective, increasing its concentration will not affect translation inhibition in *E. coli* cells.

B   This is incorrect. As chloramphenicol is rendered ineffective, increasing its incubation time will not affect translation inhibition in *E. coli* cells.

C   This is incorrect. A moderate increase in temperature will increase the translation efficiency, but will not affect translation inhibition in *E. coli* cells.

 TIP: Do not assume the answer with the least detail is incorrect.

Biological and Biochemical Foundations of Living Systems:

Passage Set III

Biological and Biochemical Foundations of Living Systems

Passage III: Questions 10–14

The protozoan that causes human malaria, *Plasmodium falciparum*, completes part of its life cycle inside human mature red blood cells (RBCs). Infected RBCs adhere to platelets, endothelial cells, and other mature RBCs. The protozoan genome contains approximately 60 *var* genes encoding transmembrane protein PfEMP1 variants, which localize to the RBC plasma membrane and bind to endothelial cells. Only one *var* gene is transcribed at a time over multiple mitotic generations, but the *var* gene that is expressed successively switches during an infection. The expressed *var* gene is located in a different place in the periphery of the nucleus than are silent *var* genes. Histone H3 on the active *var* promoter is trimethylated on lysine 4 and acetylated on lysine 9, whereas on silent *var* genes, lysine 9 of histone H3 is trimethylated.

Figure 1 shows the relative distances between expressed and silent *var* genes and either *P. falciparum* histone lysine methyltransferase PfSET10 or a telomere marker.

P. falciparum cells contain the most PfSET10 when the intraerythrocyte parasites are in an actively dividing life cycle phase. PfSET10 purified from parasites using antibodies specific for PfSET10 modifies histone H3. Figure 2 summarizes the binding activity of PfSET10 fragments.

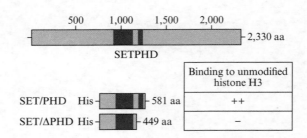

Figure 2 Testing PfSET10 domains SET10 and PHD for histone H3 binding

Source: Adapted from a paper by J. Volz, et al. Copyright 2012 by Elsevier Inc.

Figure 1 Relative localization of *var* genes with PfSET10 and telomeres (Note: In graphs, 75% of data points are below top line of boxes; thick band = median value.)

10. Of the three general cell types or cell-derived structures described in the passage as binding *P. falciparum*–infected RBCs, at least two of the three have which characteristic?

   A. They have nuclei.
   B. They are cell fragments.
   C. They are bone marrow–derived.
   D. They are connected by tight junctions.

11. The data in the passage suggest that the substrate binding domain in PfSET10 is:

   A. the SET domain.
   B. the PHD domain.
   C. the *N*-terminal domain.
   D. the *C*-terminal domain.

12. The information in the passage supports the prediction that *P. falciparum* creates unique protein trafficking structures outside the parasite itself for the trafficking of which parasite protein?

   A. PfEMP1
   B. PfSET10
   C. Histone H3
   D. Hemoglobin

13. The information in the passage suggests that PfSET10 has which function in *var* gene localization or expression? PfSET10:

   A. allows active and silent *var* genes to colocalize in the nucleus.
   B. marks the chromatin of the active *var* promoter for reexpression after mitosis.
   C. marks the chromatin of a silent *var* promoter to be expressed after mitosis.
   D. marks the chromatin of multiple *var* promoters for simultaneous expression.

14. Lysine and amino acids with similar chemical characteristics in histones most likely promote the interaction of histones with which DNA components?

   A. Purines
   B. Pyrimidines
   C. Deoxyribose
   D. Phosphate groups

Solutions for this passage begin on next page.

10. Of the three general cell types or cell-derived structures described in the passage as binding *P. falciparum*–infected RBCs, at least two of the three have which characteristic?

    A. They have nuclei.
    B. They are cell fragments.
    C. They are bone marrow–derived.
    D. They are connected by tight junctions.

Foundational Concept: 3
Complex systems of tissues and organs sense the internal and external environments of multicellular organisms and, through integrated functioning, maintain a stable internal environment within an ever-changing external environment.

Content Category: 3B
Structure and integrative functions of the main organ systems

Scientific Inquiry and Reasoning Skill: 1
Knowledge of Scientific Concepts and Principles

Key: C
The three general cell types or cell-derived structures described in the passage as having receptors that bind *P. falciparum*-infected RBCs are platelets, endothelial cells, and mature RBCs. Platelets and erythrocytes are derived from progenitors in the bone marrow.

Distractors
A   This is incorrect. Endothelial cells have nuclei, but platelets and mature RBCs do not.

B   This is incorrect. Endothelial cells and RBCs are cells, whereas platelets are cell fragments.

D   This is incorrect. Only endothelial cells are connected by tight junctions.

TIP: When questions include numbers, read the question at least twice to understand precisely what is being asked.

11. The data in the passage suggest that the substrate binding domain in PfSET10 is:

    A. the SET domain.
    B. the PHD domain.
    C. the *N*-terminal domain.
    D. the *C*-terminal domain.

Foundational Concept: 1
Biomolecules have unique properties that determine how they contribute to the structure and function of cells and how they participate in the processes necessary to maintain life.

Content Category: 1A
Structure and function of proteins and their constituent amino acids

Scientific Inquiry and Reasoning Skill: 4
Data-based and Statistical Reasoning

Key: B
According to the data in Figure 2, a PfSET10 fragment that contains the PHD domain and the SET domain binds unmodified histone H3. A fragment lacking the PHD domain but containing the SET domain does not bind unmodified histone H3. Taken together, these data best support the conclusion that the PHD domain is the substrate binding domain.

Distractors
A   This is incorrect. The observation that a fragment lacking the PHD domain but containing the SET domain does not bind unmodified histone H3 argues that the PHD domain, not the SET domain, is the substrate binding domain.

C   This is incorrect. Because a PfSET10 fragment that contains the PHD domain and the SET domain binds unmodified histone H3, the substrate binding domain is near the center of the primary structure of the protein and is not near the *N*-terminus.

D   This is incorrect. Because a PfSET10 fragment that contains the PHD domain and the SET domain binds unmodified histone H3, the substrate binding domain is near the center of the primary structure of the protein and is not near the *C*-terminus.

12. The information in the passage supports the prediction that *P. falciparum* creates unique protein trafficking structures outside the parasite itself for the trafficking of which parasite protein?

A. PfEMP1
B. PfSET10
C. Histone H3
D. Hemoglobin

Foundational Concept: 2
Highly-organized assemblies of molecules, cells, and organs interact to carry out the functions of living organisms.

Content Category: 2A
Assemblies of molecules, cells, and groups of cells within single cellular and multicellular organisms

Scientific Inquiry and Reasoning Skill: 2
Scientific Reasoning and Problem Solving

Key: A
PfEMP1 is a parasite protein that is present in the plasma membrane of the RBC that the parasite inhabits. This suggests that there must be a mechanism for transporting PfEMP1 from the parasite to the RBC plasma membrane.

Distractors
B   This is incorrect. According to the passage, PfSET10 is in the nucleus of the parasite.

C   This is incorrect. According to the passage, histone H3 is associated with *var* genes in the nucleus of the parasite.

D   This is incorrect. The parasite does digest the host RBCs hemoglobin, but this hemoglobin is not a parasite protein.

13. The information in the passage suggests that PfSET10 has which function in *var* gene localization or expression? PfSET10:

    A. allows active and silent *var* genes to colocalize in the nucleus.
    B. marks the chromatin of the active *var* promoter for reexpression after mitosis.
    C. marks the chromatin of a silent *var* promoter to be expressed after mitosis.
    D. marks the chromatin of multiple *var* promoters for simultaneous expression.

Foundational Concept: 2
Highly-organized assemblies of molecules, cells, and organs interact to carry out the functions of living organisms.

Content Category: 2C
Processes of cell division, differentiation, and specialization

Scientific Inquiry and Reasoning Skill: 2
Scientific Reasoning and Problem Solving

Key: B
According to the passage, *P. falciparum* cells contain the most PfSET10 when the intraerythrocyte parasites are in an actively dividing life cycle phase. To maintain cellular identity, there has to be a mechanism for marking genes that were transcriptionally active before mitosis for reactivation after mitosis. Because PfSET10 colocalizes with the active *var* gene, it is reasonable to hypothesize that PfSET10 methlytransferase activity is involved in this bookmarking.

Distractors

A   This is incorrect. Active and silent *var* genes do not colocalize in the nucleus.

C   This is incorrect. PfSET10 colocalizes with the active, not a silent, *var* gene. Therefore, PfSET10 is most likely not marking the chromatin of a silent *var* promoter.

D   This is incorrect. PfSET10 appears to be involved in mutually exclusive *var* gene expression.

14. Lysine and amino acids with similar chemical characteristics in histones most likely promote the interaction of histones with which DNA components?

A. Purines
B. Pyrimidines
C. Deoxyribose
D. Phosphate groups

Foundational Concept: 1
Biomolecules have unique properties that determine how they contribute to the structure and function of cells and how they participate in the processes necessary to maintain life.

Content Category: 1B
Transmission of genetic information from the gene to the protein

Scientific Inquiry and Reasoning Skill: 2
Scientific Reasoning and Problem Solving

Key: D
Lysine is a basic, positively-charged amino acid that interacts with negatively-charged phosphate groups on DNA.

Distractors

A   This is incorrect. Histones do not interact with DNA in a highly sequence-specific manner.

B   This is incorrect. Histones do not interact with DNA in a highly sequence-specific manner.

C   This is incorrect. Deoxyribose is not negatively charged.

TIP: Be prepared to identify amino acids by structure and R group classification.

Fifth Edition
The Official Guide to the MCAT® Exam
146
MCAT® is a program of the
Association of American Medical Colleges

Biological and Biochemical Foundations of Living Systems:

Passage Set IV

Fifth Edition
The Official Guide to the MCAT® Exam

MCAT® is a program of the
Association of American Medical Colleges

Biological and Biochemical Foundations of Living Systems

Passage IV: Questions 15–19

In many animals, including mice and humans, the liver quickly regenerates to its original size after a partial hepatectomy in which two-thirds of the organ is removed. Hepatocyte proliferation in response to this surgery is significantly reduced in mice with inadequate platelet activity or number.

Platelets carry 95 percent of blood serotonin, which is synthesized from tryptophan and secreted by endocrine cells in the lining of the gastrointestinal tract. Researchers experimentally tested the hypothesis that platelet serotonin is responsible for the platelets' positive effect on hepatocyte proliferation. The number of hepatocytes expressing the Ki67 protein, which is detected exclusively in the nuclei of proliferating cells, was used as a measure of liver regeneration.

Experiment 1

Wild-type mice were treated with an anti-platelet antibody that destroys 90 percent of their circulating platelets; a subset of these mice was also injected with a serotonin agonist, which mimics serotonin's actions on its receptors (Figure 1).

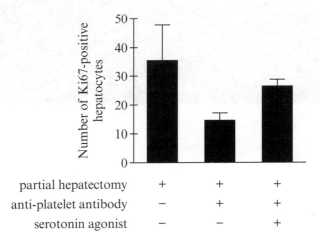

partial hepatectomy	+	+	+
anti-platelet antibody	−	+	+
serotonin agonist	−	−	+

Figure 1 Effects of platelet depletion and serotonin agonist on hepatocyte proliferation

Experiment 2

Wild-type mice were treated with antagonists of the serotonin receptors 5-HT2A and 5-HT2B, receptors that are expressed on hepatocytes and other cell types (Figure 2).

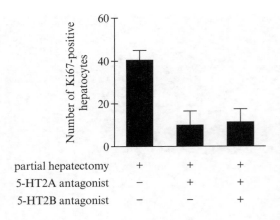

partial hepatectomy	+	+	+
5-HT2A antagonist	−	+	+
5-HT2B antagonist	−	−	+

Figure 2 Effects of serotonin receptor antagonists on hepatocyte proliferation

Experiment 3

This experiment used $TPH1^{-/-}$ mice, which lack the gastrointestinal cell enzyme TPH1 necessary to make circulating serotonin; some of the $TPH1^{-/-}$ mice were injected with a serotonin biosynthetic precursor that could be converted into serotonin and then imported into platelets (Figure 3).

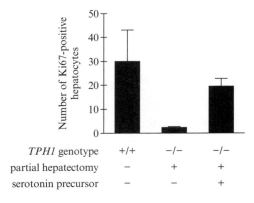

$TPH1$ genotype	+/+	−/−	−/−
partial hepatectomy	−	+	+
serotonin precursor	−	−	+

Figure 3 Effects of $TPH1^{-/-}$ genotype and serotonin precursor on hepatocyte proliferation

Source: Adapted from a paper by M. Lesurtel, et al. Copyright 2006 by the American Association for the Advancement of Science.

15. The liver synthesizes factors that act cooperatively with platelets to facilitate which physiological process?

    A. Cholesterol synthesis
    B. Glucose metabolism
    C. Blood clotting
    D. Fat digestion

16. According to the passage, platelets are LEAST likely to contain:

    A. transmembrane serotonin transporters.
    B. ribosomes.
    C. serotonin.
    D. Ki67.

17. The structure of serotonin is shown.

Where are the serotonin receptors 5-HT2A and 5-HT2B most likely to be located in hepatocytes?

    A. In the nucleus
    B. In the cytosol
    C. Embedded in the mitochondrial membrane
    D. Embedded in the cell membrane

18. Which finding, when combined with the data in the passage, is most likely to lead researchers to conclude that the 5-HT2A and 5-HT2B receptor subtypes mediate serotonin-dependent liver regeneration?

    A. Administration of 5-HT2A receptor agonist resulted in reduced Ki67 staining.
    B. RNA for seven different receptor subtypes was detectible in naïve liver tissue.
    C. Up-regulation of 5-HT2A and 5-HT2B was observed during periods of peak hepatocyte proliferation.
    D. Administration of 5-HT2C and 5-HT3 receptor antagonists reduced the number of Ki67-positive cells.

19. The amino acid precursor of serotonin is best described as having which type of R group?

    A. Nonpolar, aliphatic
    B. Polar, uncharged
    C. Aromatic
    D. Negatively charged

Solutions for this passage begin on next page.

15. The liver synthesizes factors that act cooperatively with platelets to facilitate which physiological process?

    A. Cholesterol synthesis
    B. Glucose metabolism
    C. Blood clotting
    D. Fat digestion

Foundational Concept: 3
Complex systems of tissues and organs sense the internal and external environments of multicellular organisms and, through integrated functioning, maintain a stable internal environment within an ever-changing external environment.

Content Category: 3B
Structure and integrative functions of the main organ systems

Scientific Inquiry and Reasoning Skill: 1
Knowledge of Scientific Concepts and Principles

Key: C
Platelets form a plug at the site where a blood vessel has been damaged. Blood clotting factors that have been synthesized in the liver in an inactive form then participate in a cascade that leads to a blood clot.

Distractors

A   This is incorrect. Synthesis of cholesterol is an important function of the liver. Platelets may also synthesize cholesterol, but the liver and platelets are not acting together in this process.

B   This is incorrect. The liver plays an important role in energy homeostasis by storing glucose in the form of glycogen under conditions of glucose excess and by breaking down glycogen and releasing glucose into the bloodstream under conditions of glucose limitation. The liver also synthesizes glucose from non-carbohydrate molecules. Glucose and insulin imbalances can affect the activation of platelets during coagulation, but the liver and platelets are not acting together in energy homeostasis.

D   This is incorrect. The liver synthesizes bile that emulsifies fat and facilitates its digestion in the small intestine. Platelets do not have an obvious role in this process.

TIP: Read the question in full. Noticing the word "platelets" in the sentence will directly lead to the correct answer: blood clotting. A common error would be to skim the question quickly and assume the question is asking which physiological process occurs in the liver.

Fifth Edition
The Official Guide to the MCAT® Exam
150
MCAT® is a program of the
Association of American Medical Colleges

16. According to the passage, platelets are LEAST likely to contain:

A. transmembrane serotonin transporters.
B. ribosomes.
C. serotonin.
D. Ki67.

Foundational Concept: 3
Complex systems of tissues and organs sense the internal and external environments of multicellular organisms and, through integrated functioning, maintain a stable internal environment within an ever-changing external environment.

Content Category: 3B
Structure and integrative functions of the main organ systems

Scientific Inquiry and Reasoning Skill: 2
Scientific Reasoning and Problem Solving

Key: D
Platelets are cell fragments without nuclei and therefore would not be expected to contain a protein like Ki67 that is detected exclusively in the nuclei of proliferating whole cells. Because this option presents a situation that is unlikely to be true, it is the correct answer to the question.

Distractors

A   This is incorrect. The passage states that platelets are carrying serotonin that has been synthesized outside the platelets; therefore, there must be a mechanism for transporting serotonin into platelets. Serotonin would be transported into platelets by transmembrane transporters. This option is very likely to be true; therefore, it is not the correct answer.

B   This is incorrect. Platelets are formed from large cells called megakaryocytes. Platelets consist of plasma membrane–encased megakaryocyte cytoplasm, which contains ribosomes. This option is very likely to be true; therefore, it is not the correct answer.

C   This is incorrect. A major point of the passage is that platelets carry serotonin. This option is very likely to be true; therefore, it is not the correct answer.

 TIP: If one of the options is not familiar, check the passage. The passage states the Ki67 protein is exclusively found in the nuclei of proliferating cells. As platelets are cell fragments they do not contain nuclei, therefore this is the correct answer. Failure to check the passage may have led to an incorrect choice.

17. The structure of serotonin is shown.

Where are the serotonin receptors 5-HT2A and 5-HT2B most likely to be located in hepatocytes?

    A. In the nucleus
    B. In the cytosol
    C. Embedded in the mitochondrial membrane
    D. Embedded in the cell membrane

Foundational Concept: 2
Highly-organized assemblies of molecules, cells, and organs interact to carry out the functions of living organisms.

Content Category: 2A
Assemblies of molecules, cells, and groups of cells within single cellular and multicellular organisms

Scientific Inquiry and Reasoning Skill: 2
Scientific Reasoning and Problem Solving

Key: D
The hydroxyl group and amine group of serotonin makes the molecule polar and thus, it does not readily cross the phospholipid bilayer that is the cell membrane. It is most likely that the serotonin receptors on hepatocytes are embedded within the cell membrane to facilitate serotonin transport.

Distractors

A   This is incorrect. The hydroxyl group and amine group of serotonin makes the molecule polar and thus, it does not readily cross the phospholipid bilayer of the cell membrane. Therefore, it is not likely to be located in the nucleus.

B   This is incorrect. The hydroxyl group and amine group of serotonin makes the molecule polar and thus, it does not readily cross the phospholipid bilayer of the cell membrane. Therefore, it is not likely to be located in cytosol.

C   This is incorrect. The hydroxyl group and amine group of serotonin makes the molecule polar and thus, it does not readily cross the phospholipid bilayer of the cell membrane. Therefore, it is not likely to be located in the mitochondrial membrane.

Fifth Edition
The Official Guide to the MCAT® Exam
152
MCAT® is a program of the
Association of American Medical Colleges

18. Which finding, when combined with the data in the passage, is most likely to lead researchers to conclude that the 5-HT2A and 5-HT2B receptor subtypes mediate serotonin-dependent liver regeneration?

    A. Administration of 5-HT2A receptor agonist resulted in reduced Ki67 staining.

    B. RNA for seven different receptor subtypes was detectible in naïve liver tissue.

    C. Up-regulation of 5-HT2A and 5-HT2B was observed during periods of peak hepatocyte proliferation.

    D. Administration of 5-HT2C and 5-HT3 receptor antagonists reduced the number of Ki67-positive cells.

Foundational Concept: 2

Highly-organized assemblies of molecules, cells, and organs interact to carry out the functions of living organisms.

Content Category: 2A

Assemblies of molecules, cells, and groups of cells within single cellular and multicellular organisms

Scientific Inquiry and Reasoning Skill: 4

Data-based and Statistical Reasoning

Key: C

An observed up-regulation of 5-HT2A and 5-HT2B during periods of peak hepatocyte proliferation corroborates the data presented in the passage (that administration of antagonists of 5-HT2A and 5-HT2B lead to decreased hepatocyte proliferation) and, of the options presented, is most likely to lead researchers to conclude that the 5-HT2A and 5-HT2B receptor subtypes mediate serotonin-dependent liver regeneration.

Distractors

A   This is incorrect. A reduction in Ki67 staining after administration of a 5-HT2A agonist is not consistent with the data presented in the passage.

B   This is incorrect. The presence of RNA encoding all the receptor types in the liver tissues would not lead researchers to conclude that the 5-HT2A and 5-HT2B receptor subtypes directly mediate serotonin-dependent liver regeneration.

D   This is incorrect. That 5-HT2C and 5-HT3 receptor antagonists failed to reduce the number of positive Ki67 cells is consistent with the conclusion that the 5-HT2A and 5-HT2B receptor subtypes mediate serotonin-dependent liver regeneration, but this observation is not evidence of a role of 5-HT2A and 5-HT2B in this process. Thus, this observation provides less support for the role of the 5-HT2A and 5-HT2B receptor subtypes in serotonin-dependent liver regeneration than does option C.

19. The amino acid precursor of serotonin is best described as having which type of R group?

    A. Nonpolar, aliphatic
    B. Polar, uncharged
    C. Aromatic
    D. Negatively charged

Foundational Concept: 1
Biomolecules have unique properties that determine how they contribute to the structure and function of cells and how they participate in the processes necessary to maintain life.

Content Category: 1A
Structure and function of proteins and their constituent amino acids

Scientific Inquiry and Reasoning Skill: 1
Knowledge of Scientific Concepts and Principles

Key: C
Tryptophan, the amino acid precursor of serotonin, contains an aromatic R group.

Distractors
A   This is incorrect. Tryptophan does not have a nonpolar, aliphatic R group.

B   This is incorrect. Tryptophan does not have a polar, uncharged R group.

D   This is incorrect. Tryptophan does not have a negatively charged R group.

Biological and Biochemical Foundations of Living Systems:

Passage Set V

Biological and Biochemical Foundations of Living Systems

Passage V: Questions 20–24

Traditionally, cellular differentiation and lineage commitment are thought of as robust, irreversible developmental processes. Recently, however, it has been shown that fibroblasts can be reprogrammed to a pluripotent state with a combination of transcription factors. These results have caused scientists to question whether specific transcription factors could induce other defined somatic cell fates and not just an undifferentiated state.

Scientists set out to test whether neural-lineage-specific transcription factors could convert embryonic fibroblasts from TauEGFP mice, mice engineered to express a green fluorescent protein in their neuronal tissues only, into neurons using the protocol shown in Figure 1.

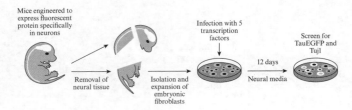

Figure 1 Experimental protocol for infecting embryonic fibroblasts from engineered TauEGFP mice

Twelve days after infection, scientists observed the presence of cells that displayed bright green fluorescence and were positive for Tuj1, a neuron-specific class III β-tubulin. These cells also expressed several neuron-specific proteins including NeuN, which binds DNA. Tests revealed that while the majority of the fluorescent cells produced the excitatory neurotransmitter glutamate ($^-OOC-CH_2-CH_2-CH(NH_2)-COOH$), a few produced the inhibitory neurotransmitter γ-aminobutyric acid (GABA) ($HOOC-CH_2-CH_2-CH_2NH_2$), much like neurons from the central nervous system.

In subsequent experiments, the scientists examined how each of the five transcription factors affected the production of Tuj1-positive cells by removing a single factor from the original 5-factor pool. The results are shown in Figure 2.

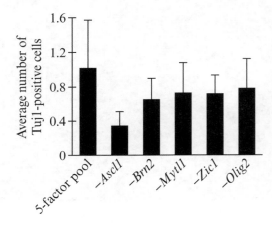

Figure 2 Average number of Tuj1-positive cells visible in a 20× field normalized to the 5-factor pool condition (Note: – indicates omission of the specified gene; error bars = standard deviation.)

Source: Adapted from a paper by T. Vierbuchen, A. Ostermeier, Z. Pang, Y. Kokubu, T. Sudhof, and M. Wenig. Copyright 2010 Macmillan Publishers, Ltd.

20. Which type of enzyme catalyzes the conversion of glutamate to GABA?

    A. Kinase
    B. Transferase
    C. Decarboxylase
    D. Dehydrogenase

21. What is the most likely reason why Tuj1 was used to assess the phenotype of cells that have incorporated the five candidate genes?

    A. Tuj1 induces expression of the TauEGFP protein.
    B. Tuj1 is expressed in fibroblasts and neurons.
    C. Tuj1 is an early marker of neural differentiation.
    D. Tuj1 is present in embryonic and adult cells in culture.

22. Of the five candidate genes, which produces a factor that most markedly increases the efficiency with which fibroblasts commit to a neuronal lineage in vitro?

    A. *Ascl1*
    B. *Brn2*
    C. *Zic1*
    D. *Olig2*

23. Does the experimental approach described in the passage yield cells that could be used in an animal model of Parkinson disease to replace dopamine-deficient neurons in the brain?

    A. Yes, because the cells obtained have the functional characteristics of nerve cells.
    B. Yes, because the cells obtained are similar to cells in the central nervous system.
    C. No, because the cells obtained may contain tumorigenic pluripotent cells.
    D. No, because the cells obtained lack the correct neurotransmitter phenotype.

24. As one step in the estimation of the efficiency of neuronal induction, scientists calculated the average number of induced cells present in 30 randomly selected 20× visual fields. Which change to this particular aspect of the experimental protocol would increase the accuracy of the estimates of efficiency?

    A. Increase the magnification of the oculars used to define the field of view.
    B. Increase the number of visual fields counted per petri dish.
    C. Select visual fields from the central portion of the petri dish where cell density is highest.
    D. Use the presence of green fluorescence to identify cells appropriate for quantification.

Solutions for this passage begin on next page.

20. Which type of enzyme catalyzes the conversion of glutamate to GABA?

    A. Kinase
    B. Transferase
    C. Decarboxylase
    D. Dehydrogenase

Foundational Concept: 1
Biomolecules have unique properties that determine how they contribute to the structure and function of cells and how they participate in the processes necessary to maintain life.

Content Category: 1A
Structure and function of proteins and their constituent amino acids

Scientific Inquiry and Reasoning Skill: 2
Scientific Reasoning and Problem Solving

Key: C
Comparison of the chemical formulas provided in the passage show that the conversion of glutamate to GABA involves the removal of a carbon from the carbon chain. These reactions are often catalyzed by decarboxylases.

Distractors

A   This is incorrect. Kinases are enzymes that modify protein targets by the transfer of phosphate groups.

B   This is incorrect. Transferases are enzymes that catalyze the transfer of functional groups between molecules.

D   This is incorrect. Dehydrogenases are enzymes that catalyze oxidation reactions.

21. What is the most likely reason why Tuj1 was used to assess the phenotype of cells that have incorporated the five candidate genes?

   A. Tuj1 induces expression of the TauEGFP protein.
   B. Tuj1 is expressed in fibroblasts and neurons.
   C. Tuj1 is an early marker of neural differentiation.
   D. Tuj1 is present in embryonic and adult cells in culture.

Foundational Concept: 2
Highly-organized assemblies of molecules, cells, and organs interact to carry out the functions of living organisms.

Content Category: 2C
Processes of cell division, differentiation, and specialization

Scientific Inquiry and Reasoning Skill: 2
Scientific Reasoning and Problem Solving

Key: C
Given that the experimental protocol described in the passage is used to convert mouse fibroblasts into functional neurons, it is reasonable to conclude that the scientists must have chosen Tuj1 because it is a reliable marker for selecting cells that, after a short time in culture, show signs of having been converted into neurons. Therefore, it must serve as an early marker for neurons.

Distractors
A   This is incorrect. Tuj1 is a tubulin protein; it is a structural protein, not a regulatory protein that could activate expression of the Tau-EGFP fusion gene.

B   This is incorrect. If Tuj1 were also expressed in fibroblasts, it would not be a useful marker for selecting reprogrammed cells (neurons) as it would be expressed in both the original cells in culture (fibroblasts) and the converted cells (neurons).

D   This is incorrect. Tuj1 is used to select for cells that have differentiated into neurons. Since fibroblasts were isolated from postnatal mice, no embryonic cells were used in the experiment, which involves the conversion of one adult cell type into another adult cell type.

TIP: A common error would be to scan the passage to look for one of the answers directly. The passage states that Tuj1 is a neuron-specific class III β-tubulin, which is not one of the options listed. However, as the researchers used Tuj1 to identify neurons twelve days after infection, Tuj1 is an early marker of neural differentiation.

22. Of the five candidate genes, which produces a factor that most markedly increases the efficiency with which fibroblasts commit to a neuronal lineage in vitro?

    A. *Ascl1*

    B. *Brn2*

    C. *Zic1*

    D. *Olig2*

Foundational Concept: 1

Biomolecules have unique properties that determine how they contribute to the structure and function of cells and how they participate in the processes necessary to maintain life.

Content Category: 1B

Transmission of genetic information from the gene to the protein

Scientific Inquiry and Reasoning Skill: 4

Data-based and Statistical Reasoning

Key: A

Tuj1-positive cells are cells derived from fibroblasts that have been reprogrammed into neurons. Figure 2 shows that when all 5 genes are present (indicated by 5 factor in the figure), the number of Tuj1-positive cells is set at 1 (100%). Omission of *Ascl1* reduces the number of these cells from 1.0 to 0.3; omission of *Brn2*, from 1.0 to 0.6; omission of *Myt1l*, from 1.0 to 0.66; omission of *Zic1*, from 1.0 to 0.66, and omission of *Olig2*, from 1.0 to 0.7. Because omission of *Ascl1* causes the biggest reduction in Tuj1-positive cells, this gene must produce a factor that most markedly increases the efficiency with which fibroblasts commit to a neuronal lineage.

Distractors

B   This is incorrect. Omission of *Brn2* reduces the number of reprogrammed neuronal cells by 40% relative to the 5-gene pool, whereas omission of *Ascl1* reduces it by 70%.

C   This is incorrect. Omission of either *Myt1l* or *Zic1* reduces the number of reprogrammed neuronal cells by 34% relative to the 5-gene pool, whereas omission of *Ascl1* reduces it by 70%.

D   This is incorrect. Omission of *Olig2* reduces the number of reprogrammed neuronal cells by 30% relative to the 5-gene pool, whereas omission of *Ascl1* reduces it by 70%.

 TIP: An easy mistake is to misinterpret the graph and associate "increase" with the highest bar on the graph. Determining which gene increases fibroblast commitment to a neuronal lineage is assessed in this case by what happens in the absence of the gene. Therefore, on this graph, the lowest bar represents the most efficient gene.

23. Does the experimental approach described in the passage yield cells that could be used in an animal model of Parkinson disease to replace dopamine-deficient neurons in the brain?

   A. Yes, because the cells obtained have the functional characteristics of nerve cells.
   B. Yes, because the cells obtained are similar to cells in the central nervous system.
   C. No, because the cells obtained may contain tumorigenic pluripotent cells.
   D. No, because the cells obtained lack the correct neurotransmitter phenotype.

Foundational Concept: 3

Complex systems of tissues and organs sense the internal and external environments of multicellular organisms and, through integrated functioning, maintain a stable internal environment within an ever-changing external environment.

Content Category: 3A

Structure and functions of the nervous and endocrine systems and ways in which these systems coordinate the organ systems

Scientific Inquiry and Reasoning Skill: 2

Scientific Reasoning and Problem Solving

Key: D

Although the cells obtained under the experimental conditions are similar to CNS neurons and may therefore be similar to neurons found in the brain, the neurons that are generated produce either glutamate or GABA. Since Parkinsonism is associated with deficiency of dopamine-producing neurons, neither of these 2 types of cells would alleviate the symptoms of this disorder.

Distractors

A   This is incorrect. It is not sufficient that the cells are functional neurons, the cells have to be dopamine-synthesizing neurons.

B   This is incorrect. It is not sufficient that the cells are similar to neurons that may be found in the brain, the cells have to be dopamine-synthesizing neurons.

C   This is incorrect. The cells obtained are differentiated neuron-like cells that are derived from differentiated fibroblasts; no pluripotent intermediate is involved in the production of the reprogrammed cells.

TIP: Try determining whether the correct answer is "yes" or "no" first. This eliminates two potential responses.

24. As one step in the estimation of the efficiency of neuronal induction, scientists calculated the average number of induced cells present in 30 randomly selected 20× visual fields. Which change to this particular aspect of the experimental protocol would increase the accuracy of the estimates of efficiency?

A. Increase the magnification of the oculars used to define the field of view.
B. Increase the number of visual fields counted per petri dish.
C. Select visual fields from the central portion of the petri dish where cell density is highest.
D. Use the presence of green fluorescence to identify cells appropriate for quantification.

Foundational Concept: 2
Highly-organized assemblies of molecules, cells, and organs interact to carry out the functions of living organisms.

Content Category: 2B
Structure, growth, physiology, and genetics of prokaryotes and viruses

Scientific Inquiry and Reasoning Skill: 3
Reasoning About the Design and Execution of Research

Key: B
Increasing the number of visual fields counted would increase the sample of cells observed from the total "population," and result in results that better approximate the true values.

Distractors
A   This is incorrect. Oculars of higher magnification would focus on a smaller area. Thus, the total area of the petri dish evaluated with high magnification oculars would be smaller than the total area evaluated with 20× oculars.

C   This is incorrect. This change would bias the scientists' sample of the population.

D   This is incorrect. This change would bias the scientists' sample of the population.

TIP: For this question, remember that research needs to be replicated and validated by other laboratories. Increasing the sample size is a simple way to improve the accuracy of the results.

Biological and Biochemical Foundations of Living Systems:

Discrete Questions

Fifth Edition
The Official Guide to the MCAT® Exam

MCAT® is a program of the
Association of American Medical Colleges

Biological and Biochemical Foundations of Living Systems

Biological and Biochemical Foundations of Living Systems Discrete (Questions 25–30)

25. Enzymes catalyze chemical reactions by stabilizing:

    A. the substrate.
    B. the product.
    C. the transition state.
    D. the equilibrium.

26. The Gibbs free energy equation can be used to predict whether a reaction will proceed spontaneously. For which relative values of ΔH and ΔS will a spontaneous reaction always occur?

    A. A positive ΔH and a negative ΔS
    B. A positive ΔH and a positive ΔS
    C. A negative ΔH and a negative ΔS
    D. A negative ΔH and a positive ΔS

27. Which type of molecule is LEAST likely to be found in a eukaryotic cell membrane?

    A. Phospholipid
    B. Cholesterol
    C. Glycoprotein
    D. Peptidoglycan

28. An epitope is a region on the surface of an antigen molecule to which a specific antibody binds. The table shows the physical and biological characteristics of several different molecules.

Molecule	Molecular weight (daltons)	Number of epitopes
Diphtheria protein	72,000	8–12
Thyroglobulin	650,000	40
Serum albumin	66,000	6–8
Ribonuclease	14,000	3
Ovalbumin	45,000	5

According to the information, which characteristics are most likely to be associated with a molecule's potential to elicit a strong immune response?

    A. High molecular weight and increased number of epitopes
    B. High molecular weight and reduced number of epitopes
    C. Low molecular weight and increased number of epitopes
    D. Low molecular weight and reduced number of epitopes

29. Increasing the volume of air that reaches the alveoli and takes part in gas exchange will cause blood pH to:

    A. increase, because the neural mechanisms that remove acid from the blood will be activated.
    B. increase, because the partial pressure of CO_2 in the blood will decrease.
    C. decrease, because the affinity of hemoglobin for oxygen will be increased.
    D. decrease, because the work associated with increased ventilation will consume more O_2.

30. Scientists have hypothesized that mitochondria evolved from aerobic heterotrophic bacteria that entered and established symbiotic relationships with primitive eukaryotic anaerobes. According to this hypothesis, the bacteria that entered primitive eukaryotic cells were able to carry out which function(s) that the primitive eukaryotic cells could not?

    A. Glycolysis
    B. Citric acid cycle and electron transport
    C. Cell division
    D. Transcription and translation

Solutions begin on next page.

25. Enzymes catalyze chemical reactions by stabilizing:

    A. the substrate.
    B. the product.
    C. the transition state.
    D. the equilibrium.

Foundational Concept: 1
Biomolecules have unique properties that determine how they contribute to the structure and function of cells and how they participate in the processes necessary to maintain life.

Content Category: 1A
Structure and function of proteins and their constituent amino acids

Scientific Inquiry and Reasoning Skill: 1
Knowledge of Scientific Concepts and Principles

Key: C
Enzymes work by stabilizing the transition state of a chemical reaction, which lowers the activation energy.

Distractors

A   This is incorrect. Stabilizing the substrate would not result in lower activation energy.

B   This is incorrect. Stabilizing the product would not result in lower activation energy.

D   This is incorrect. Enzymes do not affect the equilibrium of a reaction.

26. The Gibbs free energy equation can be used to predict whether a reaction will proceed spontaneously. For which relative values of ΔH and ΔS will a spontaneous reaction always occur?

    A. A positive ΔH and a negative ΔS
    B. A positive ΔH and a positive ΔS
    C. A negative ΔH and a negative ΔS
    D. A negative ΔH and a positive ΔS

Foundational Concept: 1
Biomolecules have unique properties that determine how they contribute to the structure and function of cells and how they participate in the processes necessary to maintain life.

Content Category: 1D
Principles of bioenergetics and fuel molecule metabolism

Scientific Inquiry and Reasoning Skill: 2
Scientific Reasoning and Problem Solving

Key: D
The Gibbs free energy equation is $\Delta G = \Delta H - T\Delta S$. In order for a reaction to occur spontaneously, the final value for ΔG must be negative. The only combination of ΔH and ΔS that will always result in a negative ΔG is a negative ΔH and a positive ΔS because of the presence of the $-T$ term.

Distractors

A   This is incorrect. A reaction with these relative thermodynamic parameters is unfavorable at all temperatures.

B   This is incorrect. A reaction with these relative thermodynamic parameters is only favorable at high temperatures.

C   This is incorrect. A reaction with these relative thermodynamic parameters is only favorable at low temperatures.

 TIP: Knowing that a negative value of the change in free energy indicates a spontaneous reaction is only the first step. The free energy equation must also be examined. Be prepared to manipulate equations to determine mathematical outcomes.

Fifth Edition
The Official Guide to the MCAT® Exam
166
MCAT® is a program of the
Association of American Medical Colleges

27. Which type of molecule is LEAST likely to be found in a eukaryotic cell membrane?

A. Phospholipid
B. Cholesterol
C. Glycoprotein
D. Peptidoglycan

Foundational Concept: 2
Highly-organized assemblies of molecules, cells, and organs interact to carry out the functions of living organisms.

Content Category: 2B
Structure, growth, physiology, and genetics of prokaryotes and viruses

Scientific Inquiry and Reasoning Skill: 1
Knowledge of Scientific Concepts and Principles

Key: D
Peptidoglycan is found in the cell walls of some bacteria, but not in the cell membranes of eukaryotes.

Distractors
A   This is incorrect. Phospholipid is found in the cell membrane of eukaryotes.

B   This is incorrect. Cholesterol is found in the cell membrane of eukaryotes.

C   This is incorrect. Glycoprotein is found in the cell membrane of eukaryotes.

TIP: Notice that this question is asking for the LEAST likely option. Phospholipid is an important component of the cell membrane but would be the incorrect answer to this question.

28. An epitope is a region on the surface of an antigen molecule to which a specific antibody binds. The table shows the physical and biological characteristics of several different molecules.

Molecule	Molecular weight (daltons)	Number of epitopes
Diphtheria protein	72,000	8–12
Thyroglobulin	650,000	40
Serum albumin	66,000	6–8
Ribonuclease	14,000	3
Ovalbumin	45,000	5

According to the information, which characteristics are most likely to be associated with a molecule's potential to elicit a strong immune response?

A. High molecular weight and increased number of epitopes
B. High molecular weight and reduced number of epitopes
C. Low molecular weight and increased number of epitopes
D. Low molecular weight and reduced number of epitopes

Foundational Concept: 3
Complex systems of tissues and organs sense the internal and external environments of multicellular organisms and, through integrated functioning, maintain a stable internal environment within an ever-changing external environment.

Content Category: 3B
Structure and integrative functions of the main organ systems

Scientific Inquiry and Reasoning Skill: 4
Data-based and Statistical Reasoning

Key: A
An epitope binds one specific antibody. Therefore, a molecule with several epitopes will bind several distinct antibody molecules. The presence of several antibodies on the surface of an antigen is expected to elicit a stronger immune response than if fewer antibodies were present. The table shows that molecules with higher molecular weights are associated with higher numbers of epitopes, which will bind a greater number of antibodies. These molecules are therefore expected to elicit a more robust immune response.

Distractors

B   This is incorrect. Molecules with a reduced number of epitopes will bind fewer antibodies, therefore generating less potential for a robust immune response.

C   This is incorrect. The table shows that molecules with a low molecular weight do not have an increased number of epitopes.

D   This is incorrect. Although from the table a low molecular weight is correlated with a reduced number of epitopes, fewer antibody recognition sites will not generate a robust immune response.

 TIP: The number of epitopes is an indicator of the potential immune response generated. Determine the correlation between epitope number and molecular weight for several molecules to confirm the correct observation.

29. Increasing the volume of air that reaches the alveoli and takes part in gas exchange will cause blood pH to:

    A. increase, because the neural mechanisms that remove acid from the blood will be activated.
    B. increase, because the partial pressure of CO_2 in the blood will decrease.
    C. decrease, because the affinity of hemoglobin for oxygen will be increased.
    D. decrease, because the work associated with increased ventilation will come more O_2.

Foundational Concept: 3

Complex systems of tissues and organs sense the internal and external environments of multicellular organisms and, through integrated functioning, maintain a stable internal environment within an ever-changing external environment.

Content Category: 3B

Structure and integrative functions of the main organ systems

Scientific Inquiry and Reasoning Skill: 2

Scientific Reasoning and Problem Solving

Key: B

Increasing the volume of air that reaches the alveoli and takes part in gas exchange will enhance O_2 uptake and CO_2 removal, thereby increasing blood pH.

Distractors

A   This is incorrect. Neural mechanisms control the rate of breathing.

C   This is incorrect. The blood pH will increase, not decrease.

D   This is incorrect. The blood pH will increase, not decrease.

 TIP: Determine whether the blood pH will increase or decrease to quickly eliminate two possible answers.

30. Scientists have hypothesized that mitochondria evolved from aerobic heterotrophic bacteria that entered and established symbiotic relationships with primitive eukaryotic anaerobes. According to this hypothesis, the bacteria that entered primitive eukaryotic cells were able to carry out which function(s) that the primitive eukaryotic cells could not?

A. Glycolysis
B. Citric acid cycle and electron transport
C. Cell division
D. Transcription and translation

Foundational Concept: 2
Highly-organized assemblies of molecules, cells, and organs interact to carry out the functions of living organisms.

Content Category: 2A
Assemblies of molecules, cells, and groups of cells within single cellular and multicellular organisms

Scientific Inquiry and Reasoning Skill: 1
Knowledge of Scientific Concepts and Principles

Key: B
According to the provided information, the primitive bacteria were aerobic and heterotrophic, whereas the primitive eukaryotes were anaerobic. If the primitive eukaryotes were anaerobic they could not exist in an oxygen-containing environment nor engage in metabolic processes requiring oxygen. Thus, the bacteria were likely to be able to carry out the oxygen-requiring reactions of the citric acid cycle and the electron transport chain while the primitive eukaryotes were not.

Distractors

A   This is incorrect. Glycolysis occurs in the cytosol and can occur under both anaerobic and aerobic conditions.

C   This is incorrect. Cell division is not dependent on aerobic metabolism.

D   This is incorrect. Transcription and translation are essential to all living organisms and would have been present in primitive eukaryotes.

Chapter 11

What Will the Chemical and Physical Foundations of Biological Systems Section Test?

The Chemical and Physical Foundations of Biological Systems section asks you to solve problems by combining your knowledge of chemical and physical foundational concepts with your scientific inquiry and reasoning skills. This section tests your understanding of the mechanical, physical, and biochemical functions of human tissues, organs, and organ systems. It also tests your knowledge of the basic chemical and physical principles that underlie the mechanisms operating in the human body and your ability to reason about and apply your understanding of these basic chemical and physical principles to living systems.

To recap from Part I, this section is designed to:

- test introductory-level biology, organic and inorganic chemistry, and physics concepts;

- test biochemistry concepts at the level taught in many colleges and universities in first-semester biochemistry courses;

- test molecular biology topics at the level taught in many colleges and universities in introductory biology sequences and first-semester biochemistry courses;

- test basic research methods and statistics concepts described by many baccalaureate faculty as important to success in introductory science courses; and

- require you to demonstrate your scientific inquiry and reasoning, research methods, and statistics skills as applied to the natural sciences.

Test Section	Number of Questions	Time
Chemical and Physical Foundations of Biological Systems	59 *(note that questions are a combination of passage-based and discrete questions)*	95 minutes

MCAT® is a program of the
Association of American Medical Colleges

Chemical and Physical Foundations of Biological Systems Distribution of Questions

Distribution of Questions by Discipline, Foundational Concept, and Scientific Inquiry and Reasoning Skill

You may wonder how much chemistry you'll see on this section of the MCAT exam, how many questions you'll get about a particular foundational concept, or how the scientific inquiry and reasoning skills will be distributed on your exam. The questions that you see are likely to be distributed in the ways described below. These are the approximate percentages of questions you'll see on a test for each discipline, foundational concept, and scientific inquiry and reasoning skill.*

Discipline:
- First-semester biochemistry, 25%
- Introductory biology, 5%
- General chemistry, 30%
- Organic chemistry, 15%
- Introductory physics, 25%

Foundational Concept:
- Foundational Concept 4, 40%
- Foundational Concept 5, 60%

Scientific Inquiry and Reasoning Skill:
- Skill 1, 35%
- Skill 2, 45%
- Skill 3, 10%
- Skill 4, 10%

*These percentages have been approximated to the nearest 5% and will vary from one test to another for a variety of reasons. These reasons include, but are not limited to, controlling for question difficulty, using groups of questions that depend on a single passage, and using unscored field-test questions on each test form.

Understanding the Foundational Concepts and Content Categories

The following are detailed explanations of each foundational concept and related content categories tested in this section. As with the Biological and Biochemical Foundations of Living Systems section, lists describing the specific topics and subtopics that define each content category for this section are provided. The same content list is provided to the writers who develop the content of the exam. An excerpt from the content list is at the top of the next page.

Excerpt from the Chemical and Physical Foundations of Biological Systems Outline

Separations and Purifications (OC, BC) ◄——————— **Topic**

- Extraction: distribution of solute between two immiscible solvents ◄——— **Subtopic**
- Distillation
- Chromatography: basic principles involved in separation process
  - ○ Column chromatography
    - ■ Gas-liquid chromatography
    - ■ High pressure liquid chromatography
  - ○ Paper chromatography
  - ○ Thin-layer chromatography
- Separation and purification of peptides and proteins (BC)
  - ○ Electrophoresis
  - ○ Quantitative analysis
  - ○ Chromatography
    - ■ Size-exclusion
    - ■ Ion-exchange
    - ■ Affinity
- Racemic mixtures, separation of enantiomers (OC)

The abbreviations found in parentheses indicate the course(s) in which undergraduate students at many colleges and universities learn about the topics and associated subtopics. The course abbreviations are

- BC: first semester of biochemistry
- BIO: two-semester sequence of introductory biology
- GC: two-semester sequence of general chemistry
- OC: two-semester sequence of organic chemistry
- PHY: two-semester sequence of introductory physics

In preparing for the MCAT exam, you will be responsible for learning the topics and associated subtopics at the levels at which they are taught at many colleges and universities in the courses listed in parentheses. A small number of subtopics have course abbreviations indicated in parentheses. In those cases, you are responsible only for learning the subtopics as they are taught in the course(s) indicated.

Using the excerpt above as an example:

- You are responsible for learning about the topic Separations and Purifications at the level at which it is taught in a typical two-semester organic chemistry sequence *and* in a typical first-semester biochemistry course.

- You are responsible for learning about the subtopic Separation and purification of peptides and proteins (and sub-subtopics) *only* at the level at which it is taught in a first-semester biochemistry course.

- You are responsible for learning about the subtopic Racemic mixtures, separation of enantiomers *only* at the level at which it is taught in a two-semester organic chemistry course.

Remember that course content at your school may differ from course content at other colleges and universities. The topics and subtopics described in this chapter may be covered in courses with titles that are different from those listed here. Your prehealth advisor and faculty are important resources for your questions about course content.

Chemical and Physical Foundations of Biological Systems

Foundational Concept 4

Complex living organisms transport materials, sense their environment, process signals, and respond to changes using processes that can be understood in terms of physical principles.

The processes that take place within organisms follow the laws of physics. They can be quantified with equations that model the behavior at a fundamental level. For example, the principles of electromagnetic radiation, and its interactions with matter, can be exploited to generate structural information about molecules or to generate images of the human body. So, too, can atomic structure be used to predict the physical and chemical properties of atoms, including the amount of electromagnetic energy required to cause ionization.

Content Categories

- *Category 4A* focuses on motion and its causes, and various forms of energy and their interconversions.

- *Category 4B* focuses on the behavior of fluids, which is relevant to the functioning of the pulmonary and circulatory systems.

- *Category 4C* emphasizes the nature of electrical currents and voltages; how energy can be converted into electrical forms that can be used to perform chemical transformations or work; and how electrical impulses can be transmitted over long distances in the nervous system.

- *Category 4D* focuses on the properties of light and sound; how the interactions of light and sound with matter can be used by an organism to sense its environment; and how these interactions can also be used to generate structural information or images.

- *Category 4E* focuses on sub-atomic particles, the atomic nucleus, nuclear radiation, the structure of the atom, and how the configuration of any particular atom can be used to predict its physical and chemical properties.

With these building blocks, medical students will be able to utilize core principles of physics to learn about the physiological functions of the respiratory, cardiovascular, and neurological systems in health and disease.

Content Category 4A: *Translational motion, forces, work, energy, and equilibrium in living systems*

The motion of any object can be described in terms of displacement, velocity, and acceleration. Objects accelerate when subjected to external forces and are at equilibrium when the net force and the net torque acting upon them are zero. Many aspects of motion can be calculated with the knowledge that energy is conserved, even though it may be converted into different forms. In a living system, the energy for motion comes from the metabolism of fuel molecules, but the energetic requirements remain subject to the same physical principles.

The content in this category covers several physics topics relevant to living systems including translational motion, forces, work, energy, and equilibrium. The topics and subtopics in this category are the following:

Translational Motion (PHY)
- Units and dimensions
- Vectors, components
- Vector addition
- Speed, velocity (average and instantaneous)
- Acceleration

Force (PHY)
- Newton's First Law, inertia
- Newton's Second Law ($F = ma$)
- Newton's Third Law, forces equal and opposite
- Friction, static and kinetic
- Center of mass

Equilibrium (PHY)
- Vector analysis of forces acting on a point object
- Torques, lever arms

Work (PHY)
- Work done by a constant force: $W = Fd \cos\theta$
- Mechanical advantage
- Work Kinetic Energy Theorem
- Conservative forces

Energy of Point Object Systems (PHY)
- Kinetic Energy: $KE = \frac{1}{2}mv^2$; units
- Potential Energy
    - $PE = mgh$ (gravitational, local)
    - $PE = \frac{1}{2}kx^2$ (spring)
- Conservation of energy
- Power, units

Periodic Motion (PHY)
- Amplitude, frequency, phase
- Transverse and longitudinal waves: wavelength and propagation speed

Please Note

Topics that appear on multiple content lists will be treated differently. Questions will focus on the topics as they are described in the narrative for the content category.

Content Category 4B: *Importance of fluids for the circulation of blood, gas movement, and gas exchange*

Fluids are featured in several physiologically important processes, including the circulation of blood, gas movement into and out of the lungs, and gas exchange with the blood. The energetic requirements of fluid dynamics can be modeled using physical equations. A thorough understanding of fluids is necessary to understand the origins of numerous forms of disease.

The content in this category covers hydrostatic pressure, fluid flow rates, viscosity, the Kinetic Molecular Theory of Gases, and the Ideal Gas Law. The topics and subtopics in this category are the following:

Fluids (PHY)
- Density, specific gravity
- Buoyancy, Archimedes' Principle
- Hydrostatic pressure
  - Pascal's Law
  - Hydrostatic pressure; $P = \rho gh$ (pressure vs. depth)
- Viscosity: Poiseuille Flow
- Continuity equation ($A \cdot v$ = constant)
- Concept of turbulence at high velocities
- Surface tension
- Bernoulli's equation
- Venturi effect, pitot tube

Circulatory System (BIO)
- Arterial and venous systems; pressure and flow characteristics

Gas Phase (GC, PHY)
- Absolute temperature, (K) Kelvin Scale
- Pressure, simple mercury barometer
- Molar volume at 0°C and 1 atm = 22.4 L/mol
- Ideal gas
  - Definition
  - Ideal Gas Law: $PV = nRT$
  - Boyle's Law: PV = constant
  - Charles' Law: V/T = constant
  - Avogadro's Law: V/n = constant
- Kinetic Molecular Theory of Gases
  - Heat capacity at constant volume and at constant pressure (PHY)
  - Boltzmann's Constant (PHY)
- Deviation of real gas behavior from Ideal Gas Law
  - Qualitative
  - Quantitative (Van der Waals' Equation)
- Partial pressure, mole fraction
- Dalton's Law relating partial pressure to composition

Fifth Edition
The Official Guide to the MCAT® Exam
177
MCAT® is a program of the
Association of American Medical Colleges

Content Category 4C: *Electrochemistry and electrical circuits and their elements*

Charged particles can be set in motion by the action of an applied electrical field, and can be used to transmit energy or information over long distances. The energy released during certain chemical reactions can be converted to electrical energy, which can be harnessed to perform other reactions or work.

Physiologically, a concentration gradient of charged particles is set up across the cell membrane of neurons at considerable energetic expense. This allows for the rapid transmission of signals using electrical impulses—changes in the electrical voltage across the membrane—under the action of some external stimulus.

The content in this category covers electrical circuit elements, electrical circuits, and electrochemistry. The topics and subtopics in this category are the following:

Electrostatics (PHY)
- Charge, conductors, charge conservation
- Insulators
- Coulomb's Law
- Electric field **E**
    - Field lines
    - Field due to charge distribution
- Electrostatic energy, electric potential at a point in space

Circuit Elements (PHY)
- Current $I = \Delta Q/\Delta t$, sign conventions, units
- Electromotive force, voltage
- Resistance
    - Ohm's Law: $I = V/R$
    - Resistors in series
    - Resistors in parallel
    - Resistivity: $\rho = R \bullet A/L$
- Capacitance
    - Parallel plate capacitor
    - Energy of charged capacitor
    - Capacitors in series
    - Capacitors in parallel
    - Dielectrics
- Conductivity
    - Metallic
    - Electrolytic
- Meters

Magnetism (PHY)
- Definition of magnetic field **B**
- Motion of charged particles in magnetic fields; Lorentz force

Electrochemistry (GC)
- Electrolytic cell
    - Electrolysis
    - Anode, cathode
    - Electrolyte
    - Faraday's Law relating amount of elements deposited (or gas liberated) at an electrode to current
    - Electron flow; oxidation, and reduction at the electrodes
- Galvanic or Voltaic cells
    - Half-reactions
    - Reduction potentials; cell potential
    - Direction of electron flow
- Concentration cell
- Batteries
    - Electromotive force, voltage
    - Lead-storage batteries
    - Nickel-cadmium batteries

Specialized Cell—Nerve Cell (BIO)
- Myelin sheath, Schwann cells, insulation of axon
- Nodes of Ranvier: propagation of nerve impulse along axon

Content Category 4D: How light and sound interact with matter

Light is a form of electromagnetic radiation—waves of electric and magnetic fields that transmit energy. The behavior of light depends on its frequency (or wavelength). The properties of light are exploited in the optical elements of the eye to focus rays of light on sensory elements. When light interacts with matter, spectroscopic changes occur that can be used to identify the material on an atomic or molecular level. Differential absorption of electromagnetic radiation can be used to generate images useful in diagnostic medicine. Interference and diffraction of light waves are used in many analytical and diagnostic techniques. The photon model of light explains why electromagnetic radiation of different wavelengths interacts differently with matter.

When mechanical energy is transmitted through solids, liquids, and gases, oscillating pressure waves known as "sound" are generated. Sound waves are audible if the sensory elements of the ear vibrate in response to exposure to these vibrations. The detection of reflected sound waves is utilized in ultrasound imaging. This non-invasive technique readily locates dense subcutaneous structures, such as bone and cartilage, and is very useful in diagnostic medicine.

The content in this category covers the properties of both light and sound and how these energy waves interact with matter. The topics and subtopics in this category are the following:

Sound (PHY)
- Production of sound
- Relative speed of sound in solids, liquids, and gases
- Intensity of sound, decibel units, log scale
- Attenuation (Damping)
- Doppler Effect: moving sound source or observer, reflection of sound from a moving object
- Pitch
- Resonance in pipes and strings
- Ultrasound
- Shock waves

Light, Electromagnetic Radiation (PHY)
- Concept of Interference; Young Double-slit Experiment
- Thin films, diffraction grating, single-slit diffraction
- Other diffraction phenomena, X-ray diffraction
- Polarization of light: linear and circular
- Properties of electromagnetic radiation
    - Velocity equals constant c, *in vacuo*
    - Electromagnetic radiation consists of perpendicularly oscillating electric and magnetic fields; direction of propagation is perpendicular to both
- Classification of electromagnetic spectrum, photon energy $E = hf$
- Visual spectrum, color

Molecular Structure and Absorption Spectra (OC)

- Infrared region
  - Intramolecular vibrations and rotations
  - Recognizing common characteristic group absorptions, fingerprint region
- Visible region (GC)
  - Absorption in visible region gives complementary color (e.g., carotene)
  - Effect of structural changes on absorption (e.g., indicators)
- Ultraviolet region
  - π-Electron and non-bonding electron transitions
  - Conjugated systems
- NMR spectroscopy
  - Protons in a magnetic field; equivalent protons
  - Spin-spin splitting

Geometrical Optics (PHY)

- Reflection from plane surface: angle of incidence equals angle of reflection
- Refraction, refractive index n; Snell's law: $n_1 \sin\theta_1 = n_2 \sin\theta_2$
- Dispersion, change of index of refraction with wavelength
- Conditions for total internal reflection
- Spherical mirrors
  - Center of curvature
  - Focal length
  - Real and virtual images
- Thin lenses
  - Converging and diverging lenses
  - Use of formula $1/p + 1/q = 1/f$, with sign conventions
  - Lens strength, diopters
- Combination of lenses
- Lens aberration
- Optical Instruments, including the human eye

Content Category 4E: *Atoms, nuclear decay, electronic structure, and atomic chemical behavior*

Atoms are classified by their *atomic number*: the number of protons in the atomic nucleus, which also includes neutrons. Chemical interactions between atoms are the result of electrostatic forces involving the electrons and the nuclei. Because neutrons are uncharged, they do not dramatically affect the chemistry of any particular type of atom, but do affect the stability of the nucleus itself.

When a nucleus is unstable, decay results from one of several different processes, which are random, but occur at well-characterized average rates. The products of nuclear decay (alpha, beta, and gamma rays) can interact with living tissue, breaking chemical bonds and ionizing atoms and molecules in the process.

The electronic structure of an atom is responsible for its chemical and physical properties. Only discrete energy levels are allowed for electrons. These levels are described individually by quantum numbers. Since the outermost, or *valence*, electrons are responsible for the strongest chemical interactions, a description of these electrons alone is a good first approximation to describe the behavior of any particular type of atom.

Mass spectrometry is an analytical tool that allows characterization of atoms or molecules, based on well recognized fragmentation patterns and the charge to mass ratio (m/z) of ions generated in the gas phase.

The content in this category covers atomic structure, nuclear decay, electronic structure, and the periodic nature of atomic chemical behavior. The topics and subtopics in this category are the following:

Atomic Nucleus (PHY, GC)
- Atomic number, atomic weight
- Neutrons, protons, isotopes
- Nuclear forces, binding energy
- Radioactive decay
    - α, β, γ decay
    - Half-life, exponential decay, semi-log plots
- Mass spectrometer

Electronic Structure (PHY, GC)
- Orbital structure of hydrogen atom, principal quantum number n, number of electrons per orbital (GC)
- Ground state, excited states
- Absorption and emission line spectra
- Use of Pauli Exclusion Principle
- Paramagnetism and diamagnetism
- Conventional notation for electronic structure (GC)
- Bohr atom
- Heisenberg Uncertainty Principle
- Effective nuclear charge (GC)
- Photoelectric effect

The Periodic Table—Classification of Elements into Groups by Electronic Structure (GC)
- Alkali metals
- Alkaline earth metals: their chemical characteristics
- Halogens: their chemical characteristics
- Noble gases: their physical and chemical characteristics
- Transition metals
- Representative elements
- Metals and non-metals
- Oxygen group

The Periodic Table—Variations of Chemical Properties with Group and Row (GC)
- Valence electrons
- First and second ionization energy
    - Definition
    - Prediction from electronic structure for elements in different groups or rows
- Electron affinity
    - Definition
    - Variation with group and row
- Electronegativity
    - Definition
    - Comparative values for some representative elements and important groups
- Electron shells and the sizes of atoms
- Electron shells and the sizes of ions

Stoichiometry (GC)
- Molecular weight
- Empirical versus molecular formula
- Metric units commonly used in the context of chemistry
- Description of composition by percent mass
- Mole concept, Avogadro's number N_A
- Definition of density
- Oxidation number
    - Common oxidizing and reducing agents
    - Disproportionation reactions
- Description of reactions by chemical equations
    - Conventions for writing chemical equations
    - Balancing equations, including redox equations
    - Limiting reactants
    - Theoretical yields

Chemical and Physical Foundations of Biological Systems

Foundational Concept 5

The principles that govern chemical interactions and reactions form the basis for a broader understanding of the molecular dynamics of living systems.

The chemical processes that take place within organisms are readily understood within the framework of the behavior of solutions, thermodynamics, molecular structure, intermolecular interactions, molecular dynamics, and molecular reactivity.

Content Categories

- *Category 5A* emphasizes the nature of solution formation, factors that affect solubility, and the properties and behavior of aqueous solutions, with special emphasis on the acid-base behavior of dissolved solutes.

- *Category 5B* focuses on molecular structure and how it affects the strength of intermolecular interactions.

- *Category 5C* emphasizes how differential intermolecular interactions can be used to effect chemical separations.

- *Category 5D* emphasizes the varied nature of biologically-relevant molecules, and how patterns of covalent bonding can be used to predict the chemical reactivity of these molecules and their structure and function within a living system.

- *Category 5E* emphasizes how relative energy dictates the overall favorability of chemical processes and the rate at which these processes can occur.

With these building blocks, medical students will be able to utilize core principles of human chemistry to learn about molecular and cellular functions in health and disease.

Content Category 5A: *Unique nature of water and its solutions*

In order to fully understand the complex and dynamic nature of living systems, it is first necessary to understand the unique nature of water and its solutions. The unique properties of water allow it to strongly interact with and mobilize many types of solutes, including ions. Water is also unique in its ability to absorb energy and buffer living systems from the chemical changes necessary to sustain life.

The content in this category covers the nature of solutions, solubility, acids, bases, and buffers. The topics and subtopics in this category are the following:

Acid/Base Equilibria (GC, BC)
- Brønsted–Lowry definition of acid, base
- Ionization of water
  - K_w, its approximate value ($K_w = [H^+][OH^-] = 10^{-14}$ at 25°C, 1 atm)
  - Definition of pH: pH of pure water
- Conjugate acids and bases (e.g., NH_4^+ and NH_3)
- Strong acids and bases (e.g., nitric, sulfuric)
- Weak acids and bases (e.g., acetic, benzoic)
  - Dissociation of weak acids and bases with or without added salt
  - Hydrolysis of salts of weak acids or bases
  - Calculation of pH of solutions of salts of weak acids or bases
- Equilibrium constants K_a and K_b: pK_a, pK_b
- Buffers
  - Definition and concepts (common buffer systems)
  - Influence on titration curves

Ions in Solutions (GC, BC)
- Anion, cation: common names, formulas and charges for familiar ions (e.g., NH_4^+ ammonium, PO_4^{3-} phosphate, SO_4^{2-} sulfate)
- Hydration, the hydronium ion

Solubility (GC)
- Units of concentration (e.g., molarity)
- Solubility product constant; the equilibrium expression K_{sp}
- Common-ion effect, its use in laboratory separations
  - Complex ion formation
  - Complex ions and solubility
  - Solubility and pH

Titration (GC)
- Indicators
- Neutralization
- Interpretation of the titration curves
- Redox titration

Content Category 5B: *Nature of molecules and intermolecular interactions*

Covalent bonding involves the sharing of electrons between atoms. If the result of such interactions is not a network solid, then the covalently bonded substance will be discrete and molecular.

The shape of molecules can be predicted based on electrostatic principles and quantum mechanics since only two electrons can occupy the same orbital. Bond polarity (both direction and magnitude) can be predicted based on knowledge of the valence electron structure of the constituent atoms. The strength of intermolecular interactions depends on molecular shape and the polarity of the covalent bonds present. The solubility and other physical properties of molecular substances depend on the strength of intermolecular interactions.

The content in this category covers the nature of molecules and includes covalent bonding, molecular structure, nomenclature, and intermolecular interactions. The topics and subtopics in this category are the following:

Covalent Bond (GC)
- Lewis Electron Dot formulas
  - Resonance structures
  - Formal charge
  - Lewis acids and bases
- Partial ionic character
  - Role of electronegativity in determining charge distribution
  - Dipole Moment
- σ and π bonds
  - Hybrid orbitals: sp^3, sp^2, sp and respective geometries
  - Valence shell electron pair repulsion and the prediction of shapes of molecules (e.g., NH_3, H_2O, CO_2)
  - Structural formulas for molecules involving H, C, N, O, F, S, P, Si, Cl
  - Delocalized electrons and resonance in ions and molecules
- Multiple bonding
  - Effect on bond length and bond energies
  - Rigidity in molecular structure
- Stereochemistry of covalently bonded molecules (OC)
  - Isomers
    - Structural isomers
    - Stereoisomers (e.g., diastereomers, enantiomers, cis/trans isomers)
    - Conformational isomers
  - Polarization of light, specific rotation
  - Absolute and relative configuration
    - Conventions for writing *R* and *S* forms
    - Conventions for writing *E* and *Z* forms

Liquid Phase—Intermolecular Forces (GC)
- Hydrogen bonding
- Dipole Interactions
- Van der Waals' Forces (London dispersion forces)

Content Category 5C: Separation and purification methods

Analysis of complex mixtures of substances—especially biologically relevant materials—typically requires separation of the components. Many methods have been developed to accomplish this task, and the method used is dependent on the types of substances which comprise the mixture. All of these methods rely on the magnification of potential differences in the strength of intermolecular interactions.

The content in this category covers separation and purification methods including: extraction, liquid and gas chromatography, and electrophoresis. The topics and subtopics in this category are the following:

Separations and Purifications (OC, BC)

- Extraction: distribution of solute between two immiscible solvents
- Distillation
- Chromatography: basic principles involved in separation process
  - Column chromatography
    - Gas-liquid chromatography
    - High pressure liquid chromatography
  - Paper chromatography
  - Thin-layer chromatography
- Separation and purification of peptides and proteins (BC)
  - Electrophoresis
  - Quantitative analysis
  - Chromatography
    - Size-exclusion
    - Ion-exchange
    - Affinity
- Racemic mixtures, separation of enantiomers (OC)

Content Category 5D: *Structure, function, and reactivity of biologically-relevant molecules*

The structure of biological molecules forms the basis of their chemical reactions including oligomerization and polymerization. Unique aspects of each type of biological molecule dictate their role in living systems, whether providing structure or information storage, or serving as fuel and catalysts.

The content in this category covers the structure, function, and reactivity of biologically-relevant molecules including the mechanistic considerations that dictate their modes of reactivity. The topics and subtopics in this category are the following:

Nucleotides and Nucleic Acids (BC, BIO)
- Nucleotides and nucleosides: composition
  - Sugar phosphate backbone
  - Pyrimidine, purine residues
- Deoxyribonucleic acid: DNA; double helix
- Chemistry (BC)
- Other functions (BC)

Amino Acids, Peptides, Proteins (OC, BC)
- Amino acids: description
  - Absolute configuration at the α position
  - Dipolar ions
  - Classification
    - Acidic or basic
    - Hydrophilic or hydrophobic
  - Synthesis of α-amino acids (OC)
    - Strecker Synthesis
    - Gabriel Synthesis
- Peptides and proteins: reactions
  - Sulfur linkage for cysteine and cystine
  - Peptide linkage: polypeptides and proteins
  - Hydrolysis (BC)
- General Principles
  - Primary structure of proteins
  - Secondary structure of proteins
  - Tertiary structure of proteins
  - Isoelectric point

The Three-Dimensional Protein Structure (BC)
- Conformational stability
  - Hydrophobic interactions
  - Solvation layer (entropy)
- Quaternary structure
- Denaturing and Folding

Non-Enzymatic Protein Function (BC)
- Binding
- Immune system
- Motor

Lipids (BC, OC)

- Description, Types
  - Storage
    - Triacyl glycerols
    - Free fatty acids: saponification
  - Structural
    - Phospholipids and phosphatids
    - Sphingolipids (BC)
    - Waxes
  - Signals/cofactors
    - Fat-soluble vitamins
    - Steroids
    - Prostaglandins (BC)

Carbohydrates (OC)

- Description
  - Nomenclature and classification, common names
  - Absolute configuration
  - Cyclic structure and conformations of hexoses
  - Epimers and anomers
- Hydrolysis of the glycoside linkage
- Keto-enol tautomerism of monosaccharides
- Disaccharides (BC)
- Polysaccharides (BC)

Aldehydes and Ketones (OC)

- Description
  - Nomenclature
  - Physical properties
- Important reactions
  - Nucleophilic addition reactions at C=O bond
    - Acetal, hemiacetal
    - Imine, enamine
    - Hydride reagents
    - Cyanohydrin
  - Oxidation of aldehydes
  - Reactions at adjacent positions: enolate chemistry
    - Keto-enol tautomerism (α-racemization)
    - Aldol condensation, retro-aldol
    - Kinetic versus thermodynamic enolate
- General principles
  - Effect of substituents on reactivity of C=O; steric hindrance
  - Acidity of α-H; carbanions

Alcohols (OC)

- Description
  - Nomenclature
  - Physical properties (acidity, hydrogen bonding)
- Important reactions
  - Oxidation
  - Substitution reactions: S_N1 or S_N2
  - Protection of alcohols
  - Preparation of mesylates and tosylates

Carboxylic Acids (OC)

- Description
  - Nomenclature
  - Physical properties
- Important reactions
  - Carboxyl group reactions
    - Amides (and lactam), esters (and lactone), anhydride formation
    - Reduction
    - Decarboxylation
  - Reactions at 2-position, substitution

Acid Derivatives (Anhydrides, Amides, Esters) (OC)

- Description
  - Nomenclature
  - Physical properties
- Important reactions
  - Nucleophilic substitution
  - Transesterification
  - Hydrolysis of amides
- General principles
  - Relative reactivity of acid derivatives
  - Steric effects
  - Electronic effects
  - Strain (e.g., β-lactams)

Phenols (OC, BC)

- Oxidation and reduction (e.g.,hydroquinones, ubiquinones): biological $2e^-$redox centers

Polycyclic and Heterocyclic Aromatic Compounds (OC, BC)

- Biological aromatic heterocycles

Content Category 5E: *Principles of chemical thermodynamics and kinetics*

The processes that occur in living systems are dynamic, and they follow the principles of chemical thermodynamics and kinetics. The position of chemical equilibrium is dictated by the relative energies of products and reactants. The rate at which chemical equilibrium is attained is dictated by a variety of factors: concentration of reactants, temperature, and the amount of catalyst (if any).

Biological systems have evolved to harness energy, and utilize it in very efficient ways to support all processes of life, including homeostasis and anabolism. Biological catalysts, known as *enzymes*, have evolved to allow all of the relevant chemical reactions required to sustain life to occur both rapidly and efficiently, and under the narrow set of conditions required.

The content in this category covers all principles of chemical thermodynamics and kinetics including enzymatic catalysis. The topics and subtopics in this category are the following:

Enzymes (BC, BIO)
- Classification by reaction type
- Mechanism
    - Substrates and enzyme specificity
    - Active site model
    - Induced-fit model
    - Cofactors, coenzymes, and vitamins
- Kinetics
    - General (catalysis)
    - Michaelis–Menten
    - Cooperativity
    - Effects of local conditions on enzyme activity
- Inhibition
- Regulatory enzymes
    - Allosteric
    - Covalently modified

Principles of Bioenergetics (BC)
- Bioenergetics/thermodynamics
    - Free energy/K_{eq}
    - Concentration
- Phosphorylation/ATP
    - ATP hydrolysis $\Delta G \ll 0$
    - ATP group transfers
- Biological oxidation–reduction
    - Half-reactions
    - Soluble electron carriers
    - Flavoproteins

Energy Changes in Chemical Reactions—Thermochemistry, Thermodynamics (GC, PHY)

- Thermodynamic system—state function
- Zeroth Law—concept of temperature
- First Law—conservation of energy in thermodynamic processes
- *PV* diagram: work done = area under or enclosed by curve (PHY)
- Second Law—concept of entropy
  - Entropy as a measure of "disorder"
  - Relative entropy for gas, liquid, and crystal states
- Measurement of heat changes (calorimetry), heat capacity, specific heat
- Heat transfer—conduction, convection, radiation (PHY)
- Endothermic/exothermic reactions (GC)
  - Enthalpy, *H*, and standard heats of reaction and formation
  - Hess' Law of Heat Summation
- Bond dissociation energy as related to heats of formation (GC)
- Free energy: *G* (GC)
- Spontaneous reactions and $\Delta G°$ (GC)
- Coefficient of expansion (PHY)
- Heat of fusion, heat of vaporization
- Phase diagram: pressure and temperature

Rate Processes in Chemical Reactions—Kinetics and Equilibrium (GC)

- Reaction rate
- Dependence of reaction rate on concentration of reactants
  - Rate law, rate constant
  - Reaction order
- Rate-determining step
- Dependence of reaction rate upon temperature
  - Activation energy
    - Activated complex or transition state
    - Interpretation of energy profiles showing energies of reactants, products, activation energy, and ΔH for the reaction
  - Use of the Arrhenius Equation
- Kinetic control versus thermodynamic control of a reaction
- Catalysts
- Equilibrium in reversible chemical reactions
  - Law of Mass Action
  - Equilibrium Constant
  - Application of Le Châtelier's Principle
- Relationship of the equilibrium constant and $\Delta G°$

Chemical and Physical Foundations of Biological Systems

Passage Set I

Sample Test Questions: Chemical and Physical Foundations of Biological Systems

Sample test questions for the Chemical and Physical Foundations of Biological Systems section are provided below. The answer key appears below each question, along with the foundational concept, the content category, and the skill the question is testing. These sample questions will give you an idea of what to expect from this section of the exam.

MCAT® is a program of the
Association of American Medical Colleges

Chemical and Physical Foundations of Biological Systems

Passage I: Questions 1–5

Catabolism of several naturally occurring amino acids proceeds by enzymatic removal of the α-amino group *via* transamination. In reactions of this type, which are catalyzed *in vivo* by transaminases, the α-amino group is transferred to the α-carbon atom of an α-keto acid. An example is shown in Figure 1.

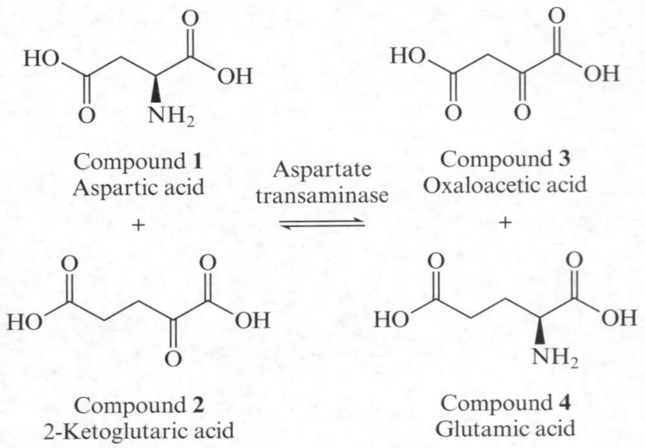

Figure 1 The aspartate transaminase reaction

All transaminases appear to follow a common reaction mechanism illustrated in Figure 2 and utilize the same prosthetic group, pyridoxal phosphate (Compound **5**). Pyridoxal phosphate acts as a carrier of the amino acid NH_2 group during the reaction.

The transaminase catalyzed reaction sequence shown in Figure 2 is reversible with $K_{eq} \sim 1.0$.

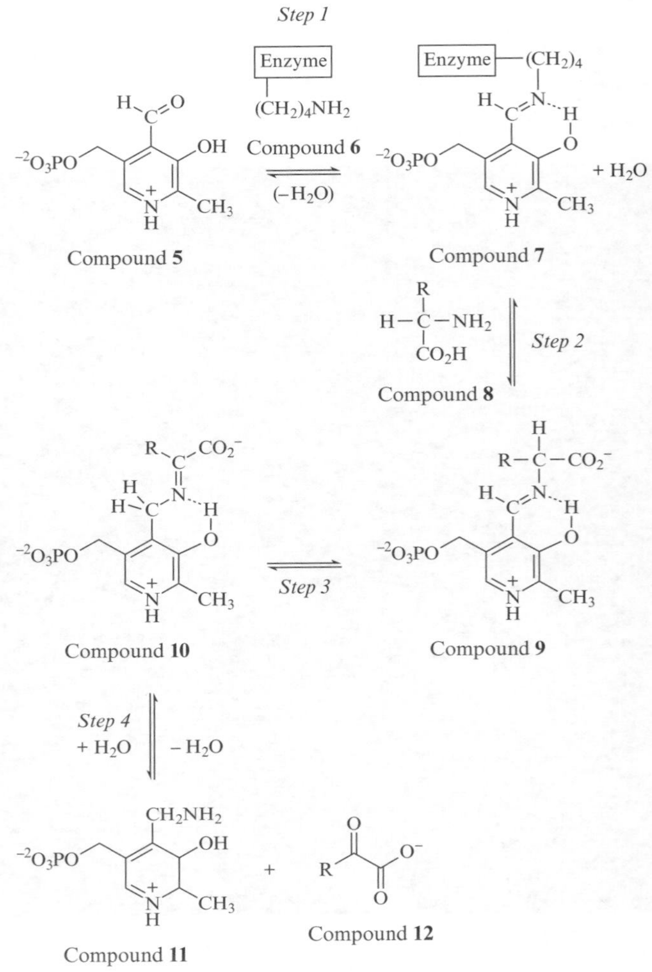

Figure 2 Intermediate steps in the transaminase reaction

Source: Adapted from A.L. Lehninger. Copyright 1975 by Worth Publishers.

1. What stereochemical designation can be assigned to naturally occurring aspartic acid?

   A. *S*
   B. *Z*
   C. *D*
   D. *E*

2. The side chain of which amino acid is used by transaminases to bind to pyridoxal phosphate in the enzyme's resting state?

   A. Val
   B. Asp
   C. Phe
   D. Lys

3. Which change to an equilibrium mixture of compounds **1–4** will increase the ratio of Compound **4** to Compound **1**?

   A. Adding Compound **3**
   B. Increasing the temperature
   C. Adding more catalyst and pyridoxal phosphate
   D. Adding Compound **2**

4. What thermodynamic and chemical changes (if any) occur during aspartate transamination (Figure 1)?

   A. Since $\Delta G < 0$, ATP is produced.
   B. Since $\Delta G = 0$, no ATP is required or produced.
   C. Since $\Delta G > 0$, ATP is required.
   D. Since $\Delta G > 0$, ATP is produced.

5. Which biological molecule can react with Compound **11** so that pyridoxal phosphate (Compound **5**) is regenerated?

   A. ATP
   B. Oxaloacetate
   C. NADH
   D. FAD$^+$

Solutions for this passage begin on next page.

1. What stereochemical designation can be assigned to naturally occurring aspartic acid?

    A. *S*
    B. *Z*
    C. *D*
    D. *E*

Foundational Concept: 5
The principles that govern chemical interactions and reactions form the basis for a broader understanding of the molecular dynamics of living systems.

Content Category: 5B
Nature of molecules and intermolecular interactions

Scientific Inquiry and Reasoning Skill: 2
Scientific Reasoning and Problem Solving

Key: A
The correct stereochemical designation can be made by using either the Fischer projection of Compound **8** (with R = CH_2CO_2H) or the perspective drawing of Compound **1**. For the Fischer projection, the priorities of the remaining three groups are $NH_2 > CO_2H > R$. This occurs in a clockwise fashion. Since the H is pointing towards the viewer in this drawing, however, the priorities would reverse to counterclockwise, or *S* when viewed with H (the lowest priority group) in the back.

Distractors
B   This designation applies to the configuration of double bonds.

C   Naturally occurring aspartic acid has an L configuration.

D   This designation applies to the configuration of double bonds.

2. The side chain of which amino acid is used by transaminases to bind to pyridoxal phosphate in the enzyme's resting state?

    A. Val
    B. Asp
    C. Phe
    D. Lys

Foundational Concept: 5
The principles that govern chemical interactions and reactions form the basis for a broader understanding of the molecular dynamics of living systems.

Content Category: 5D
Structure, function, and reactivity of biologically-relevant molecules

Scientific Inquiry and Reasoning Skill: 1
Knowledge of Scientific Concepts and Principles

Key: D
The side chain depicted in Figure 2 is $-(CH_2)_4NH_2$, which corresponds to lysine, or Lys. The resting state is shown as Compound **7** in Figure 2.

Distractors

A   This is valine whose side chain is $-CH(CH_3)_2$.

B   This is aspartic acid whose structure is shown in Figure 1.

C   This is phenylalanine whose side chain is $-C_6H_5$.

 TIP: Knowledge of the structure and properties of amino acid side chains is important to understanding enzyme reaction mechanisms.

Fifth Edition
The Official Guide to the MCAT® Exam
197
MCAT® is a program of the
Association of American Medical Colleges

3. Which change to an equilibrium mixture of compounds **1–4** will increase the ratio of Compound **4** to Compound **1**?

   A. Adding Compound **3**
   B. Increasing the temperature
   C. Adding more catalyst and pyridoxal phosphate
   D. Adding Compound **2**

Foundational Concept: 5
The principles that govern chemical interactions and reactions form the basis for a broader understanding of the molecular dynamics of living systems.

Content Category: 5E
Principles of chemical thermodynamics and kinetics

Scientific Inquiry and Reasoning Skill: 2
Scientific Reasoning and Problem Solving

Key: D
Application of Le Châtelier's principle can be used to arrive at the key. The ratio of Compound **4** to Compound **1** can be increased by removing some Compound **3** or adding Compound **2**.

Distractors

A   Removing, not adding, Compound **3** will increase the ratio of Compound **4** to Compound **1**.

B   For this reaction, since $K_{eq} = 1.0$ and the products and reactants are structurally similar, it can be assumed that the reaction is nearly thermoneutral. Changing the temperature will not change the position of equilibrium. Even if the equilibrium is disturbed by temperature changes, it is not possible from information supplied in the passage to assess in which direction the equilibrium will be shifted.

C   Adding catalyst or cofactor will only speed the rate at which equilibrium is attained, but will not affect the equilibrium concentrations of the reagents.

TIP: Chemical equilibrium is dependent on the amounts of products and reactants. Catalysts only affect kinetics or the rate at which reactions occur.

4. What thermodynamic and chemical changes (if any) occur during aspartate transamination (Figure 1)?

    A. Since $\Delta G < 0$, ATP is produced.
    B. Since $\Delta G = 0$, no ATP is required or produced.
    C. Since $\Delta G > 0$, ATP is required.
    D. Since $\Delta G > 0$, ATP is produced.

Foundational Concept: 5

The principles that govern chemical interactions and reactions form the basis for a broader understanding of the molecular dynamics of living systems.

Content Category: 5E

Principles of chemical thermodynamics and kinetics

Scientific Inquiry and Reasoning Skill: 2

Scientific Reasoning and Problem Solving

Key: B

The free energy of the reaction as written in either direction is the same since $K_{eq} = 1$, and $\Delta G = -RT\ln(K_{eq})$ and therefore $\Delta G = 0$. When a reaction is thermoneutral, ATP is neither produced nor required for the reaction to proceed.

Distractors

A   Since $K_{eq} = 1$, $\Delta G = 0$ and no ATP is required or produced.

C   Since $K_{eq} = 1$, $\Delta G = 0$ and no ATP is required or produced.

D   Since $K_{eq} = 1$, $\Delta G = 0$ and no ATP is required or produced.

 TIP: The hydrolysis of ATP generates approximately −33 kJ/mol under biological conditions. This should be considered anytime ATP is a product or reactant in a biological reaction.

5. Which biological molecule can react with Compound **11** so that pyridoxal phosphate (Compound **5**) is regenerated?

   A. ATP
   B. Oxaloacetate
   C. NADH
   D. FAD⁺

Foundational Concept: 5
The principles that govern chemical interactions and reactions form the basis for a broader understanding of the molecular dynamics of living systems.

Content Category: 5E
Principles of chemical thermodynamics and kinetics

Scientific Inquiry and Reasoning Skill: 2
Scientific Reasoning and Problem Solving

Key: B
Respondents need to connect the dots and appreciate that the sequence shown in Figure 2 accomplishes only half the net reaction shown in Figure 1. Compound **5** is regenerated from Compound **11** and a molecule of α-keto acid (such as oxaloacetate) and the cycle can continue. This was alluded to in the passage as well, when it was stated that "pyridoxal phosphate acts as a carrier of the amino acid NH_2 group during the reaction."

Distractors
A Hydrolysis of this substance is coupled to thermodynamically unfavorable reactions to allow them to occur. Since this substance is NOT an α-keto acid it will not react in the manner described.

C This is a reducing cofactor used by oxidoreductases but will not react in the manner described.

D This is an oxidizing cofactor used by oxidoreductases and will not react in the manner described.

 TIP: Use figures to work your way through problems. In Figure 2 the product or similar substance of the reaction sequence can be used to reverse the reaction and return the cofactor to its original state.

Chemical and Physical Foundations of Biological Systems

Passage Set II

Chemical and Physical Foundations of Biological Systems

Passage II: Questions 6–9

Protein molecules have strength properties as a result of their hierarchical folding patterns. An individual protein molecule in its native conformation can be mechanically unfolded using an applied external force. In an experiment, researchers attached the *C*-terminus of a modified monomeric bacteriorhodopsin protein to the tip of a flexible plane cantilever positioned inside an atomic force microscope (Figure 1).

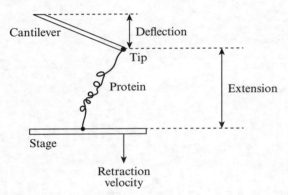

Figure 1 Experimental setup inside an atomic force microscope

This attachment was accomplished by first coating the cantilever tip with a thin layer of gold, which then binds to a thiol group in the protein. The *N*-terminus of the protein was tethered to a microscope stage that was retracted at constant velocity. The deflection of the cantilever was measured using visible laser light reflected off its surface onto a photodiode detector. The force exerted on the cantilever during the unfolding process was measured and recorded against the tip-stage distance (Figure 2).

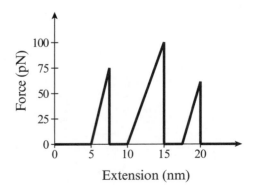

Figure 2 Correlation between exerted force and extension

The retraction velocity was varied over many experimental runs and a change in the maximum force required for unfolding was observed (Figure 3).

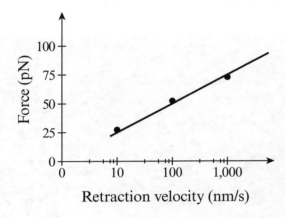

Figure 3 Dependence of the maximum exerted force on the retraction velocity

In the absence of applied force, the rate constant for unfolding of the protein was k°_{u} (Equation 1).

$$k^{\circ}_{u} = A e^{-\Delta G^{*}/k_{B}T}$$

Equation 1

The application of a force lowered the apparent free-energy barrier ΔG^{*} between the folded and unfolded conformations of the protein, which led to an increase in the rate constant $k_{u} > k^{\circ}_{u}$ for unfolding the protein.

Source: Adapted from a paper by H. Janovjak, et al. Copyright 2004 by Elsevier Inc.

6. Which wavelength of laser light can be used with the photodiode detector in the atomic force microscope?

A. 226 nm
B. 633 nm
C. 1.26 μm
D. 3.17 μm

7. What is the mechanical work done by the cantilever when the extension increases from 10 nm to 15 nm?

A. 2.00×10^{-22} J
B. 4.70×10^{-20} J
C. 2.50×10^{-19} J
D. 5.00×10^{-18} J

8. What is the mechanical power exerted on the protein when the retraction speed is 1000 nm/s?

A. 1.5×10^{-18} W
B. 7.5×10^{-17} W
C. 3.5×10^{-6} W
D. 5.5×10^{6} W

9. What are the units for the rate constant k_u discussed in the passage?

A. $M^{-1} \bullet s^{-1}$
B. $M \bullet s$
C. $M \bullet s^{-1}$
D. s^{-1}

Solutions for this passage begin on next page.

6. Which wavelength of laser light can be used with the photodiode detector in the atomic force microscope?

    A. 226 nm
    B. 633 nm
    C. 1.26 µm
    D. 3.17 µm

Foundational Concept: 4
Complex living organisms transport materials, sense their environment, process signals, and respond to changes using processes understood in terms of physical principles.

Content Category: 4D
How light and sound interact with matter

Scientific Inquiry and Reasoning Skill: 1
Knowledge of Scientific Concepts and Principles

Key: B
The wavelength of visible light is between about 400 to 750 nm. Red light in particular ranges from 620–750 nm. Helium-neon red lasers operate at 633 nm. Therefore, the only possible answer is B.

Distractors

A   This wavelength corresponds to radiation in the ultraviolet range of the electromagnetic spectrum.

C   This wavelength corresponds to radiation in the infrared range of the electromagnetic spectrum.

D   This wavelength corresponds to radiation in the infrared range of the electromagnetic spectrum.

7. What is the mechanical work done by the cantilever when the extension increases from 10 nm to 15 nm?

    A. 2.00×10^{-22} J
    B. 4.70×10^{-20} J
    C. 2.50×10^{-19} J
    D. 5.00×10^{-18} J

Foundational Concept: 4

Complex living organisms transport materials, sense their environment, process signals, and respond to changes using processes understood in terms of physical principles.

Content Category: 4A

Translational motion, forces, work, energy, and equilibrium in living systems

Scientific Inquiry and Reasoning Skill: 4

Data-based and Statistical Reasoning

Key: C

This question requires you to apply the graphical method of calculating the work done by a variable force, namely the elastic force, $W = k_s x^2/2$. Mechanical work by an elastic force is $W = k_s x^2/2 = Fx/2$. Graphically, it is the area under the force-extension graph between the corresponding data points. From Figure 2, the correct response is $\{[(100 - 0) \times 10^{-12}]N \times [(15 - 10) \times 10^{-9}]m\}/2 = 2.50 \times 10^{-19}$ J.

Distractors

A   This choice is incorrect because either the extension is used with the incorrect units: pm instead of nm.

B   This choice is incorrect because it is about 20 times larger than the correct numerical value.

D   This choice is incorrect because it is about 20 times smaller than the correct numerical value.

TIP: Common mistakes in answering this question usually consist of not using the 2 factor in the denominator and not using the correct units for the force and distance.

8. What is the mechanical power exerted on the protein when the retraction speed is 1000 nm/s?

    A. 1.5×10^{-18} W
    B. 7.5×10^{-17} W
    C. 3.5×10^{-6} W
    D. 5.5×10^{6} W

Foundational Concept: 4
Complex living organisms transport materials, sense their environment, process signals, and respond to changes using processes understood in terms of physical principles.

Content Category: 4A
Translational motion, forces, work, energy, and equilibrium in living systems

Scientific Inquiry and Reasoning Skill: 4
Data-based and Statistical Reasoning

Key: B
Power at constant speed is related to the applied force as $P = F \times v$. From Figure 3, $P = 75$ pN $\times$ 1000 nm/s = 7.5×10^{-17} W.

Distractors

A   This choice is incorrect because it is about 50 times smaller than the correct numerical value.

C   This choice is incorrect because it uses the incorrect units for the force (N instead of pN).

D   This choice is incorrect because it uses the incorrect units for the force (N instead of pN) and for the extension (m instead of nm).

 TIP: Power is energy per unit time, hence power depends on the force and the time dependence of the displacement. In this case, force varies with the displacement (i.e., extension) as shown in Figure 2, but it depends also on the speed as shown in Figure 3. Using the data in Figure 2 leads to erroneous answers.

9. What are the units for the rate constant k_u discussed in the passage?

    A. $M^{-1} \cdot s^{-1}$
    B. $M \cdot s$
    C. $M \cdot s^{-1}$
    D. s^{-1}

Foundational Concept: 5
The principles that govern chemical interactions and reactions form the basis for a broader understanding of the molecular dynamics of living systems.

Content Category: 5D
Structure, function, and reactivity of biologically-relevant molecules

Scientific Inquiry and Reasoning Skill: 2
Scientific Reasoning and Problem Solving

Key: D
The protein unfolds by a unimolecular mechanism. The rate of unfolding has units of M/s and is given by the expression Δ[unfolded protein length]$/\Delta t = k_u$[folded protein length]. The units of k_u are therefore s^{-1}.

Distractors

A   This choice is incorrect since it represents the units of a second order rate constant.

B   This choice is incorrect since a rate constant must necessarily have units of inverse time.

C   This choice is incorrect since it is the unit for a zeroth order rate constant, or the units for an overall rate expression.

Chemical and Physical Foundations of Biological Systems

Passage Set III

MCAT® is a program of the
Association of American Medical Colleges

Chemical and Physical Foundations of Biological Systems

Passage III: Questions 10–14

Selective ion transport processes help regulate the composition of a living cell. The ability of natural compounds and synthetic macrocyclic ionophores to serve as efficient agents in the transport of ions across membranes is of considerable interest. Researchers demonstrated that Compound **1** (Figure 1) allowed control of the relative rate of cation transport *in vitro*. The central portion of this molecule, known as a crown ether, selectively binds to cations based on their ionic radii.

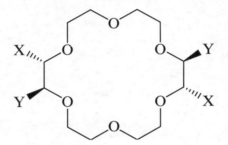

Figure 1 Structure of a synthetic macrocyclic ion transport agent featuring the 18-crown-6 backbone (Note: X = CO_2H, Y = $C(=O)N(n\text{-Pr})CH_2CH_2OCH_2CH_2N(n\text{-Pr})CO_2CH_2C_6H_5$)

Compound **1** mimicked competitive Ca^{2+}/K^+ transport coupled to H^+ antiport in a pH gradient as shown schematically in Figure 2. Compound **1** was dissolved in an organic liquid layer serving as a membrane that separated the aqueous "IN" and "OUT" solutions. With only one binding site, it extracted and transported either monovalent or divalent cations from the "IN" phase to the "OUT" phase one at a time.

Source: Adapted from A. Hriciga and J.M. Lehn, "pH Regulation of Divalent/Monovalent Ca/K Cation Transport Selectivity by a Macrocyclic Carrier Molecule." PNAS Copyright 1983 National Academcy of Sciences.

$$\left[\begin{array}{c} CO_2^- \\ CO_2H, M^+ \end{array}\right]$$

$H^+ \leftarrow$ $\leftarrow H^+$

$M^+ \rightarrow$ $[(CO_2H)_2]$ $\rightarrow M^+$

$M^{2+} \rightarrow$ $\rightarrow M^{2+}$

$2H^+ \leftarrow$ $\leftarrow 2H^+$

$$\left[\begin{array}{c} CO_2^- \\ CO_2^-, M^{2+} \end{array}\right]$$

IN   OUT

Figure 2 Schematic representation of competitive metal ion transport coupled to proton antiport in a pH gradient

All "OUT" phase solutions initially consisted of 0.1 M HCl(*aq*), and an "IN" phase solution consisted of 0.1 M $CaCl_2$(*aq*) mixed with 0.1 M KCl(*aq*) buffered at various pH values as listed in Table 1. The rate of metal cation transfer *v* was determined spectroscopically.

Table 1 Rate of Transfer *v* of Cations Across an Organic Membrane by Compound **1** at Different pH Values

Trial	pH value of "IN" phase	$v(Ca^{2+})$ (µmol/hr)	$v(K^+)$ (µmol/hr)
1	2.00	0.037	6.59
2	2.92	0.33	6.42
3	3.90	1.11	5.84
4	5.30	3.75	3.64
5	6.75	6.80	1.35
6	8.60	7.95	0.67

10. What factor can account for the relative rate of Ca^{2+} transport across the membrane as a function of pH?

A. Deprotonation of the X groups
B. Deprotonation of the Y groups
C. Protonation of the central O atoms
D. Change in ring size of the macrocyle

11. What are the configurations (R or S) of the chiral centers bonded to substituents X and Y, respectively, in Compound **1**?

A. R, R
B. R, S
C. S, R
D. S, S

12. Compound **1** remains mainly confined to the central phase during the experiments because it is:

A. hydrophilic with only polar groups.
B. hydrophilic with both polar and nonpolar groups.
C. lipophilic with only nonpolar groups.
D. lipophilic with both polar and nonpolar groups.

13. What modification of Compound **1** will favor transport of Na^+ relative to K^+?

A. Replace X with CH_3.
B. Replace Y with CH_3.
C. Increase the ring size by adding one $-CH_2CH_2O-$.
D. Decrease the ring size by removing one $-CH_2CH_2O-$.

14. Suppose that, under the experimental conditions employed, Compound **1** is "saturated" with cations. What graph depicts the expected change in rate of K^+ transport from the "IN" to the "OUT" phases at pH 2 (Trial 1 conditions) as a function of increasing K^+ ion concentration in the "IN" phase?

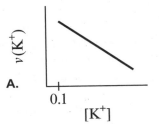

A.

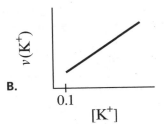

B.

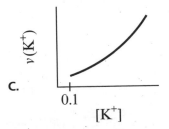

C.

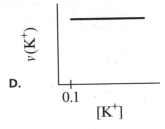

D.

Solutions for this passage begin on next page.

10. What factor can account for the relative rate of Ca^{2+} transport across the membrane as a function of pH?

A. Deprotonation of the X groups
B. Deprotonation of the Y groups
C. Protonation of the central O atoms
D. Change in ring size of the macrocyle

Foundational Concept: 5
The principles that govern chemical interactions and reactions form the basis for a broader understanding of the molecular dynamics of living systems.

Content Category: 5A
Unique nature of water and its solutions

Scientific Inquiry and Reasoning Skill: 4
Data-based and Statistical Reasoning

Key: A
The overall rate of ion transport does not change much (consider the sum of the two rates in Table 1), but the rate of Ca^{2+} increases at the expense of K^+ at high pH. This can only be due to deprotonation of the X groups. The overall entity maintains electrical neutrality by preferentially binding to a divalent cation.

Distractors

B   The Y groups will not change protonation state under the conditions of the experiment.

C   The central O atoms of the ring are not sufficiently basic to be protonated under these conditions.

D   The macrocyclic ring will be unaffected by pH changes in the range 2–9.

TIP: Remember to use the process of elimination whenever possible or necessary. pH changes in the range 2–9 can affect the protonation state of various functional groups, especially weak acids and bases such as amines or carboxylic acids, but will not affect the protonation state of other groups or change the size of the macrocyclic ring.

11. What are the configurations (*R* or *S*) of the chiral centers bonded to substituents X and Y, respectively, in Compound **1**?

A. *R, R*
B. *R, S*
C. *S, R*
D. *S, S*

Foundational Concept: 5
The principles that govern chemical interactions and reactions form the basis for a broader understanding of the molecular dynamics of living systems.

Content Category: 5B
Nature of molecules and intermolecular interactions

Scientific Inquiry and Reasoning Skill: 2
Scientific Reasoning and Problem Solving

Key: A
For the carbon atoms bonded to the Y groups, the lowest priority group is already in the back and so the ranking of the remaining groups, which occurs in a clockwise manner, gives the *R* configuration. For the carbon atoms bonded to X, the X group is in the back, and the relative rank of the remaining groups occurs in a counter-clockwise manner. When H is placed in the back, however, this would also be clockwise, or *R*.

Distractors

B   This is incorrect. The configuration of the carbon attached to the Y group is *R*.

C   This is incorrect. The configuration of the carbon attached to the X group is *R*.

D   This is incorrect. The configuration of the carbon attached to both X and Y groups is *R*.

12. Compound **1** remains mainly confined to the central phase during the experiments because it is:

   A. hydrophilic with only polar groups.
   B. hydrophilic with both polar and nonpolar groups.
   C. lipophilic with only nonpolar groups.
   D. lipophilic with both polar and nonpolar groups.

Foundational Concept: 5
The principles that govern chemical interactions and reactions form the basis for a broader understanding of the molecular dynamics of living systems.

Content Category: 5C
Separation and purification methods

Scientific Inquiry and Reasoning Skill: 1
Knowledge of Scientific Concepts and Principles

Key: D
Compound **1** mimics a membrane symport. Thus, it is lipophilic. The structure has both polar (X: carboxyl group) and nonpolar (18-crown-6 itself and Y: amide and ether) groups.

Distractors
A   The central phase is organic and separate from the aqueous phases on either side. This implies that solutes confined to it are lipophilic (hydrophobic).

B   The central phase is organic and separate from the aqueous phases on either side. This implies that solutes confined to it are lipophilic (hydrophobic).

C   Compound **1** must contain both polar and non-polar groups in order to function as an ion transporter in a hydrophobic phase.

TIP: Remember the big picture and evaluate each question in the context of the passage. The macrocycle had many polar functional groups, some ionized, but resided in the organic phase during the experiment. Overall, the molecule must be concluded to be lipophilic.

Fifth Edition
The Official Guide to the MCAT® Exam
214
MCAT® is a program of the
Association of American Medical Colleges

13. What modification of Compound **1** will favor transport of Na^+ relative to K^+?

   A. Replace X with CH_3.
   B. Replace Y with CH_3.
   C. Increase the ring size by adding one $-CH_2CH_2O-$.
   D. Decrease the ring size by removing one $-CH_2CH_2O-$.

Foundational Concept: 4
Complex living organisms transport materials, sense their environment, process signals, and respond to changes using processes understood in terms of physical principles.

Content Category: 4E
Atoms, nuclear decay, electronic structure, and atomic chemical behavior

Scientific Inquiry and Reasoning Skill: 3
Reasoning About the Design and Execution of Research

Key: D
From the passage, it was stated that K^+ is transported within the central portion of Compound **1**. Since Na^+ is chemically similar to K^+ it is reasonable to assume that there might be a way to favor its transport over K^+ by changing the size of the ring. The change necessary would be to decrease the ring size since Na^+ is smaller than K^+.

Distractors

A   This might affect overall ion transport, but should not favor Na^+ over K^+.

B   This might affect overall ion transport, but should not favor Na^+ over K^+.

C   Increasing the ring size of Compound **1** will favor transport of a larger cation, not a smaller one.

TIP: Remember to look to the passage for information useful in answering difficult questions. The passage stated that Compound **1** selectively binds to cations based on their ionic radii. This is an important clue when answering this question.

14. Suppose that, under the experimental conditions employed, Compound **1** is "saturated" with cations. What graph depicts the expected change in rate of K^+ transport from the "IN" to the "OUT" phases at pH 2 (Trial 1 conditions) as a function of increasing K^+ ion concentration in the "IN" phase?

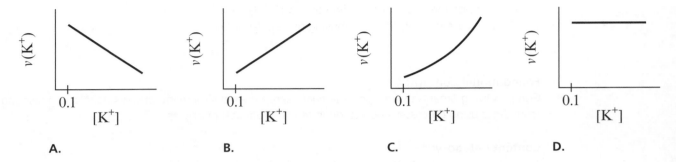

A.   **B.**   **C.**   **D.**

Foundational Concept: 5
The principles that govern chemical interactions and reactions form the basis for a broader understanding of the molecular dynamics of living systems.

Content Category: 5E
Principles of chemical thermodynamics and kinetics

Scientific Inquiry and Reasoning Skill: 4
Data-based and Statistical Reasoning

Key: D
Compound **1** acts like a catalyst for cation transport across the organic phase. If Compound **1** is saturated with substrate, increasing the substrate concentration will not increase the rate. In a plot of velocity V versus [S] (classic Michaelis–Menten kinetic treatment) the rate of cation transport is at the limiting value, called V_{max}.

Distractors
A   When a catalyst is saturated with substrate, increasing its concentration will not decrease the rate of the reaction.

B   When a catalyst is saturated with substrate, increasing its concentration will not increase the rate of the reaction.

C   When a catalyst is saturated with substrate, increasing its concentration will not increase the rate of the reaction.

   TIP: Upon reading the passage, it should be apparent that this compound is acting in a similar way to an ion transporter. This allows the information in the stem, the condition of saturation, to be interpreted in the correct context.

Fifth Edition
The Official Guide to the MCAT® Exam
216
MCAT® is a program of the
Association of American Medical Colleges

Chemical and Physical Foundations of Biological Systems

Passage Set IV

MCAT® is a program of the
Association of American Medical Colleges

Chemical and Physical Foundations of Biological Systems

Passage IV: Questions 15–19

Trinitrobenzene sulfonic acid (TNBS) is a membrane-impermeable reagent that combines with phosphatadylethanolamine (PE) as shown in Reaction 1. Upon reaction, TNBS-labeled PE molecules are frozen on the outer envelope of membranes and do not exchange with other PE molecules on the inner envelope.

Growing bacteria were treated with radioactive ^{32}P-labeled phosphate ($^{32}PO_4^{3-}$) in an effort to identify the location of PE synthesis. In this experiment newly synthesized PE will contain a ^{32}P label. When growing

bacteria are treated with a pulse of radioactive $^{32}PO_4^{3-}$ followed by immediate treatment with TNBS, almost none of the TNBS-labeled PE contained ^{32}P. In contrast, if an interval of only three minutes was allowed to elapse between the $^{32}PO_4^{3-}$ pulse and the TNBS treatment, almost 50% of the ^{32}P-labeled PE was also TNBS labeled. These results are summarized in Figure 1.

Sources: Adapted from D. Voet, J.G. Voet, and C.W. Pratt, Fundamentals of Biochemistry Copyright 2008 The Authors; J.E. Rothman and E.P. Kennedy, Proceedings of the National Academy of Sciences of the USA Copyright 1977 The National Academy of Sciences.

Reaction 1

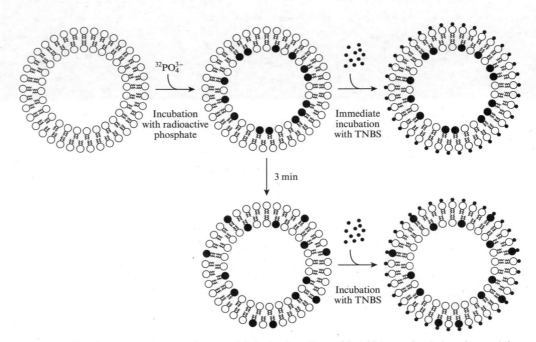

Figure 1 Summary of experiments designed to establish the location of lipid biosynthesis in a bacterial membrane; ○ = unlabeled phosphate, ● = labeled phosphate, • = TNBS molecule (attached to either ○ or ●)

15. The scientists who developed the experimental protocol described in the passage chose TNBS over many potential candidates to label PE molecules. What characteristic about the rate of reaction between TNBS and outer envelope PE molecules allowed the experiment to provide useful data? The rate of TNBS reaction with outer envelope PE molecules is:

   A. faster than the rate of exchange between inner and outer envelope PE molecules.
   B. slower than the rate of phosphate transport across the membrane.
   C. facilitated by the additional phosphate present in solution.
   D. easily measured by the method of initial rates.

16. Which statement correctly describes both PO_4^{3-} and TNBS?

   A. Both TNBS and PO_4^{3-} are hydrophobic.
   B. TNBS is hydrophobic and PO_4^{3-} is hydrophilic.
   C. PO_4^{3-} is hydrophobic and TNBS is hydrophilic.
   D. Both TNBS and PO_4^{3-} are hydrophilic.

17. In Reaction 1, what is a possible structure for either R_1 or R_2 of the reactant?

   A. CH_3
   B. NH_2
   C. $(CH_2)_{15}CH_3$
   D. $(CH_2O)_{10}CH_3$

18. The ^{32}P label was generated from naturally occurring phosphorous by:

   A. removing a neutron from the nucleus.
   B. adding a proton to the nucleus.
   C. adding three electrons to the atom.
   D. adding a neutron to the nucleus.

19. A scientist proposed that the ^{32}P label was entering PE molecules by direct exchange (swapping phosphate groups with those found in solution) and NOT through synthesis of new PE by bacterial cells. What experimental modification can show this is NOT the case?

   A. Introduce TNBS prior to pulsing with $^{32}PO_4^{3-}$.
   B. Measure the rate of incorporation of $^{32}PO_4^{3-}$ into acellular PE.
   C. Use mouse cell cultures instead of bacterial cells.
   D. Decrease the concentration of $^{32}PO_4^{3-}$ and observe the effect on incorporation rate.

Solutions for this passage begin on next page.

Fifth Edition
The Official Guide to the MCAT® Exam
219
MCAT® is a program of the
Association of American Medical Colleges

15. The scientists who developed the experimental protocol described in the passage chose TNBS over many potential candidates to label PE molecules. What characteristic about the rate of reaction between TNBS and outer envelope PE molecules allowed the experiment to provide useful data? The rate of TNBS reaction with outer envelope PE molecules is:

A. faster than the rate of exchange between inner and outer envelope PE molecules.
B. slower than the rate of phosphate transport across the membrane.
C. facilitated by the additional phosphate present in solution.
D. easily measured by the method of initial rates.

Foundational Concept: 5
The principles that govern chemical interactions and reactions form the basis for a broader understanding of the molecular dynamics of living systems.

Content Category: 5E
Principles of chemical thermodynamics and kinetics

Scientific Inquiry and Reasoning Skill: 3
Reasoning About the Design and Execution of Research

Key: A
In order for TNBS treatment to accurately determine the state of membrane phospholipids at any given time interval, the rate of the reaction must be faster than the time it takes to establish a new membrane state. Reaction with TNBS must be very fast in order to freeze the state of the membrane so that it may be analyzed.

Distractors

B   This has no effect on the usefulness regarding the location of PE synthesis based on the experimental design.

C   This is not supported by information in the passage and does not permit the experiment to provide useful data regarding the location of PE synthesis.

D   The researchers did not make kinetic measurements.

16. Which statement correctly describes both PO_4^{3-} and TNBS?

    A. Both TNBS and PO_4^{3-} are hydrophobic.
    B. TNBS is hydrophobic and PO_4^{3-} is hydrophilic.
    C. PO_4^{3-} is hydrophobic and TNBS is hydrophilic.
    D. Both TNBS and PO_4^{3-} are hydrophilic.

Foundational Concept: 5
The principles that govern chemical interactions and reactions form the basis for a broader understanding of the molecular dynamics of living systems.

Content Category: 5B
Nature of molecules and intermolecular interactions

Scientific Inquiry and Reasoning Skill: 2
Scientific Reasoning and Problem Solving

Key: D
The structure of TNBS shows that it contains three polar substituents on a benzene ring, which makes the molecule hydrophilic. Also, it does not cross the hydrophobic membrane. Phosphate is a negatively charged hydrophilic ion.

Distractors

A   Both substances bear negative charge that will interact strongly with water molecules.

B   TNBS is drawn in the figure with a negatively charged group consistent with its hydrophilicity.

C   Phosphate is a highly charged anion that interacts very strongly with water.

TIP: This question illustrates that the answer to a question often can be determined using different sets of information. If you are unsure of how the substituents affect the benzene ring, you can answer the question by reasoning about how TNBS interacts with the membrane.

17. In Reaction 1, what is a possible structure for either R_1 or R_2 of the reactant?

    A. CH_3
    B. NH_2
    C. $(CH_2)_{15}CH_3$
    D. $(CH_2O)_{10}CH_3$

Foundational Concept: 5
The principles that govern chemical interactions and reactions form the basis for a broader understanding of the molecular dynamics of living systems.

Content Category: 5D
Structure, function, and reactivity of biologically-relevant molecules

Scientific Inquiry and Reasoning Skill: 1
Knowledge of Scientific Concepts and Principles

Key: C
Because PE is a lipid, the R groups must represent the acyl chains.

Distractors

A   Methyl is not sufficiently long to be part of a phosphatadylethanolamine.

B   If R were NH_2 the group would not be a fatty acid acyl chain.

D   The acyl chains of PE molecules do not contain oxygen atoms.

18. The ^{32}P label was generated from naturally occurring phosphorous by:

    A. removing a neutron from the nucleus.
    B. adding a proton to the nucleus.
    C. adding three electrons to the atom.
    D. adding a neutron to the nucleus.

Foundational Concept: 4
Complex living organisms transport materials, sense their environment, process signals, and respond to changes using processes understood in terms of physical principles.

Content Category: 4E
Atoms, nuclear decay, electronic structure, and atomic chemical behavior

Scientific Inquiry and Reasoning Skill: 2
Scientific Reasoning and Problem Solving

Key: D
This question requires you to apply knowledge of the nuclear structure of the naturally occurring ^{31}P nucleus, and of nuclear radioactivity through the process of beta decay. The ^{32}P isotope contains an additional neutron in the nucleus compared to the naturally occurring ^{31}P nucleus, which does not change the identity of the atom. The extra neutron emits a beta particle via beta-minus decay.

Distractors
A   Removing a neutron from the ^{31}P nucleus would equalize the number of neutrons and protons, so the nucleus would not be radioactive.

B   Adding a proton to the nucleus would change the identity of the atom and would result in the creation of a positive ion.

C   Adding three electrons to the atom does not affect the radioactive properties of the nucleus.

TIP: A necessary condition for an atomic nucleus to be radioactive is that the number of protons must be different from the number of neutrons. The type of radioactivity depends on the difference between these two numbers: more protons leads to beta-plus decay, while more neutrons leads to beta-minus decay. The number of electrons in the atom does not modify the nuclear structure and its radioactive properties.

19. A scientist proposed that the ^{32}P label was entering PE molecules by direct exchange (swapping phosphate groups with those found in solution) and NOT through synthesis of new PE by bacterial cells. What experimental modification can show this is NOT the case?

A. Introduce TNBS prior to pulsing with $^{32}PO_4{}^{3-}$.
B. Measure the rate of incorporation of $^{32}PO_4{}^{3-}$ into acellular PE.
C. Use mouse cell cultures instead of bacterial cells.
D. Decrease the concentration of $^{32}PO_4{}^{3-}$ and observe the effect on incorporation rate.

Foundational Concept: 5
The principles that govern chemical interactions and reactions form the basis for a broader understanding of the molecular dynamics of living systems.

Content Category: 5D
Structure, function, and reactivity of biologically-relevant molecules

Scientific Inquiry and Reasoning Skill: 3
Reasoning About the Design and Execution of Research

Key: B
The rates of bacterial PE synthesis and any potential phosphate exchange should be different. Also, it is unlikely that phosphate would exchange from a phospholipid.

Distractors
A This would result in no incorporation of the labeled ^{32}P.

C This change is not relevant to the issue cited in the stem.

D If the enzyme responsible for PE synthesis is not saturated with $PO_4{}^{3-}$ this will result in slower incorporation regardless of the mechanism by which it takes place.

TIP: Remember that an important part of experimental design is the control experiment.

Chemical and Physical Foundations of Biological Systems

Passage Set V

MCAT® is a program of the
Association of American Medical Colleges

Chemical and Physical Foundations of Biological Systems

Passage V: Questions 20–24

Hard water contains cations that form precipitates with soap or upon boiling. The principle hardness ions are Ca^{2+}, M^{2+}, and Fe^{2+}. There are two major drawbacks of hard water.

First, the M^{2+} ions reduce the effectiveness of common soaps, which contain the sodium salts of organic acids with long carbon chains. An example is sodium stearate, $C_{17}H_{32}CO_2Na$ (MW = 306). The reaction between soaps and hardness ions yields insoluble precipitates through Reaction 1. Removal of stearate from the solution eliminates the effectiveness of the soap.

$$M^{2+}(aq) + 2NaC_{17}H_{32}CO_2(aq) \rightarrow$$
$$2Na^+(aq) + M(C_{17}H_{32}CO_2)_2(s)$$

Reaction 1

Second, hard water produces boiler scale, a layer of insoluble carbonates formed by Reaction 2 that lines the inner walls of pipes and hot-water boilers, so that the pipes' radii constantly decrease in time. Deposits of this type are especially bad in hot water and are poor conductors of heat.

$$M^{2+}(aq) + 2HCO_3^-(aq) \rightarrow$$
$$H_2O(l) + CO_2(g) + MCO_3(s)$$

Reaction 2

It is important that the cations responsible for hard water be removed before the water is heated or used for washing. Water softening, the removal of hardness ions from water, can be accomplished in several ways. One method is the ion exchange process in which water is passed through a column containing solid sodium aluminosilicates. Sodium aluminosilicates are high surface area three-dimensional extended solids with –ONa groups at the surface.

$$M^{2+}(aq) + Na_2Al_xSi_yO_z(s) \rightarrow$$
$$2Na^+(aq) + MAl_xSi_yO_z(s)$$

Reaction 3

20. The hardness ions described in the passage are:

A. alkaline earth metals.
B. strongly acidic cations.
C. formed in nature by reduction of other cations.
D. derived from atoms upon loss of two electrons.

21. What happens to the pH of a soapy solution as a result of the introduction of hardness ions?

A. The pH increases as [H⁺] increases.
B. The pH is not changed since no acid-base reaction occurs.
C. The pH decreases as [OH⁻] decreases.
D. The effect on pH depends on the identity M²⁺.

22. Soaps are chemically modified natural products that can be derived from all of the following EXCEPT:

A. fatty acids.
B. cholesterols.
C. triacylglycerols.
D. phospholipids.

23. A pump is used to force an aqueous solution through a pipe at high temperature according to Poiseuille's Law:

$$\text{Flow rate} = \frac{\Delta P \pi r^4}{8L\eta}$$

where ΔP is the pressure difference applied by the pump, r is the radius of the pipe, L is the length of the pipe, and η is the viscosity of the solution. Which graph depicts the rate of energy consumed over time in order to maintain constant flow through a pipe subject to boiler scale?

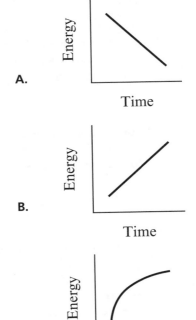

A.

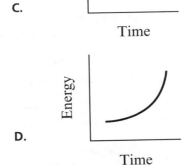

B.

C.

D.

24. Which experimental approach can be used to analyze the metal content of soapy precipitate produced by Reaction 1? Dissolve the solid in a known volume of:

A. 0.1 M NaHCO₃(aq), then titrate with standardized 0.1 M HCl(aq) using an indicator.
B. 0.1 M NaOH(aq), then titrate with standardized 0.1 M HCl(aq) using an indicator.
C. 0.1 M NaCl(aq), then titrate with standardized 0.1 M NaOH(aq) using an indicator.
D. 0.1 M HCl(aq), then titrate with standardized 0.1 M NaOH(aq) using an indicator.

Solutions for this passage begin on next page.

20. The hardness ions described in the passage are:

    A. alkaline earth metals.
    B. strongly acidic cations.
    C. formed in nature by reduction of other cations.
    D. derived from atoms upon loss of two electrons.

Foundational Concept: 4

Complex living organisms transport materials, sense their environment, process signals, and respond to changes using processes understood in terms of physical principles.

Content Category: 4E

Atoms, nuclear decay, electronic structure, and atomic chemical behavior

Scientific Inquiry and Reasoning Skill: 1

Knowledge of Scientific Concepts and Principles

Key: D

All the ions described in the passage have a +2 charge, meaning they lost two electrons.

Distractors

A Fe^{2+} is a transition metal cation.

B   None of the cations mentioned are strongly acidic. Small, highly charged cations such as Al^{3+} are strongly acidic.

C   This is not necessarily the case and is especially unlikely for M^{2+} and Ca^{2+} which can be easily derived from the metals by reaction with acidic solutions or oxygen in the atmosphere.

TIP: Evaluate each response carefully. Not all M^{2+} ions are alkaline earth cations. An M^{2+} cation can only be formed from an atom by the loss of two electrons, however.

21. What happens to the pH of a soapy solution as a result of the introduction of hardness ions?

  A. The pH increases as $[H^+]$ increases.
  B. The pH is not changed since no acid-base reaction occurs.
  C. The pH decreases as $[OH^-]$ decreases.
  D. The effect on pH depends on the identity M^{2+}.

Foundational Concept: 5

The principles that govern chemical interactions and reactions form the basis for a broader understanding of the molecular dynamics of living systems.

Content Category: 5A

Unique nature of water and its solutions

Scientific Inquiry and Reasoning Skill: 2

Scientific Reasoning and Problem Solving

Key: C

Removal of weak bases such as RCO_2^- results in a decrease in pH, and a decrease in $[OH^-]$.

Distractors

A   Since $pH = -\log[H^+]$, an increase in $[H^+]$ results in a decrease in pH.

B   An acid-base reaction does occur. Moreover this reaction will affect the pH of the solution since weak bases are eliminated from solution.

D   The effect on pH is always the same for the three cations listed.

TIP: Often, useful information is concealed in the passage and must be interpreted properly. In this case, the passage stated that the sodium salts of organic acids represent soaps, which means that the conjugate bases of organic acids are what is in solution with the hardness ions.

22. Soaps are chemically modified natural products that can be derived from all of the following EXCEPT:

 A. fatty acids.
 B. cholesterols.
 C. triacylglycerols.
 D. phospholipids.

Foundational Concept: 5
The principles that govern chemical interactions and reactions form the basis for a broader understanding of the molecular dynamics of living systems.

Content Category: 5D
Structure, function, and reactivity of biologically-relevant molecules

Scientific Inquiry and Reasoning Skill: 2
Scientific Reasoning and Problem Solving

Key: B
While cholesterols are hydrocarbons found in cell membranes, they are not structurally similar to fatty acids.

Distractors

A   Fatty acids are RCO_2H which can easily be converted to soaps RCO_2Na by the addition of NaOH.

C   Triacylglycerols contain RCO_2^- groups that can be released by hydrolysis and precipitated as soap.

D   Phospholipids also contain RCO_2^- groups that can be released by hydrolysis and precipitated as soap.

 TIP: Reasoning about biochemical molecules will often require you to compare different structural forms of the same class of molecules.

23. A pump is used to force an aqueous solution through a pipe at high temperature according to Poiseuille's Law:

$$\text{Flow rate} = \frac{\Delta P \pi r^4}{8 L \eta}$$

where ΔP is the pressure difference applied by the pump, r is the radius of the pipe, L is the length of the pipe, and η is the viscosity of the solution. Which graph depicts the rate of energy consumed over time in order to maintain constant flow through a pipe subject to boiler scale?

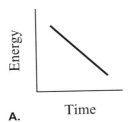

A.

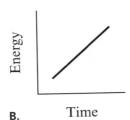

B.

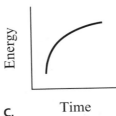

C.

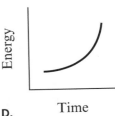

D.

Foundational Concept: 4
Complex living organisms transport materials, sense their environment, process signals, and respond to changes using processes understood in terms of physical principles.

Content Category: 4B
Importance of fluids for the circulation of blood, gas movement, and gas exchange

Scientific Inquiry and Reasoning Skill: 4
Data-based and Statistical Reasoning

Key: D
The energy consumed by the pump is used to create the pressure difference that maintains the viscous flow through the pipe. For a constant flow to occur while the pipe's diameter decreases, the pressure difference should increase in time. According to Poiseuille's Law, at constant flow rate, the pressure difference is inversely proportional to the radius of the pipe to the fourth power. The energy used is equal to the work done in moving the fluid, hence is proportional to the pressure difference. In other words, energy is inversely proportional to the radius of the pipe to the fourth power. As the radius decreases in time, the energy used increases more due to the fourth power dependence of the radius. In other words, more power (energy per unit time) is required to maintain the same flow through a pipe with decreased radius. Hence, the only choice that depicts such a power increase that is getting larger in time is shown in graph D.

Distractors

A   Energy used cannot decrease in time, as more energy is required to push the fluid through a narrowing pipe.

B   This graph shows that the power used is constant in time, as the slope of the graph is constant. This is inconsistent with the fact that the pipe radius decreases in time, hence a larger pressure difference is needed for the same flow.

C   According to the graph, the power required (i.e., the slope of the graph) is decreasing in time, to the point where it becomes zero (the graph becomes asymptotically horizontal). This is inconsistent with the fact that the pipe radius decreases, and the pressure applied must increase.

TIP: The question requires a thorough understanding of the notion of viscous flow and power, that is, work rate or energy rate, as a function of time. It is important to note that the constant flow requirement imposes a certain relationship between the pipe radius and the pressure applied, which is not linear. Because the energy used to keep the flow constant and its rate, namely the power, are also dependent on the pressure difference, the relationship between the energy used (and the corresponding power) and the pipe radius that changes in time is also nonlinear.

24. Which experimental approach can be used to analyze the metal content of soapy precipitate produced by Reaction 1? Dissolve the solid in a known volume of:

A. 0.1 M NaHCO$_3$(aq), then titrate with standardized 0.1 M HCl(aq) using an indicator.
B. 0.1 M NaOH(aq), then titrate with standardized 0.1 M HCl(aq) using an indicator.
C. 0.1 M NaCl(aq), then titrate with standardized 0.1 M NaOH(aq) using an indicator.
D. 0.1 M HCl(aq), then titrate with standardized 0.1 M NaOH(aq) using an indicator.

Foundational Concept: 5
The principles that govern chemical interactions and reactions form the basis for a broader understanding of the molecular dynamics of living systems.

Content Category: 5A
Unique nature of water and its solutions

Scientific Inquiry and Reasoning Skill: 3
Reasoning About the Design and Execution of Research

Key: D
The soapy precipitate is the salt of a weak base. Addition of HCl will generate the free fatty acid which can then be neutralized by NaOH. The difference in the number of moles of HCl and NaOH required to reach the endpoint gives the number of moles of RCO$_2$ which can then be used to calculate the mass present in the solid and the percentage of the metal content.

Distractors
A   Since the precipitate will not be broken up in this approach the results of the titration are likely to be complicated.

B   The precipitate will not be broken up in this approach and the addition of NaOH will result in a spike in pH with no discernible equivalence point.

C   The solution will quickly rise in pH and no equivalence point can be obtained using this approach.

 TIP: It is often useful to eliminate those distractors that represent incorrect interpretation of concepts. For instance, choice C does not represent a titration and can immediately be removed from consideration.

Chemical and Physical Foundations of Biological Systems

Discrete Questions

MCAT® is a program of the
Association of American Medical Colleges

Chemical and Physical Foundations of Biological Systems

Chemical and Physical Foundations of Biological Systems Discrete (Questions 25–30)

25. The overall reaction for glycolysis:
Glucose + 2NAD$^+$ + 2ADP + 2P$_i$ →
2Pyruvate + 2NADH + 2H$^+$ + 2ATP + 2H$_2$O

can be broken down into two separate processes (reactions 1 and 2).

Glucose + 2NAD$^+$ → 2Pyruvate + 2NADH + 2H$^+$

Reaction 1: $\Delta G° = -146$ kJ/mol

ADP + P$_i$ → ATP + H$_2$O

Reaction 2: $\Delta G° = +30.5$ kJ/mol

What is $\Delta G°$ for glycolysis?

A. −207.0 kJ/mol
B. −176.5 kJ/mol
C. −85.0 kJ/mol
D. −54.5 kJ/mol

---

26. Positron Emission Spectroscopy (PET) imaging involves injecting a patient with a positron (anti-electron) emitting isotope. The emission of positrons occurs during:

A. alpha decay.
B. alpha absorption.
C. gamma absorption.
D. beta decay.

27. The pressure and volume changes that occur during a cycle of breathing are illustrated graphically in the figure shown.

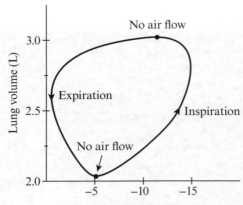

What does the area within the curve represent?

A. Work done
B. Oxygen removed
C. Lung volume change
D. Air pressure change

---

28. Human speech is generated in the vocal cords as the lungs push air past them. What property of the vocal cords is changed so that the frequency of sound can be altered?

A. Volume
B. Density
C. Tension
D. Number

---

29. If sounds produced by the human vocal cords are approximated as waves on a string fixed at both ends, and the average length of a vocal cord is 15 mm, what is the fundamental frequency of the sound? (Note: Use 3 m/s for the speed of sound through the vocal cord.)

A. 10 Hz
B. 100 Hz
C. 1000 Hz
D. 10,000 Hz

30. A researcher measures the initial rate ($V_0 = \Delta[P]/\Delta t$) of an enzymatically catalyzed reaction at a variety of substrate concentrations $[S]_0$.

$$S \xrightarrow{\text{enzyme}} P$$

Which graph best represents the observed relationship between $[S]_0$ versus V_0?

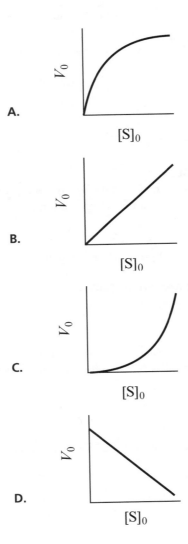

A.

B.

C.

D.

Solutions begin on next page.

25. The overall reaction for glycolysis:

$$Glucose + 2NAD^+ + 2ADP + 2P_i \rightarrow 2Pyruvate + 2NADH + 2H^+ + 2ATP + 2H_2O$$

can be broken down into two separate processes (reactions 1 and 2).

$$Glucose + 2NAD^+ \rightarrow 2Pyruvate + 2NADH + 2H^+$$

Reaction 1: $\Delta G° = -146$ kJ/mol

$$ADP + P_i \rightarrow ATP + H_2O$$

Reaction 2: $\Delta G° = +30.5$ kJ/mol

What is $\Delta G°$ for glycolysis?

    A. -207.0 kJ/mol
    B. -176.5 kJ/mol
    C. -85.0 kJ/mol
    D. -54.5 kJ/mol

Foundational Concept: 5
The principles that govern chemical interactions and reactions form the basis for a broader understanding of the molecular dynamics of living systems.

Content Category: 5E
Principles of chemical thermodynamics and kinetics

Scientific Inquiry and Reasoning Skill: 4
Data-based and Statistical Reasoning

Key: C
Glycolysis is the net sum of Reaction 1 and two rounds of Reaction 2. The overall free energy change can therefore be calculated as (-146 kJ/mol) + 2(30.5 kJ/mol) = -85 kJ/mol.

Distractors

A   This is the result if you subtract 2 × $\Delta G°$ for Reaction 2 instead of adding it.

B   This is the result if you subtract $\Delta G°$ for Reaction 2 from $\Delta G°$ for Reaction 1.

D   This is the result if you add 3 × $\Delta G°$ for Reaction 2 to $\Delta G°$ for Reaction 1.

26. Positron Emission Spectroscopy (PET) imaging involves injecting a patient with a positron (anti-electron) emitting isotope. The emission of positrons occurs during:

   A. alpha decay.
   B. alpha absorption.
   C. gamma absorption.
   D. beta decay.

Foundational Concept: 4
Complex living organisms transport materials, sense their environment, process signals, and respond to changes using processes understood in terms of physical principles.

Content Category: 4E
Atoms, nuclear decay, electronic structure, and atomic chemical behavior

Scientific Inquiry and Reasoning Skill: 1
Knowledge of Scientific Concepts and Principles

Key: D
Beta decay is the decay in which a beta particle (electron or positron) is emitted from a heavy-atom nucleus.

Distractors

A   During alpha decay, alpha particles (He nuclei) are emitted by the heavy-atom nuclei.

B   During alpha absorption, alpha particles (He nuclei) are absorbed by the target atoms.

C   Absorption of gamma rays consists of the process in which high energy photons (also called gamma ray photons) are absorbed by target atoms.

27. The pressure and volume changes that occur during a cycle of breathing are illustrated graphically in the figure shown.

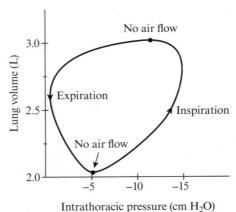

What does the area within the curve represent?

A. Work done
B. Oxygen removed
C. Lung volume change
D. Air pressure change

Foundational Concept: 5
The principles that govern chemical interactions and reactions form the basis for a broader understanding of the molecular dynamics of living systems.

Content Category: 5E
Principles of chemical thermodynamics and kinetics

Scientific Inquiry and Reasoning Skill: 4
Data-based and Statistical Reasoning

Key: A
This question requires you to interpret graphically a thermodynamic process and the area it encloses when represented in pressure-volume coordinates. The area under a curve that represents graphically the relationship of two physical variables (one independent and the other dependent) has the physical dimension of the product of the measurement units of the variables. In this case, a thermodynamic process is shown in *PV* coordinates, hence the area under the curve has the dimensions of $[N/m^2] \times [m^3] = [N \times m] = [J]$. The unit of joule (J) is used for energy and work.

Distractors

B   The quantity of oxygen removed is not measured in units of work or energy.

C   Lung volume change is shown on the vertical axis of coordinates.

D   Air pressure change is shown on the horizontal axis.

TIP: This type of question can be answered using dimensional analysis, by computing the product of the units of measurement of the quantities shown on the two axes of coordinates, as expressed in the International System of Units (SI).

28. Human speech is generated in the vocal cords as the lungs push air past them. What property of the vocal cords is changed so that the frequency of sound can be altered?

   A. Volume
   B. Density
   C. Tension
   D. Number

Foundational Concept: 4
Complex living organisms transport materials, sense their environment, process signals, and respond to changes using processes understood in terms of physical principles.

Content Category: 4D
How light and sound interact with matter

Scientific Inquiry and Reasoning Skill: 2
Scientific Reasoning and Problem Solving

Key: C
The frequency of the sound produced in vibrating cords and strings (such as vocal cords) of fixed length is proportional to the propagation speed of the sound through the cord. In turn, the propagation speed of a transverse wave (such as the sound wave in the vocal cords) is directly proportional to the tension applied along the cord.

Distractors

A   A change in the volume of the vocal cords cannot affect the sound frequency because the frequency only depends on the propagation speed (for a fixed-length cord), and the speed is independent of the volume.

B   A change in the density of the vocal cords cannot affect the sound frequency because the frequency only depends on the propagation speed (for a fixed-length cord), and the speed is independent of the density, as it propagates as a transverse wave through the cords.

D   The number of vocal cords used in generating the speech is constant.

29. If sounds produced by the human vocal cords are approximated as waves on a string fixed at both ends, and the average length of a vocal cord is 15 mm, what is the fundamental frequency of the sound? (Note: Use 3 m/s for the speed of sound through the vocal cord.)

A. 10 Hz
B. 100 Hz
C. 1000 Hz
D. 10,000 Hz

Foundational Concept: 4
Complex living organisms transport materials, sense their environment, process signals, and respond to changes using processes understood in terms of physical principles.

Content Category: 4D
How light and sound interact with matter

Scientific Inquiry and Reasoning Skill: 2
Scientific Reasoning and Problem Solving

Key: B
This question requires you to apply knowledge of sound production by vibrating cords and strings, and to identify the physical properties of such cords and their relationship with sound characteristics: frequency, propagation speed, and amplitude. In particular, the relationship between the sound speed and frequency for a string fixed at both ends must be used. The fundamental frequency of a vibrating string is given by $f = v/(2L) = (3 \text{ m/s})/(30 \times 10^{-3} \text{ m}) = 1/10^{-2}$ Hz = 100 Hz.

Distractors

A   This incorrect answer results from using the length of the vocal cords as 15 cm.

C   This incorrect answer results from using the sound speed as 30 m/s.

D   This incorrect answer results from using the length of the vocal cords as 1.5 mm and the sound speed as 30 m/s.

TIP: The frequency of the sound generated by vibrating strings fixed at both ends can be confused with the frequency of the sound generated by strings fixed at one end only, or generated in tubes open at both ends. While all cases have in common that frequency is proportional to the ratio between the propagation speed and the length of the vibrating media, the proportionality constant and the number of harmonics is specific to each case.

Fifth Edition
The Official Guide to the MCAT® Exam
240
MCAT® is a program of the
Association of American Medical Colleges

30. A researcher measures the initial rate ($V_0 = \Delta[P]/\Delta t$) of an enzymatically catalyzed reaction at a variety of substrate concentrations $[S]_0$.

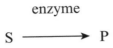

$$S \longrightarrow P$$

Which graph best represents the observed relationship between $[S]_0$ versus V_0?

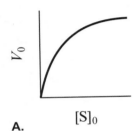

A.

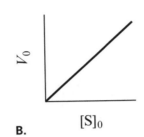

B.

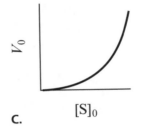

C.

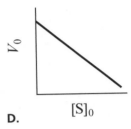

D.

Foundational Concept: 5
The principles that govern chemical interactions and reactions form the basis for a broader understanding of the molecular dynamics of living systems.

Content Category: 5E
Principles of chemical thermodynamics and kinetics

Scientific Inquiry and Reasoning Skill: 1
Knowledge of Scientific Concepts and Principles

Key: A
For enzymatically catalyzed processes, the reaction rate will level off with increasing concentration of substrate as the enzyme becomes the bottleneck for the reaction. This is called saturation kinetics.

Distractors

B   Unlike first-order processes, increasing the concentration of substrate will not linearly increase the rate.

C   Unlike second- or third-order processes, where increasing the substrate concentration can cause a squaring or tripling of the initial rate, enzymatically catalyzed reactions will not show such increases.

D   In general, increasing the concentration of a reactant will increase the rate of its reaction.

Chapter 12

What Will the Psychological, Social, and Biological Foundations of Behavior Section Test?

The Psychological, Social, and Biological Foundations of Behavior section asks you to solve problems by combining your knowledge of foundational concepts with your scientific inquiry and reasoning skills. This section tests your understanding of the ways psychological, social, and biological factors influence perceptions and reactions to the world; behavior and behavior change; what people think about themselves and others; the cultural and social differences that influence well-being; and the relationships between social stratification, access to resources, and well-being.

The Psychological, Social, and Biological Foundations of Behavior section emphasizes concepts that tomorrow's doctors need to know in order to serve an increasingly diverse population and have a clear understanding of the impact of behavior on health. Further, it communicates the need for future physicians to be prepared to deal with the human and social issues of medicine.

To recap from Part I, this section is designed to:

- test psychology, sociology, and biology concepts that provide a solid foundation for learning in medical school about the behavioral and sociocultural determinants of health;

- test concepts taught at many colleges and universities in first-semester psychology and sociology courses;

- test biology concepts that relate to mental processes and behavior that are taught at many colleges and universities in introductory biology;

- test basic research methods and statistics concepts described by many baccalaureate faculty as important to success in introductory science courses; and

- require you to demonstrate your scientific inquiry and reasoning, research methods, and statistics skills as applied to the social and behavioral sciences.

Test Section	Number of Questions	Time
Psychological, Social, and Biological Foundations of Behavior	59 *(note that questions are a combination of passage-based and discrete questions)*	95 minutes

Psychological, Social, and Biological Foundations of Behavior Distribution of Questions

Distribution of Questions by Discipline, Foundational Concept, and Scientific Inquiry and Reasoning Skill

You may wonder how much psychology, sociology, and biology you'll see on this section of the MCAT exam, how many questions you'll get about a particular foundational concept, or how the scientific inquiry and reasoning skills will be distributed on your exam. The questions that you see are likely to be distributed in the ways described below. These are the approximate percentages of questions you'll see on a test for each discipline, foundational concept, and scientific inquiry and reasoning skill.*

Discipline:
- Introductory psychology, 65%**
- Introductory sociology, 30%
- Introductory biology, 5%

Foundational Concept:
- Foundational Concept 6, 25%
- Foundational Concept 7, 35%
- Foundational Concept 8, 20%
- Foundational Concept 9, 15%
- Foundational Concept 10, 5%

Scientific Inquiry and Reasoning Skill:
- Skill 1, 35%
- Skill 2, 45%
- Skill 3, 10%
- Skill 4, 10%

---

*These percentages have been approximated to the nearest 5% and will vary from one test to another for a variety of reasons. These reasons include, but are not limited to, controlling for question difficulty, using groups of questions that depend on a single passage, and using unscored field-test questions on each test form.

**Please note that about 5% of this test section will include psychology questions that are biologically relevant. This is in addition to the discipline target of 5% for introductory biology specified for this section.

Understanding the Foundational Concepts and Content Categories

The following are detailed explanations of each foundational concept and related content category tested by the Psychological, Social, and Biological Foundations of Behavior section. As with the natural sciences sections, content lists describing specific topics and subtopics that define each content category are provided. The same content list is provided to the writers who develop the content of the exam. Here is an excerpt from the content list:

Excerpt from the Psychological, Social, and Biological Foundations of Behavior Outline

Self-presentation and Interacting with Others (PSY, SOC) ◄——— **Topic**

- Expressing and detecting emotion ◄——————— **Subtopic**
  - The role of gender in the expression and detection of emotion
  - The role of culture in the expression and detection of emotion
- Presentation of self
  - Impression management
  - Front stage vs. back stage self (Dramaturgical approach) (SOC)
- Verbal and nonverbal communication
- Animal signals and communication (PSY, BIO)

The abbreviations found in parentheses indicate the course(s) in which undergraduate students at many colleges and universities learn about the topics and associated subtopics. The course abbreviations are

- PSY: one semester of introductory psychology
- SOC: one semester of introductory sociology
- BIO: two-semester sequence of introductory biology

In preparing for the MCAT exam, you will be responsible for learning the topics and associated subtopics at the levels at which they are taught in the courses listed in parentheses. A small number of subtopics have course abbreviations indicated in parentheses. In those cases, you are responsible only for learning the subtopics as they are taught in the course(s) indicated.

Using the excerpt above as an example,

- You are responsible for learning about the topic Self-presentation and Interacting with Others at the level at which it is taught in a typical introductory psychology course *and* in a typical introductory sociology course.
- You are responsible for learning about the sub-subtopic Front stage vs. back stage self (Dramaturgical approach) *only* at the level at which it is taught in a typical introductory sociology course.
- You are responsible for learning about the subtopic Animal signals and communication at the level at which it is taught in a typical introductory psychology course *and* in a typical introductory biology course.

Remember that course content at your school may differ from course content at other colleges and universities. The topics and subtopics described in this chapter may be covered in courses with titles that are different from those listed here. Your prehealth advisor and faculty are important resources for your questions about course content.

Psychological, Social, and Biological Foundations of Behavior

Foundational Concept 6

Biological, psychological, and sociocultural factors influence the ways that individuals perceive, think about, and react to the world.

The way in which we sense, perceive, think about, and react to stimuli affects our experiences. Foundational Concept 6 focuses on these components of experience, starting with the initial detection and perception of stimuli through cognition, and continuing to emotion and stress.

Content Categories

- *Category 6A* focuses on the detection and perception of sensory information.

- *Category 6B* focuses on cognition, including our ability to attend to the environment, think about and remember what we experience, and use language to communicate with others.

- *Category 6C* focuses on how we process and experience emotion and stress.

With these building blocks, medical students will be able to learn about the ways in which cognitive and perceptual processes influence their understanding of health and illness.

Content Category 6A: *Sensing the environment*

Psychological, sociocultural, and biological factors affect our sensation and perception of the world. All sensory processing begins with first detecting a stimulus in the environment through sensory cells, receptors, and biological pathways.

After collecting sensory information, we then interpret and make sense of it. Although sensation and perception are distinct functions, they are both influenced by psychological, social, and biological factors and therefore become almost indistinguishable in practice. This complexity is illuminated by examining human sight, hearing, touch, taste, and smell.

The content in this category covers sensation and perception across all human senses. The topics and subtopics in this category are the following:

Sensory Processing (PSY, BIO)
- Sensation
  - Threshold
  - Weber's Law (PSY)
  - Signal detection theory (PSY)
  - Sensory adaptation
  - Psychophysics
- Sensory receptors
  - Sensory pathways
  - Types of sensory receptor

Vision (PSY, BIO)
- Structure and function of the eye
- Visual processing
  - Visual pathways in the brain
  - Parallel processing (PSY)
  - Feature detection (PSY)

Hearing (PSY, BIO)
- Structure and function of the ear
- Auditory processing (e.g., auditory pathways in the brain)
- Sensory reception by hair cells

Other Senses (PSY, BIO)
- Somatosensation (e.g., pain perception)
- Taste (e.g., taste buds/chemoreceptors that detect specific chemicals)
- Smell
  - Olfactory cells/chemoreceptors that detect specific chemicals
  - Pheromones (BIO)
  - Olfactory pathways in the brain (BIO)
- Kinesthetic sense (PSY)
- Vestibular sense

Perception (PSY)
- Bottom-up/top-down processing
- Perceptual organization (e.g., depth, form, motion, constancy)
- Gestalt principles

Content Category 6B: *Making sense of the environment*

The way we think about the world depends on our awareness, thoughts, knowledge, and memories. It is also influenced by our ability to solve problems, make decisions, form judgments, and communicate. Psychological, sociocultural, and biological influences determine the development and use of these different yet convergent processes.

Biological factors underlie the mental processes that create our reality, shape our perception of the world, and influence the way we perceive and react to every aspect of our lives.

The content in this category covers critical aspects of cognition—including consciousness, cognitive development, problem solving and decision making, intelligence, memory, and language. The topics and subtopics in this category are the following:

Attention (PSY)
- Selective attention
- Divided attention

Cognition (PSY)
- Information-processing model
- Cognitive development
  - Piaget's stages of cognitive development
  - Cognitive changes in late adulthood
  - Role of culture in cognitive development
  - Influence of heredity and environment on cognitive development
- Biological factors that affect cognition (PSY, BIO)
- Problem solving and decision making
  - Types of problem solving
  - Barriers to effective problem solving
  - Approaches to problem solving
  - Heuristics and biases (e.g., overconfidence, belief perseverance)
- Intellectual functioning
  - Theories of intelligence
  - Influence of heredity and environment on intelligence
  - Variations in intellectual ability

Consciousness (PSY)
- States of consciousness
  - Alertness (PSY, BIO)
  - Sleep
    - Stages of sleep
    - Sleep cycles and changes to sleep cycles
    - Sleep and circadian rhythms (PSY, BIO)
    - Dreaming
    - Sleep–wake disorders
  - Hypnosis and meditation
- Consciousness-altering drugs
  - Types of consciousness-altering drugs and their effects on the nervous system and behavior
  - Drug addiction and the reward pathway in the brain

Memory (PSY)

- Encoding
    - Process of encoding information
    - Processes that aid in encoding memories
- Storage
    - Types of memory storage (e.g., sensory, working, long-term)
    - Semantic networks and spreading activation
- Retrieval
    - Recall, recognition, and relearning
    - Retrieval cues
    - The role of emotion in retrieving memories (PSY, BIO)
    - Processes that aid retrieval
- Forgetting
    - Aging and memory
    - Memory dysfunctions (e.g., Alzheimer disease, Korsakof syndrome)
    - Decay
    - Interference
    - Memory construction and source monitoring
- Changes in synaptic connections underlie memory and learning (PSY, BIO)
    - Neural plasticity
    - Memory and learning
    - Long-term potentiation

Language (PSY)

- Theories of language development (e.g., Learning, Nativist, Interactionist)
- Influence of language on cognition
- Brain areas that control language and speech (PSY, BIO)

Content Category 6C: Responding to the world

We experience a barrage of environmental stimuli throughout the course of our lives. In many cases, environmental stimuli trigger physiological responses, such as an elevated heart rate, increased perspiration, or heightened feelings of anxiety. How we perceive and interpret these physiological responses is complex and influenced by psychological, sociocultural, and biological factors.

Emotional responses, such as feelings of happiness, sadness, anger, or stress are often born out of our interpretation of this interplay of physiological responses. Our experience with emotions and stress not only affects our behavior, but also shapes our interactions with others.

The content in this category covers the basic components and theories of emotion and their underlying psychological, sociocultural, and biological factors. It also addresses stress, stress outcomes, and stress management. The topics and subtopics in this category are the following:

Emotion (PSY)
- Three components of emotion (i.e., cognitive, physiological, behavioral)
- Universal emotions (i.e., fear, anger, happiness, surprise, disgust, and sadness)
- Adaptive role of emotion
- Theories of emotion
    - James–Lange theory
    - Cannon–Bard theory
    - Schachter–Singer theory
- The role of biological processes in perceiving emotion (PSY, BIO)
    - Brain regions involved in the generation and experience of emotions
    - The role of the limbic system in emotion
    - Emotion and the autonomic nervous system
    - Physiological markers of emotion (signatures of emotion)

Stress (PSY)
- The nature of stress
    - Appraisal
    - Different types of stressors (e.g., cataclysmic events, personal)
    - Effects of stress on psychological functions
- Stress outcomes/response to stressors
    - Physiological (PSY, BIO)
    - Emotional
    - Behavioral
- Managing stress (e.g., exercise, relaxation, spirituality)

Psychological, Social, and Biological Foundations of Behavior

Foundational Concept 7

Biological, psychological, and sociocultural factors influence behavior and behavior change.

Human behavior is complex and often surprising, differing across individuals in the same situation and within an individual across different situations. A full understanding of human behavior requires knowledge of the interplay between psychological, sociocultural, and biological factors that are related to behavior. This interplay has important implications for the way we behave and the likelihood of behavior change.

Foundational Concept 7 focuses on individual and social determinants of behavior and behavior change.

Content Categories

- *Category 7A* focuses on the individual psychological and biological factors that affect behavior.

- *Category 7B* focuses on how social factors, such as groups and social norms, affect behavior.

- *Category 7C* focuses on how learning affects behavior, as well as the role of attitude theories in behavior and behavior change.

With these building blocks, medical students will be able to learn how behavior can either support health or increase risk for disease.

Content Category 7A: *Individual influences on behavior*

A complex interplay of psychological and biological factors shapes behavior. Biological structures and processes serve as the pathways by which bodies carry out activities. They also affect predispositions to behave in certain ways, shape personalities, and influence the likelihood of developing psychological disorders. Psychological factors also affect behavior, and consequently, health and well-being.

The content in this category covers biological bases of behavior, including the effect of genetics and how the nervous and endocrine systems affect behavior. It also addresses how personality, psychological disorders, motivation, and attitudes affect behavior. Some of these topics are learned in the context of non-human animal species. The topics and subtopics in this category are the following:

Biological Bases of Behavior (PSY, BIO)
- The nervous system
  - Neurons (e.g., the reflex arc)
  - Neurotransmitters
  - Structure and function of the peripheral nervous system
  - Structure and function of the central nervous system
    - The brain
      - Forebrain
      - Midbrain
      - Hindbrain
      - Lateralization of cortical functions
      - Methods used in studying the brain
    - The spinal cord
- Neuronal communication and its influence on behavior (PSY)
- Influence of neurotransmitters on behavior (PSY)
- The endocrine system
  - Components of the endocrine system
  - Effects of the endocrine system on behavior
- Behavioral genetics
  - Genes, temperament, and heredity
  - Adaptive value of traits and behaviors
  - Interaction between heredity and environmental influences
- Influence of genetic and environmental factors on the development of behaviors
  - Experience and behavior (PSY)
  - Regulatory genes and behavior (BIO)
  - Genetically based behavioral variation in natural populations
- Human physiological development (PSY)
  - Prenatal development
  - Motor development
  - Developmental changes in adolescence

Personality (PSY)
- Theories of personality
  - Psychoanalytic perspective
  - Humanistic perspective
  - Trait perspective
  - Social cognitive perspective

- o Biological perspective
- o Behaviorist perspective
- Situational approach to explaining behavior

Psychological Disorders (PSY)
- Understanding psychological disorders
  - o Biomedical vs. biopsychosocial approaches
  - o Classifying psychological disorders
  - o Rates of psychological disorders
- Types of psychological disorders
  - o Anxiety disorders
  - o Obsessive–compulsive disorder
  - o Trauma- and stressor-related disorders
  - o Somatic symptom and related disorders
  - o Bipolar and related disorders
  - o Depressive disorders
  - o Schizophrenia
  - o Dissociative disorders
  - o Personality disorders
- Biological bases of nervous system disorders (PSY, BIO)
  - o Schizophrenia
  - o Depression
  - o Alzheimer disease
  - o Parkinson disease
  - o Stem cell-based therapy to regenerate neurons in the central nervous system (BIO)

Motivation (PSY)
- Factors that influence motivation
  - o Instinct
  - o Arousal
  - o Drives (e.g., negative feedback systems) (PSY, BIO)
  - o Needs
- Theories that explain how motivation affects human behavior
  - o Drive reduction theory
  - o Incentive theory
  - o Other theories (e.g., cognitive, need-based)
- Biological and sociocultural motivators that regulate behavior (e.g., hunger, sex drive, substance addiction)

Attitudes (PSY)
- Components of attitudes (i.e., cognitive, affective, and behavioral)
- The link between attitudes and behavior
  - o Processes by which behavior influences attitudes (e.g., foot-in-the door phenomenon, role-playing effects)
  - o Processes by which attitudes influence behavior
  - o Cognitive dissonance theory

Content Category 7B: *Social processes that influence human behavior*

Many social processes influence human behavior; in fact, the mere presence of other individuals can influence our behavior. Groups and social norms also exert influence over our behavior. Oftentimes, social processes influence our behavior through unwritten rules that define acceptable and unacceptable behavior in society.

Our understanding of groups and social norms is learned through the process of socialization. What we learn about the groups and society to which we belong affects our behavior and influences our perceptions and interactions with others.

The content in this category covers how the presence of others, group decision-making processes, social norms, and socialization shape our behavior. The topics and subtopics in this category are the following:

How the Presence of Others Affects Individual Behavior (PSY)
- Social facilitation
- Deindividuation
- Bystander effect
- Social loafing
- Social control (SOC)
- Peer pressure (PSY, SOC)
- Conformity (PSY, SOC)
- Obedience (PSY, SOC)

Group Decision-making Processes (PSY, SOC)
- Group polarization (PSY)
- Groupthink

Normative and Non-normative Behavior (SOC)
- Social norms (PSY, SOC)
  - Sanctions (SOC)
  - Folkways, mores, and taboos (SOC)
  - Anomie (SOC)
- Deviance
  - Perspectives on deviance (e.g., differential association, labeling theory, strain theory)
- Aspects of collective behavior (e.g., fads, mass hysteria, riots)

Socialization (PSY, SOC)
- Agents of socialization (e.g., the family, mass media, peers, workplace)

Fifth Edition
The Official Guide to the MCAT® Exam
254
MCAT® is a program of the
Association of American Medical Colleges

Content Category 7C: *Attitude and behavior change*

Learning is a relatively permanent change in behavior brought about by experience. There are a number of different types of learning, which include habituation as well as associative, observational, and social learning.

Although people can learn new behaviors and change their attitudes, psychological, environmental, and biological factors influence whether those changes will be short-term or long-term. Understanding how people learn new behaviors, change their attitudes, and the conditions that affect learning helps us understand behavior and our interactions with others.

The content in this category covers learning and theories of attitude and behavior change. This includes the elaboration likelihood model and social cognitive theory. The topics and subtopics in this category are the following:

Habituation and Dishabituation (PSY)

Associative Learning (PSY)
- Classical conditioning (PSY, BIO)
  - Neutral, conditioned, and unconditioned stimuli
  - Conditioned and unconditioned response
  - Processes: acquisition, extinction, spontaneous recovery, generalization, discrimination
- Operant conditioning (PSY, BIO)
  - Processes of shaping and extinction
  - Types of reinforcement: positive, negative, primary, conditional
  - Reinforcement schedules: fixed-ratio, variable-ratio, fixed-interval, variable-interval
  - Punishment
  - Escape and avoidance learning
- The role of cognitive processes in associative learning
- Biological processes that affect associative learning (e.g., biological predispositions, instinctive drift) (PSY, BIO)

Observational Learning (PSY)
- Modeling
- Biological processes that affect observational learning
  - Mirror neurons
  - Role of the brain in experiencing vicarious emotions
- Applications of observational learning to explain individual behavior

Theories of Attitude and Behavior Change (PSY)
- Elaboration likelihood model
- Social cognitive theory
- Factors that affect attitude change (e.g., changing behavior, characteristics of the message and target, social factors)

Psychological, Social, and Biological Foundations of Behavior

Foundational Concept 8

Psychological, sociocultural, and biological factors influence the way we think about ourselves and others, as well as how we interact with others.

The connection between how people think about themselves and others is complex and affects social interactions. The interplay between thoughts about ourselves, thoughts about others, and our biology has important implications for our sense of self and interpersonal relationships.

Foundational Concept 8 focuses on the physical, cognitive, and social components of our identity, as well as how these components influence the way we think about and interact with others.

Content Categories

- *Category 8A* focuses on the notion of self and identity formation.
- *Category 8B* focuses on the attitudes and beliefs that affect social interaction.
- *Category 8C* focuses on the actions and processes underlying social interactions.

With these building blocks, medical students will be able to learn how to communicate and collaborate with patients and other members of the health care team.

Fifth Edition
The Official Guide to the MCAT® Exam
256
MCAT® is a program of the
Association of American Medical Colleges

Content Category 8A: *Self-identity*

The *self* refers to the thoughts and beliefs we have about ourselves. Our notion of self is complex and multifaceted. It includes gender, racial, and ethnic identities, as well as beliefs about our ability to accomplish tasks and exert control over different situations.

Our notion of self develops over time and is shaped by a variety of factors, including society, culture, individuals and groups, and our unique experiences. How we view ourselves influences our perceptions of others, and by extension, our interactions with them.

The content in this category covers the notions of self-concept and identity, along with the role of self-esteem, self-efficacy, and locus of control in the development of self-concept. Identity formation, including developmental stages and the social factors that affect identity formation, is also covered here. Theories are included to provide historical context for the field of identity formation. The topics and subtopics in this category are the following:

Self-Concept, Self-Identity, and Social Identity (PSY, SOC)
- The role of self-esteem, self-efficacy, and locus of control in self-concept and self-identity (PSY)
- Different types of identities (e.g., race/ethnicity, gender, age, sexual orientation, class)

Formation of Identity (PSY, SOC)
- Theories of identity development (e.g., gender, moral, psychosexual, social)
- Influence of social factors on identity formation
    - Influence of individuals (e.g., imitation, looking-glass self, role-taking)
    - Influence of groups (e.g., reference group)
- Influence of culture and socialization on identity formation

Content Category 8B: Social thinking

Social thinking refers to the ways in which we view others and our environment, as well as how we interpret others' behaviors. A variety of factors—personality, environment, and culture—factor into the beliefs and attitudes we develop.

Our beliefs and attitudes about others and the environment also shape the way we interact with each other. To interact with others, we need to interpret different aspects of a situation, including our perception of ourselves, the behavior of others, and the environment.

The content in this category covers our attitudes about others and how those attitudes develop, including how perceptions of culture and environment affect attributions of behavior. It also covers how our attitudes about different groups—prejudice, stereotypes, stigma, and ethnocentrism—may influence our interactions with group members. The topics and subtopics in this category are the following:

Attributing Behavior to Persons or Situations (PSY)
- Attributional processes (e.g., fundamental attribution error, role of culture in attributions)
- How self-perceptions shape our perceptions of others
- How perceptions of the environment shape our perceptions of others

Prejudice and Bias (PSY, SOC)
- Processes that contribute to prejudice
  - Power, prestige, and class (SOC)
  - The role of emotion in prejudice (PSY)
  - The role of cognition in prejudice (PSY)
- Stereotypes
- Stigma (SOC)
- Ethnocentrism (SOC)
  - Ethnocentrism vs. cultural relativism

Processes Related to Stereotypes (PSY)
- Self-fulfilling prophecy
- Stereotype threat

Content Category 8C: *Social interactions*

Humans are social beings by nature. Though the sentiment is simple, the actions and processes underlying and shaping our social interactions are not.

The changing nature of social interaction is important for understanding the mechanisms and processes through which people interact with each other, both individually and within groups. A variety of factors—environment, culture, and biology—affect how we present ourselves to others and how we treat them. For example, perceptions of prejudice and stereotypes can lead to acts of discrimination, whereas positive attitudes about others can lead to the provision of help and social support.

The content in this category covers the mechanisms of self-presentation and social interaction including expressing and detecting emotion, impression management, communication, the biological underpinning of social behavior, and discrimination. The topics and subtopics in this category are the following:

Elements of Social Interaction (PSY, SOC)
- Status (SOC)
    - Types of status (e.g., achieved, ascribed)
- Role
    - Role conflict and role strain (SOC)
    - Role exit (SOC)
- Groups
    - Primary and secondary groups (SOC)
    - In-group vs. out-group
    - Group size (e.g., dyads, triads) (SOC)
- Networks (SOC)
- Organizations (SOC)
    - Formal organization
    - Bureaucracy
        - Characteristics of an ideal bureaucracy
        - Perspectives on bureaucracy (e.g., iron law of oligarchy, McDonaldization)

Self-presentation and Interacting with Others (PSY, SOC)
- Expressing and detecting emotion
    - The role of gender in the expression and detection of emotion
    - The role of culture in the expression and detection of emotion
- Presentation of self
    - Impression management
    - Front stage vs. back stage self (Dramaturgical approach) (SOC)
- Verbal and nonverbal communication
- Animal signals and communication (PSY, BIO)

Social Behavior (PSY)

- Attraction
- Aggression
- Attachment
- Altruism
- Social support (PSY, SOC)
- Biological explanations of social behavior in animals (PSY, BIO)
    - Foraging behavior (BIO)
    - Mating behavior and mate choice
    - Applying game theory (BIO)
    - Altruism
    - Inclusive fitness (BIO)

Discrimination (PSY, SOC)

- Individual vs. institutional discrimination (SOC)
- The relationship between prejudice and discrimination
- How power, prestige, and class facilitate discrimination (SOC)

Psychological, Social, and Biological Foundations of Behavior

Foundational Concept 9

Cultural and social differences influence well-being.

Social structure and demographic factors influence peoples' health and well-being. Knowledge about basic sociological theories, social institutions, culture, and demographic characteristics of societies is important to understand how these factors shape peoples' lives and their daily interactions.

Foundational Concept 9 focuses on social variables and processes that influence our lives.

Content Categories

- *Category 9A* focuses on the link between social structures and human interactions.
- *Category 9B* focuses on the demographic characteristics and processes that define a society.

With these building blocks, medical students will be able to learn about the ways in which patients' social and demographic backgrounds influence their perceptions of health and disease, the health care team, and therapeutic interventions.

Content Category 9A: *Understanding social structure*

Social structure organizes all human societies. Elements of social structure include social institutions and culture. These elements are linked in a variety of ways and shape our experiences and interactions with others—a process that is reciprocal.

The content in this category provides a foundation for understanding social structure and the various forms of interactions within and among societies. It includes theoretical approaches to studying society and social groups, specific social institutions relevant to student preparation for medical school, and the construct of culture. The topics and subtopics in this category are the following:

Theoretical Approaches (SOC)
- Microsociology vs. macrosociology
- Functionalism
- Conflict theory
- Symbolic interactionism
- Social constructionism
- Exchange-rational choice
- Feminist theory

Social Institutions (SOC)
- Education
    - Hidden curriculum
    - Teacher expectancy
    - Educational segregation and stratification
- Family (PSY, SOC)
    - Forms of kinship (SOC)
    - Diversity in family forms
    - Marriage and divorce
    - Violence in the family (e.g., child abuse, elder abuse, spousal abuse) (SOC)
- Religion
    - Religiosity
    - Types of religious organizations (e.g., churches, sects, cults)
    - Religion and social change (e.g., modernization, secularization, fundamentalism)
- Government and economy
    - Power and authority
    - Comparative economic and political systems
    - Division of labor
- Health and medicine
    - Medicalization
    - The sick role
    - Delivery of health care
    - Illness experience
    - Social epidemiology

Culture (PSY, SOC)

- Elements of culture (e.g., beliefs, language, rituals, symbols, values)
- Material vs. symbolic culture (SOC)
- Culture lag (SOC)
- Culture shock (SOC)
- Assimilation (SOC)
- Multiculturalism (SOC)
- Subcultures and countercultures (SOC)
- Mass media and popular culture (SOC)
- Evolution and human culture (PSY, BIO)
- Transmission and diffusion (SOC)

Content Category 9B: Demographic characteristics and processes

In order to understand the structure of a society, it is important to understand the demographic characteristics and processes which define it. Knowledge of the demographic structure of societies and an understanding of how societies change helps us to comprehend the distinct processes and mechanisms through which social interaction occurs.

The content in this category covers the important demographic variables at the core of understanding societies, and also includes concepts related to demographic shifts and social change. The topics and subtopics in this category are the following:

Demographic Structure of Society (PSY, SOC)
- Age
    - Aging and the life course
    - Age cohorts (SOC)
    - Social significance of aging
- Gender
    - Sex versus gender
    - The social construction of gender (SOC)
    - Gender segregation (SOC)
- Race and ethnicity (SOC)
    - The social construction of race
    - Racialization
    - Racial formation
- Immigration status (SOC)
    - Patterns of immigration
    - Intersections with race and ethnicity
- Sexual orientation

Demographic Shifts and Social Change (SOC)
- Theories of demographic change (i.e., Malthusian theory and demographic transition)
- Population growth and decline (e.g., population projections, population pyramids)
- Fertility, migration, and mortality
    - Fertility and mortality rates (e.g., total, crude, age-specific)
    - Patterns in fertility and mortality
    - Push and pull factors in migration
- Social movements
    - Relative deprivation
    - Organization of social movements
    - Movement strategies and tactics
- Globalization
    - Factors contributing to globalization (e.g., communication technology, economic interdependence)
    - Perspectives on globalization
    - Social changes in globalization (e.g., civil unrest, terrorism)
- Urbanization
    - Industrialization and urban growth
    - Suburbanization and urban decline
    - Gentrification and urban renewal

Psychological, Social, and Biological Foundations of Behavior

Foundational Concept 10

Social stratification and access to resources influence well-being.

Social stratification and inequality affect all human societies, and shape the lives of all individuals by affording privileges to some and positioning others at a disadvantage.

Foundational Concept 10 focuses on the aspects of social inequality that influence how we interact with one another, as well as how we approach our health and the health care system.

Content Category

- *Category 10A* focuses on a broad understanding of social class, including theories of stratification, social mobility, and poverty.

With these building blocks, medical students will be able to learn about the ways in which social and economic factors can affect access to care and the probability of maintaining health and recovering from disease.

Content Category 10A: *Social inequality*

Barriers to the access of institutional resources exist for the segment of the population that is disenfranchised or lacks power within a given society. Barriers to access might include language, geographic location, socioeconomic status, immigration status, and racial/ethnic identity. Institutionalized racism and discrimination are also factors which prevent some groups from obtaining equal access to resources. An understanding of the barriers to the access of institutional resources, informed by perspectives such as social justice, is essential to address health and health care disparities.

The content in this category covers spatial inequality, the structure and patterns of social class, and health disparities in relation to class, race/ethnicity, and gender. The topics and subtopics in this category are the following:

Spatial Inequality (SOC)
- Residential segregation
- Neighborhood safety and violence
- Environmental justice (location and exposure to health risks)

Social Class (SOC)
- Aspects of social stratification
  - Social class and socioeconomic status
  - Class consciousness and false consciousness
  - Cultural capital and social capital
  - Social reproduction
  - Power, privilege, and prestige
  - Intersectionality (e.g., race, gender, age)
  - Socioeconomic gradient in health
  - Global inequalities
- Patterns of social mobility
  - Intergenerational and intragenerational mobility
  - Vertical and horizontal mobility
  - Meritocracy
- Poverty
  - Relative and absolute poverty
  - Social exclusion (segregation and isolation)

Health Disparities (SOC) (e.g., class, gender, and race inequalities in health)

Health Care Disparities (SOC) (e.g., class, gender, and race inequalities in health care)

Psychological, Social, and Biological Foundations of Behavior

Passage Set I

Sample Test Questions: Psychological, Social, and Biological Foundations of Behavior

Sample test questions for the Psychological, Social, and Biological Foundations of Behavior section are provided below. The answer key appears below each question, along with the foundational concept, the content category, and the skill the question is testing. These sample questions will give you an idea of what to expect from this section of the exam.

Psychological, Social, and Biological Foundations of Behavior

Passage I: Questions 1–6

Homophily—the tendency of social contacts to be similar to one another—can have widespread effects on behavior. A recent study examined how similarity in social networks affects health-related behavior, such as a healthy diet. The investigators recruited participants from an online fitness program and divided them into two groups: 1) a homophilous social network, in which participants were matched with health buddies according to age, gender, and body mass index (BMI), and 2) an unstructured social network, in which participants were matched with health buddies at random. Each participant received a notification that their health buddy had started using an Internet-based diet diary, which could be used to share diet information among buddies. The participants had to decide whether to adopt an Internet-based diet diary themselves. Figure 1 shows the results of this study.

In follow-up experiments, the researchers pursued several questions regarding health-related behaviors and attitudes. First, they considered factors that might increase the likelihood that subjects would adopt the diet diary. Second, they examined how participants view their own BMI and that of other individuals, hypothesizing that the self-serving bias could account for these views. Third, they explored the relationship between cognitive dissonance and health-related behaviors. To answer these questions, the researchers gave the participants a survey that assessed the extent to which the participants view exercise and a good diet as important.

Source: Adapted from D. Centola, "An Experimental Study of Homophily in the Adoption of Health Behavior." Copyright 2011 Science.

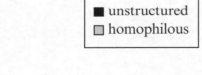

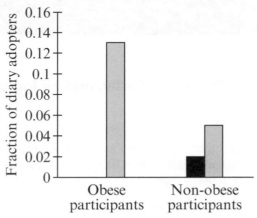

Figure 1 Fraction of obese and non-obese participants who adopted a diary

1. Which conclusion is best supported by the findings in Figure 1?

   A. Non-obese participants experience more cognitive dissonance than obese participants.
   B. Participants experience more cognitive dissonance in homophilous groups.
   C. Non-obese participants conform more than obese participants.
   D. Participants conform more in homophilous groups.

2. How could the researchers use the foot-in-the-door technique to increase the participants' likelihood of adopting a diet diary?

   A. Encourage the participants to sign a petition in support of diet diaries.
   B. Have the participants personally interact with the health buddy who adopted the diet diary.
   C. Tell the participants that the health buddy who adopts the diet diary is a trustworthy health expert.
   D. Tell the participants that by agreeing to be in the study, they have agreed to cooperate with the researchers.

3. Which statement is NOT compatible with the hypothesis that the self-serving bias can account for participants' explanations of their body weights?

   A. Obese participants view their unhealthy weight as a result of having too many fast food restaurants near home.
   B. Non-obese participants view their healthy weight as a result of having strong willpower.
   C. Obese participants view their unhealthy weight as a result of not having time to exercise regularly.
   D. Non-obese participants view their healthy weight as a result of not having any fast food restaurants near their home.

4. All the participants in the study are given information regarding the benefits of a healthy diet. According to the cognitive dissonance theory, which hypothetical finding is most likely?

   A. Obese participants will change their unhealthy eating behaviors.
   B. Non-obese participants will change their unhealthy eating behaviors.
   C. Obese participants will question the validity of the information provided.
   D. Non-obese participants will overemphasize the importance of the information provided.

5. If the study were modified to investigate the effect of homophily on the changes in participants' exercise patterns as well as their likelihood of adopting an Internet-based diary, how would this change the design of the study?

   A. A new independent variable would be added.
   B. A new dependent variable would be added.
   C. Levels of an existing independent variable would increase.
   D. The study would become an experimental study.

6. In helping to explain the results of the study, which other concept would be most similar to a homophilous social network?

   A. Reference group
   B. Secondary group
   C. Out-group
   D. Social group

   Solutions for this passage begin on next page.

1. Which conclusion is best supported by the findings in Figure 1?

    A. Non-obese participants experience more cognitive dissonance than obese participants.

    B. Participants experience more cognitive dissonance in homophilous groups.

    C. Non-obese participants conform more than obese participants.

    D. Participants conform more in homophilous groups.

Foundational Concept: 7

Biological, psychological, and sociocultural factors influence behavior and behavior change.

Content Category: 7B

Social processes that influence human behavior

Scientific Inquiry and Reasoning Skill: 4

Data-based and Statistical Reasoning

Key: D

The question requires identifying the concept that is assessed in the study as conformity and combining this information with the numeric information in Figure 1. The "Fraction of diary adopters" refers to the fraction of participants who adopted a diary after they were told that their buddy had started using one, which is an example of conformity. The figure shows that all participants conform more in homophilous groups (indicated by the gray bars).

Distractors

A   Misidentifies the concept that is being assessed as cognitive dissonance.

B   Misidentifies the concept that is being assessed as cognitive dissonance.

C   Suggests that non-obese participants conform more than obese participants, but this is not correct across all conditions. Figure 1 shows that in the homophilous condition, obese participants conform more than non-obese participants.

TIP: When a passage includes a figure or table that reports study results, such as the bar graph in the above passage, be prepared to respond to a question that requires an understanding of the findings along with a concept that is relevant to the study. The first sample question applies a concept that is assessed in the study (conformity) with the findings that are represented in the figure.

2. How could the researchers use the foot-in-the-door technique to increase the participants' likelihood of adopting a diet diary?

A. Encourage the participants to sign a petition in support of diet diaries.
B. Have the participants personally interact with the health buddy who adopted the diet diary.
C. Tell the participants that the health buddy who adopts the diet diary is a trustworthy health expert.
D. Tell the participants that by agreeing to be in the study, they have agreed to cooperate with the researchers.

Foundational Concept: 7
Biological, psychological, and sociocultural factors influence behavior and behavior change.

Content Category: 7A
Individual influences on behavior

Scientific Inquiry and Reasoning Skill: 1
Knowledge of Scientific Concepts and Principles

Key: A
The foot-in-the-door technique refers to convincing individuals to make a small commitment toward a cause, because this small commitment increases the likelihood of a larger commitment toward the same cause in the future. Option A is an example of this. If the participants make a small commitment toward diet diaries (signing a petition), according to the foot-in-the-door technique, they will be more likely to adopt a diet diary in the future.

Distractors

B   This is incorrect. It describes a situation that can plausibly increase the likelihood of adopting a diet diary but is not an example for the foot-in-the-door technique.

C   This is incorrect. It gives an example of how the peripheral route to persuasion can be used to increase the participants' likelihood of adopting a diet diary.

D   This is incorrect. It suggests that compliance can be used to increase the likelihood of adopting a diet diary.

TIP: To answer this question, it is especially important to keep in mind that the distractors can be plausible. All the distractors for this question can possibly increase the participants' likelihood of adopting a diet diary. C describes a method for increasing participants' likelihood of using a diet diary by manipulating the credibility of other individuals who use diet diaries, an effective method that you may be familiar with from your psychology coursework. The question requires distinguishing among the different techniques that can be used to change participants' behavior and picking the technique specified in the question.

3. Which statement is NOT compatible with the hypothesis that the self-serving bias can account for participants' explanations of their body weights?

A. Obese participants view their unhealthy weight as a result of having too many fast food restaurants near home.

B. Non-obese participants view their healthy weight as a result of having strong willpower.

C. Obese participants view their unhealthy weight as a result of not having time to exercise regularly.

D. Non-obese participants view their healthy weight as a result of not having any fast food restaurants near their home.

Foundational Concept: 8
Psychological, sociocultural, and biological factors influence the way we think about ourselves and others as well as how we interact with others.

Content Category: 8B
Social thinking

Scientific Inquiry and Reasoning Skill: 2
Scientific Reasoning and Problem Solving

Key: D
Self-serving bias suggests that when explaining their own behavior, individuals attribute positive behaviors to internal, stable sources, but attribute negative behaviors to external sources. A non-obese individual would attribute his or her healthy weight to an internal, stable source, such as strong willpower. However, a non-obese individual would not attribute his or her healthy weight to an external source, such as not having any fast food restaurants near home. Therefore, D is incompatible with the self-serving bias.

Distractors

A   This is compatible with the self-serving bias. An obese individual is likely to attribute his or her obesity to an external source (availability of fast food).

B   This is compatible with the self-serving bias. A non-obese individual is likely to attribute his or her obesity to an internal source (strong willpower).

C   This is compatible with the self-serving bias. An obese individual is likely to attribute his or her obesity to an external source (not having time to exercise).

 TIP: Be especially careful when responding to NOT questions. In this instance, finding the right answer requires selecting the option that is NOT compatible with the self-serving bias.

4. All the participants in the study are given information regarding the benefits of a healthy diet. According to the cognitive dissonance theory, which hypothetical finding is most likely?

A. Obese participants will change their unhealthy eating behaviors.
B. Non-obese participants will change their unhealthy eating behaviors.
C. Obese participants will question the validity of the information provided.
D. Non-obese participants will overemphasize the importance of the information provided.

Foundational Concept: 7
Biological, psychological, and sociocultural factors influence behavior and behavior change.

Content Category: 7A
Individual influences on behavior

Scientific Inquiry and Reasoning Skill: 2
Scientific Reasoning and Problem Solving

Key: C
C is correct. According to the cognitive dissonance theory, when an individual's attitudes are incongruent with his or her behavior, this leads to cognitive dissonance. To eliminate cognitive dissonance, the individual can either change his or her attitudes or his or her behavior. The theory posits that individuals are more likely to adjust their attitudes to align with their behavior than the other way around. Therefore, obese participants are likely to question the importance of the information provided.

Distractors

A This is incorrect because it is not the most likely outcome. It suggests that obese participants will change their behavior to align with their attitudes when there is a discrepancy between their attitudes and behaviors.

B This is incorrect because non-obese participants are less likely than obese participants to experience cognitive dissonance and change their behavior due to cognitive dissonance.

D This is incorrect because non-obese participants are less likely than obese participants to experience cognitive dissonance and change their attitudes due to cognitive dissonance.

 TIP: Most and least likely questions require extra attention because they require ranking the likelihood of multiple options that are potentially correct. Answering this particular question requires making two important judgments: 1) That obese individuals are more likely to experience cognitive dissonance if presented information regarding the importance of a healthy diet, as they are more likely to have unhealthy eating habits, and 2) that people who experience dissonance are more likely to change their attitudes than their behaviors.

5. If the study were modified to investigate the effect of homophily on the changes in participants' exercise patterns as well as their likelihood of adopting an Internet-based diary, how would this change the design of the study?

    A. A new independent variable would be added.
    B. A new dependent variable would be added.
    C. Levels of an existing independent variable would increase.
    D. The study would become an experimental study.

Foundational Concept: 7
Biological, psychological, and sociocultural factors influence behavior and behavior change.

Content Category: 7B
Social processes that influence human behavior

Scientific Inquiry and Reasoning Skill: 3
Reasoning About the Design and Execution of Research

Key: B
B is correct. "Changes in exercise patterns" corresponds to a new dependent variable because the researchers are interested in the effect of homophily (independent variable) on exercise, along with adopting an Internet-based diary.

Distractors
A   This is incorrect because "changes in exercise patterns" is not an example of adding another independent variable because the researchers are not interested in the effect of changes in exercise patterns on another variable.

C   This is incorrect because measuring changes in exercise patterns introduces a new variable to the study rather than changing the levels of an existing variable.

D   This is incorrect because adding a new variable does not render a study experimental.

TIP: Scientific Inquiry and Reasoning Skill 3 questions may be based upon understanding basic terms and distinctions associated with research methods. This question requires knowing how to distinguish independent and dependent variables. Other fundamental distinctions that are helpful include knowing the difference between reliability and validity and knowing the relationship between a sample and a population. Refer to the Skill 3 narrative description for other important information about methods.

Fifth Edition
The Official Guide to the MCAT® Exam
274
MCAT® is a program of the
Association of American Medical Colleges

6. In helping to explain the results of the study, which other concept would be most similar to a homophilous social network?

    A. Reference group
    B. Secondary group
    C. Out-group
    D. Social group

Foundational Concept: 8
Psychological, sociocultural, and biological factors influence the way we think about ourselves and others as well as how we interact with others.

Content Category: 8C
Social interactions

Scientific Inquiry and Reasoning Skill: 1
Knowledge of Scientific Concepts and Principles

Key: A
A is correct. A reference group is defined as "any group that individuals use as a standard for evaluating themselves and their own behavior," and is similar to the mechanism behind the effect of the "homophilous" group in the study.

Distractors

B   This is incorrect because secondary group refers to a formal, impersonal group.

C   This is incorrect because an out-group is defined as a group that people do not feel connected to.

D   This is incorrect because a social group, which is a general term that refers to a collection of people with common identity and regular interaction, is not as specific as a reference group.

TIP: Remember to read the question carefully. The use of "most similar" in this question means that the correct answer will be the closest concept to a homophilous network among the options. Although a homophilous network could be a social group in some settings, a reference group is the term that is most conceptually similar based on the results of the study.

Psychological, Social, and Biological Foundations of Behavior

Passage Set II

MCAT® is a program of the
Association of American Medical Colleges

Psychological, Social, and Biological Foundations of Behavior

Passage II: Questions 7–10

Low birth weight is a risk factor associated with less favorable health and developmental outcomes later in childhood and adolescence. In the United States, low birth weight is disproportionately prevalent among racial and ethnic minority groups and has been linked to specific environmental and social characteristics of neighborhoods.

Using data from approximately 100,000 live births in Chicago, a study found low birth weight to be related to the presence of environmental stressors, such as high violent crime rates, and to a scarcity of social resources, such as limited reciprocal exchange among neighbors. In addition to these neighborhood characteristics, the investigators discovered a spatial distribution to birth weight, observing that mean birth weight in a given neighborhood was systematically related to mean birth weight in adjacent neighborhoods.

Another study used data from a national sample of approximately 1.2 million live births in the United States to investigate the relationship between residential segregation and birth weight for various racial and ethnic groups. The researchers found that increased racial/ethnic segregation reduced the chances of low birth weight among Asian American mothers, but marginally increased low birth weight among African American mothers. Moreover, low birth weight among Asian American mothers was less frequent if mothers resided in metropolitan areas in which Asian American enclaves tended to be clustered. No evidence of a similar clustering effect was found for African American or Hispanic/Latina mothers. Table 1 displays the percentage of low-birth-weight infants by race/ethnicity of the mother in segregated neighborhoods.

Table 1 Percentage of Low-Weight Births in Segregated Neighborhoods by Race/Ethnicity

Maternal Race/Ethnicity	Percentage of Low-Weight Births
Hispanic/Latina	5.29%
Asian American	6.10%
African American	11.05%

Sources: Adapted from J. Morenoff, "Neighborhood Mechanisms and the Spatial Dynamics of Birth Weight."
Copyright 2003 University of Chicago Press. E. Walton, "Residential Segregation and Birth Weight among Racial
and Ethnic Minorities in the United States." Copyright 2009 American Sociological Association.

7. A study finds that low birth weight is associated with delayed cognitive development in childhood. Based on this result and the studies in the passage, children born to women living in which neighborhoods are likely to be at greater risk of falling behind in elementary school?

A. Asian American enclaves
B. Neighborhoods next to Asian American enclaves
C. Neighborhoods with extensive reciprocal exchange
D. Neighborhoods with high rates of violent crime

8. Which concept is most relevant for explaining the relationship between social resources and birth-weight outcomes that was found in the first study in the passage?

A. Poverty
B. Heredity
C. Social networks
D. Socialization

9. A researcher wants to determine whether the findings from the first study are also influenced by psychological responses to stress. To test this idea, a random sample of mothers from the first study is later given a stress assessment. What is the flaw in this research design?

A. The dependent variable is temporally prior to measurement of the independent variable.
B. The independent variable is temporally prior to measurement of the dependent variable.
C. The updated sample contains too little variation to draw reliable conclusions.
D. The updated sample is not representative of the population of mothers.

10. Which independent variable is most relevant for a study that investigates the possible impact of primary groups on the outcome measure discussed in the passage?

A. Family structure
B. Religious affiliation
C. Occupational status
D. Population density

Solutions for this passage begin on next page.

7. A study finds that low birth weight is associated with delayed cognitive development in childhood. Based on this result and the studies in the passage, children born to women living in which neighborhoods are likely to be at greater risk of falling behind in elementary school?

  A.   Asian American enclaves
  B.   Neighborhoods next to Asian American enclaves
  C.   Neighborhoods with extensive reciprocal exchange
  D.   Neighborhoods with high rates of violent crime

Foundational Concept: 10
Social stratification affects access to resources and well-being.

Content Category: 10A
Social inequality

Scientific Inquiry and Reasoning Skill: 2
Scientific Reasoning and Problem Solving

Key: D
In this question, information from both studies in the passage is used to set up a scenario involving an additional psychological factor. Identifying the correct answer relies on knowledge that scholastic achievement can be affected by cognitive development. D is correct because environmental stressors (such as high violent crime rates) are associated with an increased risk of low-weight births.

Distractors

A   This is incorrect because the second study in the passage suggests that low birth weight is less frequent in metropolitan areas with clusters of Asian American enclaves.

B   This is incorrect because proximity to an Asian American enclave, although seemingly related to the second study in the passage, is not a factor that is specifically identified in the study.

C   This is incorrect because limited reciprocal exchange is identified as a factor associated with low birth weight. Extensive reciprocal exchange, on the other hand, is more likely to be a protective factor.

TIP: Passages will often include more than one study from an area of research. Some questions will only be relevant to a particular study from the passage. However, other questions will require consideration of both studies together. This could include responding to questions that ask you to identify a contrast in the way a concept is used across the studies, to propose a hypothesis that is derived from findings of the studies, or to point out an element of research design that differs between the studies. When reading a passage with more than one study, it can help to start thinking about the similarities and differences in how the studies are described.

8. Which concept is most relevant for explaining the relationship between social resources and birth-weight outcomes that was found in the first study in the passage?

A. Poverty
B. Heredity
C. Social networks
D. Socialization

Foundational Concept: 8
Psychological, sociocultural, and biological factors influence the way we think about ourselves and others as well as how we interact with others.

Content Category: 8C
Social interactions

Scientific Inquiry and Reasoning Skill: 1
Knowledge of Scientific Concepts and Principles

Key: C
Option C is correct because reciprocal exchange, as it is described as a social resource with the first study in the passage, is best identified as a social network process.

Distractors

A   This is incorrect because the description of the study in the passage specifically mentions a lack of social resources but does not refer to a lack of material resources. It is possible that poverty is a contributing factor, but it was not specifically identified in the passage.

B   This is incorrect because, although a genetic component is possible with low birth weight, the passage is specifically about social and environmental associations.

D   This is incorrect because socialization refers to the lifelong process by which norms and values are learned, and thus does not specifically address a social resource (such as reciprocal exchange).

TIP: Questions that test Scientific Inquiry and Reasoning Skill 1 may ask about the relationship between concepts. This question requires consideration of which concept among the options (all of which are covered by the Psychological, Social, and Biological Foundations of Behavior content list) is most relevant to information presented in the context of a study from the passage (about social resources and reciprocal exchange).

9. A researcher wants to determine whether the findings from the first study are also influenced by psychological responses to stress. To test this idea, a random sample of mothers from the first study is later given a stress assessment. What is the flaw in this research design?

    A. The dependent variable is temporally prior to measurement of the independent variable.
    B. The independent variable is temporally prior to measurement of the dependent variable.
    C. The updated sample contains too little variation to draw reliable conclusions.
    D. The updated sample is not representative of the population of mothers.

Foundational Concept: 6
Biological, psychological, and sociocultural factors influence the ways that individuals perceive, think about, and react to the world.

Content Category: 6C
Responding to the world

Scientific Inquiry and Reasoning Skill: 3
Reasoning About the Design and Execution of Research

Key: A
Hypothesized factors must be temporally prior to their assumed effects. Option A is correct because the hypothesized factor (mediating factor of psychological response to stress) was assessed after the outcome of interest (birth weight).

Distractors

B   This is incorrect because it identifies the correct time order of variables, so would not present a flaw.

C   This is incorrect because the sample was randomly constructed so is not likely to present a flaw. In addition, the implied references to variability and reliability in the option are used imprecisely.

D   This is incorrect because, as with option C, the sample is not the primary flaw in the design. Instead, the use of a random sample is likely to help ensure the representativeness of the sample.

10. Which independent variable is most relevant for a study that investigates the possible impact of primary groups on the outcome measure discussed in the passage?

    A. Family structure
    B. Religious affiliation
    C. Occupational status
    D. Population density

Foundational Concept: 8

Psychological, sociocultural, and biological factors influence the way we think about ourselves and others as well as how we interact with others.

Content Category: 8C

Social interactions

Scientific Inquiry and Reasoning Skill: 1

Knowledge of Scientific Concepts and Principles

Key: A

Primary groups include the family. Thus, a variable measuring family structure would be most relevant to assessing the impact of primary groups.

Distractors

B   This is incorrect because religious affiliation can encompass both primary groups and secondary groups.

C   This is incorrect because occupational status does not clearly address the distinction between primary and secondary groups. Instead, occupational status is more relevant for social status or social roles.

D   This is incorrect because the group distinctions, such as the difference between primary and secondary groups, are conceptually distinct from demographic concepts like population density.

TIP: When a question asks about a specific term, think about any other terms that are related. Knowing the main distinction between closely related terms can help to arrive at the correct answer. This question asks about primary groups, which are usually understood in contrast to secondary groups. Remember that primary groups are typically close and long-lasting, whereas secondary groups are considered impersonal and temporary. With this contrast in mind, the correct answer is more apparent.

Psychological, Social, and Biological Foundations of Behavior

Passage Set III

MCAT® is a program of the
Association of American Medical Colleges

Psychological, Social, and Biological Foundations of Behavior

Passage III: Questions 11–15

When rats are placed in a cage with a running wheel and their food intake is restricted to one hour per day, they begin to exercise excessively and reduce their eating significantly. Under these circumstances, they die of starvation within ten days. This phenomenon is called activity-based anorexia (ABA). Control rats that are on the same restricted food schedule without access to a running wheel adjust their eating and typically gain weight.

ABA is often studied as an animal model of exercise addiction. Exercise stimulates the release of endorphins. The increase in endorphins is hypothesized to play a role in exercise addiction. In Study 1, a group of rats were trained to press a lever for the self-administration of heroin. Afterwards, half of the rats were ABA-induced. The researchers found that ABA-induced rats reduced their heroin intake. In Study 2, rats were placed either in cages with running wheels or cages without running wheels. Half of each group had 1-hour access to food per day and the other half had 24-hour access to food. After seven days, these rats were injected with naloxone, a chemical that binds to the endorphin receptors and blocks their functioning. The rats were then monitored for responses typically associated with opiate withdrawal in laboratory animals. Figure 1 presents the results of Study 2.

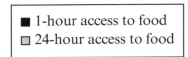

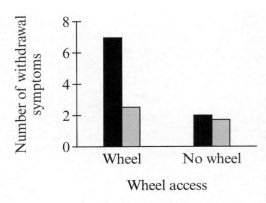

Figure 1 Withdrawal symptoms as a function of wheel and food access

Source: Adapted from R.B. Kanarek, K.E. D'Anci, N. Jurdak, and W.F. Mathes, "Running and Addiction: Precipitated withdrawal in a Rat Model of Activity-based Anorexia." Copyright 2009 Behavioral Neuroscience.

11. A hot water tail-flick test measures the time it takes rats to remove their tail when it is dipped in hot water. Rats housed with a running wheel exhibit a delayed response in the test. Based on this response, which type of sensory receptors are most likely negatively regulated by exercise?

   A. Baroreceptors
   B. Nociceptors
   C. Mechanoreceptors
   D. Chemoreceptors

12. According to the hypothesis presented in the passage, which drug is most likely to cause a decline in the wheel-running behavior of ABA-induced rats?

   A. Alcohol
   B. Cocaine
   C. Marijuana
   D. Morphine

13. Based on the passage, ABA-induced rats are most likely to demonstrate:

   A. increased sensitivity to the effects after running in their wheels.
   B. increased sensitivity to pain over time.
   C. withdrawal symptoms if they are prevented from running in their wheels.
   D. withdrawal symptoms if they are injected with opiates.

14. Which statement provides the most likely explanation for the results in Figure 1?

   A. ABA-induced rats show a decrease in withdrawal symptoms because an opioid agonist mimicked the effects of wheel-running.
   B. Rats with 24-hour access to food show a decrease in withdrawal symptoms because an opioid agonist increased the reinforcement value of food.
   C. ABA-induced rats show an increase in withdrawal symptoms because an opioid antagonist interfered with the effects of wheel-running.
   D. Non-ABA-induced rats show an increase in withdrawal symptoms because an opioid antagonist enhanced the effects of wheel-running.

15. What type of learning is taking place in Study 1?

   A. Operant conditioning
   B. Classical conditioning
   C. Social learning
   D. Observational learning

Solutions for this passage begin on next page.

11. A hot water tail-flick test measures the time it takes rats to remove their tail when it is dipped in hot water. Rats housed with a running wheel exhibit a delayed response in the test. Based on this response, which type of sensory receptors are most likely negatively regulated by exercise?

  A. Baroreceptors
  B. Nociceptors
  C. Mechanoreceptors
  D. Chemoreceptors

Foundational Concept: 6
Biological, psychological, and sociocultural factors influence the ways that individuals perceive, think about, and react to the world.

Content Category: 6A
Sensing the environment

Scientific Inquiry and Reasoning Skill: 2
Scientific Reasoning and Problem Solving

Key: B
Exposure to hot water activates pain receptors (nociceptors); a delayed response indicates that nociceptors are negatively regulated.

Distractors
A   There is no indication that pressure was measured.

C   There is no indication that touch was measured.

D   There is no indication that chemical changes were measured.

12. According to the hypothesis presented in the passage, which drug is most likely to cause a decline in the wheel-running behavior of ABA-induced rats?

    A. Alcohol
    B. Cocaine
    C. Marijuana
    D. Morphine

Foundational Concept: 6
Biological, psychological, and sociocultural factors influence the ways that individuals perceive, think about, and react to the world.

Content Category: 6B
Making sense of the environment

Scientific Inquiry and Reasoning Skill: 2
Scientific Reasoning and Problem Solving

Key: D
D is correct. The hypothesis suggests that exercise addiction results from the fact that exercise increases endorphin levels. If this neurotransmitter is stimulated by a drug, then ABA-induced rats would be less likely to run in their wheels (because their endorphin levels would be elevated by an alternative method). The only drug in the list that is an endorphin agonist is D, morphine.

Distractors

A   This is incorrect because alcohol is not directly associated with increases in endorphin levels.

B   This is incorrect because cocaine is not directly associated with increases in endorphin levels.

C   This is incorrect because marijuana is not directly associated with increases in endorphin levels.

13. Based on the passage, ABA-induced rats are most likely to demonstrate:

    A. increased sensitivity to the effects after running in their wheels.
    B. increased sensitivity to pain over time.
    C. withdrawal symptoms if they are prevented from running in their wheels.
    D. withdrawal symptoms if they are injected with opiates.

Foundational Concept: 6
Biological, psychological, and sociocultural factors influence the ways that individuals perceive, think about, and react to the world.

Content Category: 6B
Making sense of the environment

Scientific Inquiry and Reasoning Skill: 2
Scientific Reasoning and Problem Solving

Key: C
C is correct. Rats that have developed exercise addiction should experience withdrawal symptoms if they are hindered from running in their wheels. The running behavior leads to an increase in endorphins which, according to the passage, leads to exercise addiction. Preventing the running behavior is likely to lead to withdrawal, as it would interfere with the increase in endorphins that the ABA-induced rats are addicted to.

Distractors
A   This is incorrect because after running in their wheels, the ABA-induced rats likely have high levels of endorphins and will not be especially sensitive to the effects of endorphin agonists.

B   This is incorrect. ABA-induced rats are not likely to become more sensitive to pain over time, especially because the running behavior results in an increase in endorphins, which are natural painkillers.

D   This is incorrect because opiates are endorphin agonists and will not lead to withdrawal symptoms for the ABA-induced rats.

TIP: Some questions require reasoning about multiple introductory psychology concepts and considering how they relate to each other in the context provided by the passage. Answering this question requires combining the information from the passage (regarding the exercise addiction of the ABA-induced rats and the role of endorphins in this process) with introductory psychology knowledge on the effects of opiates on endorphins. It also requires reasoning about how another introductory psychology concept, withdrawal, fits in with this interaction.

Fifth Edition
The Official Guide to the MCAT® Exam
290
MCAT® is a program of the
Association of American Medical Colleges

14. Which statement provides the most likely explanation for the results in Figure 1?

    A. ABA-induced rats show a decrease in withdrawal symptoms because an opioid agonist mimicked the effects of wheel-running.

    B. Rats with 24-hour access to food show a decrease in withdrawal symptoms because an opioid agonist increased the reinforcement value of food.

    C. ABA-induced rats show an increase in withdrawal symptoms because an opioid antagonist interfered with the effects of wheel-running.

    D. Non-ABA-induced rats show an increase in withdrawal symptoms because an opioid antagonist enhanced the effects of wheel-running.

Foundational Concept:
Biological, psychological, and sociocultural factors influence the ways that individuals perceive, think about, and react to the world.

Content Category: 6B
Making sense of the environment

Scientific Inquiry Reasoning Skill: 4

Key: A
C is correct. ABA-induced rats (the rats with restricted access to food and access to a running wheel) show increased withdrawal symptoms because naloxone, an opioid antagonist, likely interferes with the physiological effects of wheel-running.

Distractors

A   ABA-induced rats (the rats with restricted access to food and access to a running wheel) do not show a decrease in withdrawal symptoms.

B   The drug used in the study, naloxone, is an opioid antagonist.

D   Non-ABA-induced rats do not show an increase in withdrawal symptoms.

15. What type of learning is taking place in Study 1?

A. Operant conditioning
B. Classical conditioning
C. Social learning
D. Observational learning

Foundational Concept: 7
Biological, psychological, and sociocultural factors influence behavior and behavior change.

Content Category: 7C
Attitude and behavior change

Scientific Inquiry and Reasoning Skill: 1
Knowledge of Scientific Concepts and Principles

Key: A
A is correct. In Study 1, the frequency of pressing the lever increases because it results in the delivery of heroin, which is an example of operant conditioning through positive reinforcement.

Distractors
B This is incorrect because classical conditioning does not involve a change in behavior due to the behavior's outcome.

C This is incorrect because social learning refers to learning through observing a model.

D This is incorrect because observational learning, like social learning, refers to learning through a model.

Psychological, Social, and Biological Foundations of Behavior

Passage Set IV

MCAT® is a program of the
Association of American Medical Colleges

Psychological, Social, and Biological Foundations of Behavior

Passage IV: Questions 16–20

Black men are less likely than White men and Black women to attend healthcare appointments. In a number of studies, this has been linked to mistrust toward healthcare professionals. A study examined several factors that might account for the medical mistrust that Black men experience. Black male participants were recruited through advertisements placed in Michigan and Georgia. The researchers collected information on several variables that might predict participants' level of medical mistrust. Because help-seeking behavior might be perceived as incompatible with the traditional male gender identity, researchers surveyed the participants on their endorsement of male gender roles. Participants also completed questionnaires assessing neuroticism, experiences with racism, the nature of recent healthcare experiences, and the degree of medical mistrust they experienced. The researchers found that recent experiences with racism in any setting, as well as a strong male identity, increased the likelihood of medical mistrust. Furthermore, recent unpleasant healthcare experiences reduced the frequency of participants' seeking healthcare in the future.

These results suggest that if medical mistrust is to be reduced, it is necessary for healthcare professionals to pay close attention to their interactions with Black men. Related studies showed that when interacting with Black patients, doctors are less likely to assume a patient-centered communication style, which involves focusing on the patients' needs, concerns, and satisfaction. Based on these findings, a follow-up experiment was designed to investigate whether the doctor's communication style caused a difference in the patients' levels of mistrust.

Source: Adapted from W.P. Hammond, "Psychosocial correlates of Medical Mistrust Among Black Men." Copyright 2010 American Journal of Community Psychology.

16. According to the passage, one of the reasons Black men have medical mistrust is because seeking help violates their:

    A. gender schema.
    B. gender script.
    C. gender conditioning.
    D. gender adaptation.

17. Which operationalization is most appropriate for the independent variable of the proposed follow-up experiment?

    A. Level of mistrust, established by an inventory that measures participants' medical mistrust
    B. Level of mistrust, established by independent judges who rate participants' medical mistrust
    C. Type of communication, established by training a doctor who is also a confederate to use patient–centered communication or a communication style that is not patient centered
    D. Type of communication, established by giving doctors in the study an inventory that assesses whether their communication style is patient-centered or not

18. The tendency of doctors to use a physician-centered communication style more often with Black patients is an example of:

    A. prejudice.
    B. stereotyping.
    C. discrimination.
    D. ethnocentrism.

19. Based on the passage, unpleasant healthcare experiences act as:

    A. positive reinforcement.
    B. negative reinforcement.
    C. positive punishment.
    D. negative punishment.

20. Another researcher reviews the study described in the passage and suggests that the medical mistrust experienced by Black men can be explained, in part, by the concept of institutional discrimination. Which statement best describes that concept?

    A. Discrimination is not systematic, except when observed within institutions.
    B. If they have a history of unfair treatment, institutions are labeled as discriminatory.
    C. When several individuals exhibit prejudiced attitudes within an institution, then that institution will also be discriminatory.
    D. As opposed to discriminatory acts committed by individuals, there are institutional policies that disadvantage certain groups and favor others.

Solutions for this passage begin on next page.

16. According to the passage, one of the reasons Black men have medical mistrust is because seeking help violates their:

    A. gender schema.
    B. gender script.
    C. gender conditioning.
    D. gender adaptation.

Foundational Concept: 8
Psychological, sociocultural, and biological factors influence the way we think about ourselves and others as well as how we interact with others.

Content Category: 8A
Self-identity

Scientific Inquiry and Reasoning Skill: 1
Knowledge of Scientific Concepts and Principles

Key: A
A is correct. According to the passage, seeking help is viewed as incompatible with the male identity. The cognitions regarding what constitutes the male identity are an example of schemas.

Distractors

B   This is incorrect because a script is organized information regarding the order of actions that are appropriate to a familiar situation.

C   This is incorrect because gender conditioning is a term that does not refer to an actual concept.

D   This is incorrect because gender adaptation is a term that does not refer to an actual concept.

Fifth Edition
The Official Guide to the MCAT® Exam
296
MCAT® is a program of the
Association of American Medical Colleges

17. Which operationalization is most appropriate for the independent variable of the proposed follow-up experiment?

   A. Level of mistrust, established by an inventory that measures participants' medical mistrust

   B. Level of mistrust, established by independent judges who rate participants' medical mistrust

   C. Type of communication, established by training a doctor who is also a confederate to use patient-centered communication or a communication style that is not patient-centered

   D. Type of communication, established by giving doctors in the study an inventory that assesses whether their communication style is patient-centered or not

Foundational Concept: 8
Psychological, sociocultural, and biological factors influence the way we think about ourselves and others as well as how we interact with others.

Content Category: 8C
Social interactions

Scientific Inquiry and Reasoning Skill: 3
Reasoning About the Design and Execution of Research

Key: C
C is correct. The researchers are interested in the effect of type of communication on level of mistrust; therefore, type of communication is the independent variable. To establish a causal relationship between the two variables, the independent variable needs to be manipulated, as described in C, by training the doctor to adopt different communication styles.

Distractors

A   This is incorrect because level of mistrust is the dependent variable.

B   This is incorrect because level of mistrust is the dependent variable.

D   This is incorrect because the operational definition provided does not involve manipulating the independent variable.

TIP: Answering this question involves making two judgments. The first is establishing which variable (type of communication or level of mistrust) is the independent variable. The second is selecting the appropriate operational definition for this independent variable. Both C and D offer operational definitions for type of communication that are plausible; however, only C offers an operational definition that involves the researchers manipulating type of communication directly. Direct manipulation of the independent variable is a necessary condition for an experiment.

18. The tendency of doctors to use a physician-centered communication style more often with Black patients is an example of:

    A. prejudice.
    B. stereotyping.
    C. discrimination.
    D. ethnocentrism.

Foundational Concept: 8
Psychological, sociocultural, and biological factors influence the way we think about ourselves and others as well as how we interact with others.

Content Category: 8C
Social interactions

Scientific Inquiry and Reasoning Skill: 1
Knowledge of Scientific Concepts and Principles

Key: C
C is correct. The communication style assumed by the doctors is an example of discrimination because it suggests that the doctors are behaving differently based on the patients' racial background.

Distractors

A   This is incorrect because prejudice describes attitudes, not behaviors.

B   This is incorrect because stereotypes refer to cognitions regarding social groups, not behaviors toward social groups.

D   This is incorrect because ethnocentrism refers to the assumption that one's own culture is superior to other cultures.

19. Based on the passage, unpleasant healthcare experiences act as:

A. positive reinforcement.
B. negative reinforcement.
C. positive punishment.
D. negative punishment.

Foundational Concept: 7
Biological, psychological, and sociocultural factors influence behavior and behavior change.

Content Category: 7C
Attitude and behavior change

Scientific Inquiry and Reasoning Skill: 1
Knowledge of Scientific Concepts and Principles

Key: C
C is correct. According to the passage, negative healthcare experiences reduce the frequency of seeking health care. This suggests that negative healthcare experiences punish seeking health care. It is positive punishment as opposed to negative, because it involves introducing an unpleasant experience rather than removing a pleasant stimulus.

Distractors

A   This is incorrect because positively reinforced behaviors increase in frequency.

B   This is incorrect because negatively reinforced behaviors increase in frequency.

D   This is incorrect because the punisher described in the passage involves introducing an unpleasant experience rather than removing a pleasant stimulus (which is involved in negative punishment).

TIP: Telling apart positive and negative reinforcement, as well as positive and negative punishment, can be tricky. When deciding whether an outcome acts as reinforcement or punishment, an important factor is what happens to the response. Reinforced responses increase in frequency and punished responses decrease in frequency. When telling apart whether a reinforcer (or a punisher) is positive or negative, consider whether the reinforcer (or the punisher) involves introducing a stimulus or taking away a stimulus. A positive reinforcer involves introducing a desirable/appetitive stimulus (for example, response results in the delivery of food). A negative reinforcer involves removing an undesirable/aversive stimulus (for example, response results in the termination of an electric shock). A positive punisher involves introducing an undesirable/aversive stimulus (for example, response results in the delivery of an electric shock). A negative punisher involves removing a desirable/appetitive stimulus (for example, response results in the termination of access to food).

20. Another researcher reviews the study described in the passage and suggests that the medical mistrust experienced by Black men can be explained, in part, by the concept of institutional discrimination. Which statement best describes that concept?

    A. Discrimination is not systematic, except when observed within institutions.

    B. If they have a history of unfair treatment, institutions are labeled as discriminatory.

    C. When several individuals exhibit prejudiced attitudes within an institution, then that institution will also be discriminatory.

    D. As opposed to discriminatory acts committed by individuals, there are institutional policies that disadvantage certain groups and favor others.

Foundational Concept: 8

Psychological, sociocultural, and biological factors influence the way we think about ourselves and others as well as how we interact with others.

Content Category: 8C

Social interactions

Scientific Inquiry and Reasoning Skill: 1

Knowledge of Scientific Concepts and Principles

Key: D

D is correct. Medical mistrust could be considered part of a general mistrust in institutions (for example, medicine, government, economy) that some social groups experience. Of the options, D is the best description of institutional discrimination, since it identifies the contrast with individual discrimination.

Distractors

A   This is incorrect because discrimination is not considered random, and so the contrast is not accurate.

B   This is incorrect because a history of unfair treatment is imprecise as a description of institutional discrimination. The option does not address the distinction with individual discrimination.

C   This is incorrect because institutional discrimination is not an additive process. This option also misses the distinction between prejudice (attitude) and discrimination (behavior).

 TIP: When a question includes the use of "best" (such as with "best describes" in the above question), pay close attention to the distinctions between options. Some options may include plausible elements (such as option B), but do not provide the best description of the concept. In this question, the correct answer identifies the main contrast that is associated with the concept of institutional discrimination.

Psychological, Social, and Biological Foundations of Behavior

Passage Set V

Psychological, Social, and Biological Foundations of Behavior

Passage V: Questions 21–24

People who experience head trauma undergo a period of adjustment, which includes cognitive, social, and personality changes. The most frequent complaints after a head injury are memory deficits and headaches. Types of head injuries vary widely, but the two most common sites of injury are the frontal and temporal lobes. Frontal lobe syndrome usually involves the inability to plan and reason and can result in loss of insight. In temporal lobe syndrome, the most common symptoms are irritability and hostility. Soon after a head injury, general overall intelligence stabilizes. Regaining memory is typically slower. Sometimes, people do not regain their memories of events that happened just prior to a head injury.

A research scientist developed a new drug that may help reduce memory loss for events that occurred during childhood and for events that occurred immediately before a head injury. The researcher gave the drug to two subjects, Person A and Person B, who experienced brain injuries in car accidents. Person A was initially in a coma and sustained damage to the brain stem region. Person B sustained trauma to the frontal lobes and prefrontal cortex. They were given the drug twice per day for 20 days. Both subjects were administered memory tests for events that occurred during childhood and immediately before the head injury. Memory tests were administered before and after taking the drug. Figure 1 summarizes the results of this study.

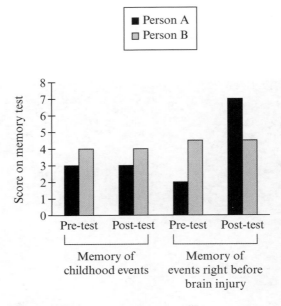

Figure 1 Memory scores before and after taking an experimental drug for recall of different events.

Source: Adapted from Fundamentals of Human Neuropsychology. Copyright 2009 Worth Publishers.

21. After taking the experimental drug, Person A showed an improvement in:

    A. anterograde memory.
    B. retrograde memory.
    C. semantic memory.
    D. short-term memory.

22. At the time of the car accidents, which component of the nervous system of both Person A and Person B was NOT likely to be activated?

    A. sympathetic nervous system.
    B. parasympathetic nervous system.
    C. peripheral nervous system.
    D. central nervous system.

23. While Person A was in a coma, researchers considered stimulating her brain to bring her out of the comatose state. The researchers would most likely have stimulated the:

    A. Wernicke's area.
    B. parietal lobes.
    C. reticular activating system.
    D. somatosensory cortex.

24. Which conclusion is supported by Figure 1?

    A. Person A showed improvement in both types of memory at post-test.
    B. Person B showed improvement in memory for childhood events at post-test.
    C. Both Person A and Person B showed improvement in both types of memory at post-test.
    D. Person A showed improvement in memory for events right before the brain injury at post-test.

Solutions for this passage begin on next page.

21. After taking the experimental drug, Person A showed an improvement in:

    A. anterograde memory.
    B. retrograde memory.
    C. semantic memory.
    D. short-term memory.

Foundational Concept: 6
Biological, psychological, and sociocultural factors influence the ways that individuals perceive, think about, and react to the world.

Content Category: 6B
Making sense of the environment

Scientific Inquiry and Reasoning Skill: 4
Data-based and Statistical Reasoning

Key: B
B is correct. Retrograde memory refers to the ability to remember the information before brain injury. Figure 1 shows that Person A showed a considerable increase in memory for events right before brain injury during the post-test.

Distractors

A   This is incorrect because anterograde memory refers to the ability to form long-term memories after brain injury.

C   This is incorrect because semantic memory (for example, knowledge of facts) was not tested.

D   This is incorrect because short-term memory was not tested.

TIP: This question is an example of one that tests both reading a graph and translating the variables on the graph to psychological terms. To arrive at the correct answer, first, the condition that improved after the administration of the drug needs to be identified (Person A's memory for events right before brain injury). Second, the psychological term that matches this condition needs to be identified (retrograde memory).

Fifth Edition
The Official Guide to the MCAT® Exam
304
MCAT® is a program of the
Association of American Medical Colleges

22. At the time of the car accidents, which component of the nervous system of both Person A and Person B was NOT likely to be activated?

    A. sympathetic nervous system.
    B. parasympathetic nervous system.
    C. peripheral nervous system.
    D. central nervous system.

Foundational Concept: 7
Biological, psychological, and sociocultural factors influence behavior and behavior change.

Content Category: 7A
Individual influences on behavior

Scientific Inquiry and Reasoning Skill: 1
Knowledge of Scientific Concepts and Principles

Key: B
B is correct. The parasympathetic nervous system is an energy conserving (rest-and-digest) system and is not likely to be activated at the time of a stressful event.

Distractors

A   This is incorrect because the sympathetic system activation is involved in the stress response and is likely to be activated at the time of a stressful event.

C   This is incorrect because the sympathetic nervous system is a part of the peripheral nervous system, and therefore, the peripheral nervous system will be activated at the time of a stressful event.

D   This is incorrect because the reticular activating system (part of the central nervous system) will be activated at the time of a stressful event.

23. While Person A was in a coma, researchers considered stimulating her brain to bring her out of the comatose state. The researchers would most likely have stimulated the:

   A. Wernicke's area.
   B. parietal lobes.
   C. reticular activating system.
   D. somatosensory cortex.

Foundational Concept: 7
Biological, psychological, and sociocultural factors influence behavior and behavior change.

Content Category: 7A
Individual influences on behavior

Scientific Inquiry and Reasoning Skill: 1
Knowledge of Scientific Concepts and Principles

Key: C
C is correct. The reticular activating system is involved in controlling alertness and is most likely to be stimulated to bring someone out of a coma.

Distractors

A   This is incorrect, as Wernicke's area is involved mostly in speech processing.

B   This is incorrect, as the parietal lobes do not directly control alertness.

D   This is incorrect, as the somatosensory cortex is involved in receiving the sensory signals from the skin.

TIP: Although most brain regions do not directly correspond to a single function, some brain regions have established associations with specific behavioral functions. Familiarize yourself with these associations (for example, vision—occipital cortex, language—the left hemisphere, or memory—hippocampus).

24. Which conclusion is supported by Figure 1?

    A. Person A showed improvement in both types of memory at post-test.
    B. Person B showed improvement in memory for childhood events at post-test.
    C. Both Person A and Person B showed improvement in both types of memory at post-test.
    D. Person A showed improvement in memory for events right before the brain injury at post-test.

Foundational Concept: 6
Biological, psychological, and sociocultural factors influence the ways that individuals perceive, think about, and react to the world.

Content Category: 6B
Making sense of the environment

Scientific Inquiry and Reasoning Skill: 4
Data-based and Statistical Reasoning

Key: D
D is correct. Figure 1 shows that Person A showed an improvement in memory for events right before the injury at post-test.

Distractors

A   This is incorrect because Person A's memory for childhood events did not improve at post-test.

B   This is incorrect because Person B's memory for childhood events is the same at pre-test and post-test.

C   This is incorrect because both Person A and Person B did not show improvement in both types of memory. The only improvement was seen in Person A's memory for events right before brain injury.

TIP: Questions that test Scientific Inquiry and Reasoning Skill 4 may ask about interpreting data presented in a figure or a table, such as the bar graph that is in the passage. Becoming familiar with common ways in which data are represented in figures and tables can help with answering these types of questions. Be sure to read the figure or table caption and pay close attention to the legend and axes labels. Misunderstanding or misreading an important aspect of a table or figure could lead to selecting the wrong answer.

Psychological, Social, and Biological Foundations of Behavior

Discrete Questions

Psychological, Social, and Biological Foundations of Behavior

Psychological, Social, and Biological Foundations of Behavior Discrete (Questions 25–30)

25. A team of researchers wanted to test whether the James–Lange theory of emotional arousal could explain subjects' physical and emotional experiences while they viewed clips from a horror film. Which of the following scenarios is most consistent with the James–Lange theory?

   A. The participants felt general excitement and simultaneously experienced physical symptoms of autonomic arousal, such as a racing heart.
   B. The participants experienced physical symptoms of autonomic arousal, such as a racing heart, and then they reported that they felt afraid.
   C. The participants felt fear, and then began to experience physical symptoms of autonomic arousal, such as a racing heart.
   D. The participants showed physical symptoms of autonomic arousal, such as a racing heart, and then they reported that they felt general excitement.

26. Anxious about a nagging illness, a patient feels ignored by a doctor who is struggling to catch up with patient examinations on a very busy day. The doctor misinterprets the discomfort and agitation of the patient as hostility. Which sociological paradigm can best explain this scenario?

   A. Functionalism
   B. Conflict Theory
   C. Symbolic Interactionism
   D. Social Constructionism

27. A teacher rewards his students by distributing plastic chips. Students receive a chip for each instance of desirable behavior. At the end of each month, they can exchange their chips for prizes. The teacher sees major decreases in undesirable behaviors as a result of this system, which is known as:

   A. aversive conditioning.
   B. operant extinction.
   C. a token economy.
   D. an unconditioned stimulus.

28. A researcher interested in memory of novel words shows participants unrelated words printed on a card, one after the other. Participants see 20 words in total, wait for 2 minutes, and then are asked to write down all of the words they can remember. The researcher finds that 95% of the subjects remember the first three words. This finding is an example of:

   A. the recency effect.
   B. proactive interference.
   C. the primacy effect.
   D. retroactive interference.

29. Researchers conducted an experiment to study Weber's Law. Going from 10- to 12-pound weights created the just noticeable difference for one participant. For this participant, how many pounds need to be added to a 20-pound weight to create the just noticeable difference?

   A. 1 pound
   B. 2 pounds
   C. 4 pounds
   D. 8 pounds

30. Which aspect of equality is considered a requirement in a meritocracy?

   A. Equality of opportunity
   B. Equality of talent
   C. Equality of skill
   D. Equality of outcome

Solutions begin on next page.

25. A team of researchers wanted to test whether the James–Lange theory of emotional arousal could explain subjects' physical and emotional experiences while they viewed clips from a horror film. Which of the following scenarios is most consistent with the James–Lange theory?

A. The participants felt general excitement and simultaneously experienced physical symptoms of autonomic arousal, such as a racing heart.

B. The participants experienced physical symptoms of autonomic arousal, such as a racing heart, and then they reported that they felt afraid.

C. The participants felt fear, and then began to experience physical symptoms of autonomic arousal, such as a racing heart.

D. The participants showed physical symptoms of autonomic arousal, such as a racing heart, and then they reported that they felt general excitement.

Foundational Concept: 6
Biological, psychological, and sociocultural factors influence the ways that individuals perceive, think about, and react to the world.

Content Category: 6C
Responding to the world

Scientific Inquiry and Reasoning Skill: 2
Scientific Reasoning and Problem Solving

Key: B
B is correct. According to the James–Lange theory, physiological arousal precedes the identification of emotion. An individual first experiences the physiological symptoms of a given emotion and then labels this emotion.

Distractors

A   This is incorrect because the James–Lange theory posits that physiological symptoms precede emotional experience. A is more compatible with the Cannon–Bard theory of emotion.

C   This is incorrect because it suggests that the emotional labeling precedes physiological symptoms.

D   This is incorrect because the James–Lange theory of emotion suggests that physiological symptoms are recognized as a specific emotion, not as generalized excitement.

 TIP: To answer this question, knowing the premises of alternative theories of emotion is very useful. Recognizing how another theory explains emotion allows eliminating option A.

26. Anxious about a nagging illness, a patient feels ignored by a doctor who is struggling to catch up with patient examinations on a very busy day. The doctor misinterprets the discomfort and agitation of the patient as hostility. Which sociological paradigm can best explain this scenario?

   A. Functionalism
   B. Conflict Theory
   C. Symbolic Interactionism
   D. Social Constructionism

Foundational Concept: 9
Cultural and social differences influence well-being.

Content Category: 9A
Understanding social structure

Scientific Inquiry and Reasoning Skill: 1
Knowledge of Scientific Concepts and Principles

Key: C
C is the correct answer since the scenario concerns the inter-subjective negotiation of symbols or meanings, which is indicative of symbolic interactionist theory.

Distractors

A   This is incorrect because functionalism is considered a macro-level theory that understands social phenomena in terms of their function for society.

B   This is incorrect because conflict theory focuses on the differences in material resources among groups in society.

D   This is incorrect because social constructionism bridges the micro and macro levels but places more emphasis on how concepts emerge (such as illness), as opposed to understanding social interactions.

TIP: Depending on the context of a question or the passage, sociological theories are sometimes identified in slightly different ways (for example, as Functionalism or Functionalist theory) or with different descriptors (for example, as a paradigm, a theory, or an approach). Familiarity with the main premises of each theory will help when navigating the slight variations in how a theory is identified or labeled.

27. A teacher rewards his students by distributing plastic chips. Students receive a chip for each instance of desirable behavior. At the end of each month, they can exchange their chips for prizes. The teacher sees major decreases in undesirable behaviors as a result of this system, which is known as:

    A. aversive conditioning.
    B. operant extinction.
    C. a token economy.
    D. an unconditioned stimulus.

Foundational Concept: 7
Biological, psychological, and sociocultural factors influence behavior and behavior change.

Content Category: 7C
Attitude and behavior change

Scientific Inquiry and Reasoning Skill: 1
Knowledge of Scientific Concepts and Principles

Key: C
C is correct. Rewarding individuals with secondary reinforcers that can be exchanged for appetitive stimuli is typical of a token economy.

Distractors

A   This is incorrect because the students are being trained by positive reinforcement, not punishment.

B   This is incorrect because although operant learning is taking place, the stem specifies the acquisition of desirable behaviors, not extinction.

D   This is incorrect because unconditioned stimuli are involved in classical conditioning, not operant conditioning.

 TIP: It is important to read the options carefully, and not select options that contain only part of the correct answer, such as "operant extinction" in this question. Although the type of learning that is being used is operant conditioning, B is incorrect, because the example in the question does not focus on extinction specifically.

28. A researcher interested in memory of novel words shows participants unrelated words printed on a card, one after the other. Participants see 20 words in total, wait for 2 minutes, and then are asked to write down all of the words they can remember. The researcher finds that 95% of the subjects remember the first three words. This finding is an example of:

    A. the recency effect.
    B. proactive interference.
    C. the primacy effect.
    D. retroactive interference.

Foundational Concept: 6
Biological, psychological, and sociocultural factors influence the ways that individuals perceive, think about, and react to the world.

Content Category: 6B
Making sense of the environment

Scientific Inquiry and Reasoning Skill: 1
Knowledge of Scientific Concepts and Principles

Key: C
Improved memory for earlier information is an example of the primacy effect.

Distractors

A   This is incorrect because the recency effect refers to improved memory for the later information that is still in working memory.

B   This is incorrect because proactive interference refers to earlier information interfering with memory for later information.

D   This is incorrect because retroactive interference refers to later information interfering with memory for earlier information.

29. Researchers conducted an experiment to study Weber's Law. Going from 10- to 12-pound weights created the just noticeable difference for one participant. For this participant, how many pounds need to be added to a 20-pound weight to create the just noticeable difference?

    A. 1 pound
    B. 2 pounds
    C. 4 pounds
    D. 8 pounds

Foundational Concept: 6
Biological, psychological, and sociocultural factors influence the ways that individuals perceive, think about, and react to the world.

Content Category: 6A
Sensing the environment

Scientific Inquiry and Reasoning Skill: 2
Scientific Reasoning and Problem Solving

Key: C
C is correct. Weber's Law states that just noticeable difference is a ratio of the existing stimulus intensity. Two pounds are 1/5 of 10 pounds and they create the just noticeable difference for 10 pounds. To create the just noticeable difference for 20 pounds, 4 pounds (1/5 of 20 pounds) are needed.

Distractors
A   This is incorrect because it suggests that a smaller amount of change will lead to the just noticeable difference in a more intense stimulus, whereas the amount of change needed to produce the just noticeable difference increases as the original stimulus intensity increases.

B   This is incorrect because it suggests that the intensity needed to create the just noticeable difference is constant.

D   This is incorrect because it suggests an intensity that is greater than the minimum needed to create the just noticeable difference.

Fifth Edition
The Official Guide to the MCAT® Exam
315
MCAT® is a program of the
Association of American Medical Colleges

30. Which aspect of equality is considered a requirement in a meritocracy?

  A. Equality of opportunity
  B. Equality of talent
  C. Equality of skill
  D. Equality of outcome

Foundational Concept: 10
Social stratification affects access to resources and well-being.

Content Category: 10A
Social inequality

Scientific Inquiry and Reasoning Skill: 1
Knowledge of Scientific Concepts and Principles

Key: A
A meritocracy is when societal rewards, status, and positions are awarded to individuals based on their own ability and work (that is, merit). In order for a meritocracy to operate, everyone within the society would need the same opportunity to succeed, so that rewards are actually based (primarily) on merit.

Distractors

B   This is incorrect because a meritocracy is not when everyone has the same level of talent.

C   This is incorrect because a meritocracy is not when everyone has the same level of skill.

D   This is incorrect because a meritocracy is not when everyone experiences the same outcome.

Chapter 13

What Will the Critical Analysis and Reasoning Skills Section Test?

The Critical Analysis and Reasoning Skills section of the MCAT exam will be similar to many of the verbal reasoning tests you have taken in your academic career. It includes passages and questions that test your ability to understand what you read. You may find this section to be unique in several ways, though, because it has been developed specifically to measure the analysis and reasoning skills you will need to be successful in medical school. The Critical Analysis and Reasoning Skills section achieves this goal by asking you to read and think about passages from a wide range of disciplines in the social sciences and humanities, followed by a series of questions that lead you through the process of comprehending, analyzing, and reasoning about the material you have read.

Critical Analysis and Reasoning Skills passages are relatively short, typically between 500 and 600 words, but they are complex, often thought-provoking pieces of writing with sophisticated vocabulary and, at times, intricate writing styles. Everything you need to know to answer test questions is in the passages and the questions themselves. No additional coursework or specific knowledge is required to do well on the Critical Analysis and Reasoning Skills section, but you, as the test taker, may find yourself needing to read the passages and questions in ways that are different from the reading required in the textbooks you used in most prehealth courses or on tests like the SAT Reading Test. Passages for the Critical Analysis and Reasoning Skills section—even those written in a conversational or opinionated style—are often multifaceted and focus on the relationships between ideas or theories. The questions associated with the passages will require you to assess the content, but you will also need to consider the authors' intentions and tones and the words they used to express their points of view.

To recap from Part I, this section is designed to:

- test your comprehension, analysis, and reasoning skills by asking you to critically analyze information provided in passages;

- include content from ethics, philosophy, studies of diverse cultures, population health, and a wide range of social sciences and humanities disciplines; and

- provide all the information you need to answer questions in the passages and questions themselves.

Test Section	Number of Questions	Time
Critical Analysis and Reasoning Skills	53 *(note that questions are all passage-based)*	90 minutes

MCAT® is a program of the
Association of American Medical Colleges

Critical Analysis and Reasoning Skills Distribution of Questions

Distribution of Questions by Critical Analysis and Reasoning Skill and Passages in the Humanities and Social Sciences

You may wonder how many questions you'll get testing a particular critical analysis and reasoning skill or how many humanities or social science passages you'll see on the test. The questions that you see are likely to be distributed in the ways described below.*

Critical Analysis and Reasoning Skill:
- Foundations of Comprehension, 30%
- Reasoning Within the Text, 30%
- Reasoning Beyond the Text, 40%

Passage Content:
- Humanities, 50%
- Social Sciences, 50%

*These percentages have been approximated to the nearest 5% and will vary from one test to another for a variety of reasons. These reasons include, but are not limited to, controlling for question difficulty, using groups of questions that depend on a single passage, and using unscored field-test questions on each test form.

Introduction and Overview of the Critical Analysis and Reasoning Skills Section

All passages in the Critical Analysis and Reasoning Skills section of the MCAT exam consist of multiple paragraphs and require thoughtful reading. As you read, it's important to grasp the meaning of each paragraph and also to identify the relationships across all the paragraphs. Additionally, you will need to attend to the author's stated and unstated assumptions and to the rhetorical choices he or she has made to develop stance, voice, and style. This section includes nine passages followed by 5 to 7 questions for a total of 53 questions. As such, while thoughtful reading is very important for your success, it's also important to read quickly and efficiently.

The questions following the passages require their own focused kinds of reading, analyzing, and reasoning because many ask you to think about the passages from different perspectives or to question the author's statements, judge the relevance of the author's examples, or consider crucial facts that might challenge the author's assertions.

What Is the Content of the Passages?

Passages in the Critical Analysis and Reasoning Skills section are excerpted from the kinds of books, journals, and magazines that college students are likely to read. Passages from the social sciences and humanities disciplines might present interpretations, implications, or applications of historical accounts, theories, observations, or trends of human society as a whole, specific population groups, or specific countries.

Of these two types of passages (social sciences and humanities), social sciences passages tend to be more factual and scientific in tone. For example, a social sciences passage might discuss how basic psychological and sociological assumptions help scholars reconstruct patterns of prehistoric civilizations from ancient artifacts. Humanities passages often focus on the relationships between ideas and are more likely to be written in a conversational or opinionated style. Therefore, you should keep in mind the tone and word choice of the author in addition to the passage assertions themselves. Humanities passages might describe the ways art reflects historical or social change or how the philosophy of ethics has adapted to prevailing technological changes.

Critical Analysis and Reasoning Skills passages come from a variety of humanities and social sciences disciplines.

Humanities

Passages in the humanities are drawn from a variety of disciplines, including (but not limited to):

- Architecture
- Art
- Dance
- Ethics
- Literature
- Music
- Philosophy
- Popular Culture
- Religion
- Theater
- Studies of Diverse Cultures*

---

* Depending on the focus of the text, a Studies of Diverse Cultures passage could be classified as belonging to either the Humanities or Social Sciences.

Social Sciences

Social sciences passages are also drawn from a variety of disciplines, including (but not limited to):

- Anthropology
- Archaeology
- Economics
- Education
- Geography
- History
- Linguistics
- Political Science
- Population Health
- Psychology
- Sociology
- Studies of Diverse Cultures**

What Kinds of Analysis Skills Does the Critical Analysis and Reasoning Skills Section Require?

The Critical Analysis and Reasoning Skills section assesses three broad critical analysis and reasoning skills. Questions in this section will ask you to determine the overall meaning of the text, to summarize, evaluate, and critique the "big picture," and to synthesize, adapt, and reinterpret concepts you processed and analyzed. The questions following Critical Analysis and Reasoning Skills passages lead you through this complex mental exercise of finding meaning within each text and then reasoning beyond the text to expand the initial meaning. The analysis and reasoning skills on which you will be tested mirror those that mature test takers use to make sense of complex materials. The skills assessed in the Critical Analysis and Reasoning Skills section are represented in the graphic, and each skill is explained in the following sections.

Foundations of Comprehension

- Understanding the basic components of the text
- Inferring meaning from rhetorical devices, word choice, and text structure

Reasoning Within the Text

- Integrating different components of the text to increase comprehension

Reasoning Beyond the Text

- Applying or extrapolating ideas from the passage to new contexts
- Assessing the impact of introducing new factors, information, or conditions to ideas from the passage

---

** Depending on the focus of the text, a Studies of Diverse Cultures passage could be classified as belonging to either the Humanities or Social Sciences.

Foundations of Comprehension

The topics of some passages in the Critical Analysis and Reasoning Skills section will be familiar; some will not. Explanations, illustrative examples, and definitions of significant specialized terms in these passages will help you develop the strong basic foundation needed for answering all the questions you encounter in this section of the MCAT exam.

Additionally, some questions may ask you about the overall meaning of information in the passages or the author's central themes or ideas; others may ask you to select the definitions of specific words or phrases as they are used in context. These kinds of questions help you build the foundation that will allow you to think in new ways about concepts or facts presented in the passages. Paragraph numbers may be included in questions to help you locate relevant portions of the text.

Two sets of skills are the basis of the Foundations of Comprehension questions on the Critical Analysis and Reasoning Skills section.

Understanding the Basic Components of the Text

The most fundamental questions on the Critical Analysis and Reasoning Skills section ask about the basic components of the passages. Comprehension questions at this level may ask you to provide a general overview of the passage or to focus on specific portions of the text. You may be asked to identify the author's thesis, the main point or theme of the passage, examples, or something slightly more complex, such as portions of the passage where the author digresses from the central theme.

In responding to these questions, you need to be able to recognize the purpose of different portions of the target passage: what is the thesis statement, what examples support the main idea, and what statements pose an argument or assumption? An author distinguishes sections of text that indicate the existence of a sustained train of thought, as opposed to an isolated detail, with rhetorical labels such as "for example," "therefore," or "consequently."

You will also need to be able to recognize when an author seems to have drawn upon multiple sources to support a thesis or when he or she presents different points of view in the single passage. It's also important to attend to perspective: does the author present his or her own perspective, or does he or she use verbatim quotations or restatements from the perspective of other sources?

Inferring Meaning from Rhetorical Devices, Word Choice, and Text Structure

Questions may also require you to infer meanings that can't be determined from a superficial reading of the text, such as meanings that the author has implied but did not state directly. You may have to determine how the author has structured the text—for example, through cause-and-effect relationships for discussions in the behavioral sciences, chronologically for historical discussions, or point-and-counterpoint for political science pieces. Identifying the structure should help you understand the passage and determine its purpose. To do that, you will need to understand how the parts of a text fit together via these different kinds of relationships.

You may also need to attend to specific subtle and nuanced rhetorical decisions an author has made to shape his or her ideas, arguments, or discussions and perhaps to complicate a passage's meaning. For example, questions may ask you to explain paradoxes, a highlighted word or phrase, or an unexpected transition in ideas. To answer these questions, look for clues in the context around the specific sections of the passage. You may be asked to identify points of view, other than the author's, presented indirectly through authorial summaries or paraphrases. An author's choice about tone (e.g., humorous, authoritative, satirical) also contributes to—or obscures—meaning, and tone can often communicate the purpose for which a passage is written (e.g., to persuade, instruct, inform, entertain). For example, a satirical piece may at first seem merely entertaining, but a closer examination often reveals that its purpose is actually to persuade.

Some questions at this level may ask about information not specifically stated in the passage, and you must make assumptions based on what the author merely hints at through his or her use of connotative language or figures of speech. Look for the author's expressed point of view and the extent to which he or she uses summaries or paraphrases to introduce others' points of view.

The ending of passages is also fair game for questions at this level. Does the passage have a definitive solution, a partial resolution, or a call for additional research? Does it end with a dramatic rhetorical statement or a joke that leaves unanswered questions? Again, considering these questions requires you to understand how the different parts of the passage fit together to support the central thesis of the author.

Reasoning Within the Text

Questions that test Reasoning Within the Text differ from those assessing Foundations of Comprehension in that they ask you to integrate separate passage components into a more generalized and complex interpretation of passage meaning. Questions assessing Reasoning Within the Text will direct your attention to an argument, claim, or theme presented in the passage and then ask you to judge the passage according to specific criteria. The criteria could be the logic and plausibility of the passage text, the soundness of its arguments, the reasonableness of its conclusions, the appropriateness of its generalizations, or the credibility of the author and the sources he or she cites. The questions require you to dig beneath the passage's surface as you examine evidence, biases, faulty notions of causality, and irrelevant information and to determine the significance of and relationships among different parts of a passage. Additionally, some questions may require that you analyze the author's language, stance, and purpose. For example, plausible-sounding, transitional phrases may in fact be tricky. If read quickly, the words appear to make a legitimate connection between parts of a passage; however, when subjected to scrutiny, the links they appear to have established may fall apart.

This may sound like a long list of possible critical and analysis skills to have mastered, but they are skills you probably already possess and use every day. Similar to your reactions when you hear someone trying to convince you about something, persuade you to think a particular way, or sell you something, these questions often invite you to doubt and then judge the author's intentions and credibility. Questioning an author is a legitimate and often necessary analysis strategy that can serve test takers well when making sense of complex text. Answering these questions requires looking beyond contradictions or omission of facts or details to find clues such as vague or evasive terms or language that sounds self-aggrandizing, overblown, or otherwise suspect within the context of the passage. Credible sources—essayists, scientists, lecturers, even pundits—should be both authoritative and objective and should clearly demonstrate expertise. Blatant, one-sided arguments and rigid points of view are easy to identify, but some authors are more nuanced in presenting biased ideas in the guise of objectivity. The key to identifying bias lies in identifying the author's *treatment* of ideas, which you achieve by analyzing and evaluating different aspects of the passage. For example, an author who uses demeaning stereotypes or derogatory labels is not likely to be a source of objective, judicious analysis.

It's important to remember that Reasoning Within the Text questions do not ask you to provide your own personal opinion. You may, in fact, disagree with the author's overall conclusion yet find that the conclusion is a reasonable inference from the limited information provided in the passage. If you happen to know some obscure fact or anecdote outside the scope of the passage that could invalidate the author's conclusion, ignore it. The content of the passage or new information introduced by the questions should be the only sources on which you base your responses. Achieving a good score on the Critical Analysis and Reasoning Skills section depends on this!

Reasoning Beyond the Text

The final category, Reasoning Beyond the Text, requires you to use one of two analysis or reasoning skills, which in a way can be thought of as two sides of a single coin. Questions assessing the first set of skills ask you to *apply or extrapolate* information or ideas presented in the passage to a new or novel situation—for example, extending information the author presents beyond the actual context of the passage.

The second set of skills involves considering new information presented in a test question, mentally *integrating* this new information into the passage content, and then *assessing* the potential impact of introducing the new elements into the actual passage. Reasoning about new, hypothetical elements should cause you to synthesize passage content anew and alter your interpretation of the passage in some plausible way.

Application and integration questions elicit some of the same kinds of thinking. Both types deal with changes caused by combinations or comparisons, and both test your mental flexibility. They do differ, however, and their distinct requirements are explained in more detail below. Remember, though, that as with questions assessing different levels of analysis and reasoning, you must still use only the content of the passages and the new information in the questions to determine your answers. Keep avoiding the temptation to bring your existing knowledge to bear in answering these questions.

Applying or Extrapolating Ideas from the Passage to New Contexts

Virtually all questions assessing application or extrapolation skills ask you how the information or ideas presented in the passage could be extended to other areas or fields. This is the kind of high-level analysis and reasoning skill scientists or theoreticians use when they consider a set of facts or beliefs and create new knowledge by combining the "givens" in new ways. Of course, these combinations may or may not result in a successful combination or outcome.

For each application question, the passage material is the "given," and the test question provides specific directions about how the passage information might be applied to a new situation or how it might be used to solve a problem outside the specific context of the passage. As the test taker, your first task is to analyze the choices offered in the four response options so that you can gauge the likely outcome of applying the existing passage content to the specified new context. Each response option will yield a different result, but each test question has only one defensible and demonstrably correct response option.

The correct answer is the one option that presents the most likely and most reasonable outcome, based only on the information provided in the passage and question. The questions do not assess your personal ability to apply information or solve problems, only your ability to apply information from the question to the passage you have read. For example, if a question asks you to determine the author's likely response to four hypothetical situations, you would choose the response most consistent with what the author has already said or done according to the text of the passage. In determining the correct response, rule out the options that do not fit or are incongruent with the context (e.g., framework, perspective, scenario) created by the passage material.

Application questions sometimes require selection of a response option that is most *analogous* to some relationship in the passage. Here the parameters are broad. Likeness is measured not by inherent similarity but by analogy. Questions dealing with analogies test the ability to identify a fundamental common feature that seemingly different things or processes share. This may sometimes require translating a figurative comparison into equivalent sets of literal terms. However, the task always requires looking beneath surface imagery to discern underlying relationships or paradigms.

Assessing the Impact of Incorporating New Factors, Information, or Conditions to Ideas from the Passage

The essential difference between application and incorporation skills is that the two-part purpose of incorporation questions is to introduce a specific piece of information for you to consider and ask you to assess how ideas in the passage might be affected by its introduction. The premise of these questions is that ideas and information in the passages are potentially malleable, not a fixed framework, as in application questions.

In some incorporation questions, you must find the best answer to a "what if" question by reinterpreting and reassessing passage content with the additional fact or idea introduced by the question. Does the new information support or contradict the inherent logic of the passage? Could the new information coexist with what is already in the passage, or would it negate an aspect of the author's argument? If the latter is the case, the question could ask what modifications or alterations might need to be made to the passage content to accommodate the new element introduced by the question. Remember, the passage should be considered malleable.

Other forms of incorporation questions may ask you to think about a possible logical relationship that might exist between the passage content and the facts or assertions included in the answer options. The task is to select the one option that, if added to the passage content, would result in the *least* amount of change. The correct response option will present the situation or argument that is most similar to what is outlined in the passage. In other words, you must determine which new fact or assertion would least alter the central thesis the passage has developed.

Sample Skills Passage and Questions

How will the MCAT exam ask you to demonstrate each of the critical analysis and reasoning skills? The sample passage and questions that follow provide some examples.

Passage

The exhibition, The Garry Winogrand Game of Photography, was a reminder of why so many people consider Winogrand to be one of the great American photographers of the twentieth century. Although they continue to acquire further layers of historical specificity, his street photographs, many of them shot in Midtown Manhattan in the 1950s and 1960s, have lost none of their kinetic immediacy; the best of his animal photographs provide sly, incisive views of the human condition; his pictures from the American road grab the wheel from Walker Evans and Robert Frank to send the genre on an unpredictable detour; in photographing all manner of public events, from antiwar demonstrations to art-world parties to political press conferences, Winogrand added significantly to the pictorial record of midcentury United States history. With his liking for seemingly random compositions and his famous tilted-frame effect, Winogrand made photographs that initially struck many viewers as devoid of formal strengths. Now, however, we can appreciate the subtlety and unexpectedness of his framing and the complex interplay he often achieves between anecdote and form.

In putting together the exhibition, one of the curators, Richard Misrach, decided to focus on an aspect of Winogrand's work to which little attention had been given: the color slides. Winogrand began shooting color photos in the 1950s and continued doing so until the late 1960s. He never explained why he stopped shooting in color, but the difficulty and expense of making color prints and their instability may have contributed to his decision.

Misrach was especially drawn to the photographs Winogrand made at boxing matches in the 1950s, and his selections for the exhibition included eighteen boxing shots. In each, the fighters' bodies are isolated against dark backgrounds and often fragmented by the out-of-focus, quasi-abstract ropes cutting across the frame. In one amazing, weirdly off-center shot, a boxer doubling up from a body blow appears to be ascending into the surrounding void.

This small selection whetted one's appetite for seeing more images from Winogrand's color work. However, it was the slides that caused some of the most heated arguments among curators. Bill Jay objected to the slides being shown in any format because they had never been edited by Winogrand. While the prints in the archive had already been chosen for enlargement by the photographer from contact sheets, Jay pointed out, the slides had undergone no such process. Jay insisted that the archive's hoard of thousands of slides and unproofed negatives should be used only for research and never published or exhibited.

Misrach came to his own defense by saying that if "curatorial laws" were followed, the "real hidden treasures" of the archive would never be seen by anyone. He also observed that Winogrand gave his photographs, slides, and negatives to the Center for Creative Photography without conditions, which implies permission to show and publish the work. If Winogrand didn't want the photographs in his archive to be seen, Misrach argued, he could have simply destroyed them. Indeed, as others remarked, some photographers have sought to exert control over the future of their work by destroying negatives. Furthermore, some curators argued for the importance of posthumous discoveries of artists' work. And taking the discussion into a wider realm, one curator argued that the "artist is not always in the best position to judge his or her work," citing the example of author Franz Kafka asking Max Brod to destroy his manuscripts and how Brod had ignored the request, to the world's benefit.

Source: Adapted from R. Rubinstein, Snap Judgments: Exploring the Winogrand Archive. Copyright 2002 by Brant Publications, Inc.

MCAT® is a program of the
Association of American Medical Colleges

Questions

Foundations of Comprehension Example: Foundations of Comprehension questions test two skills: 1) understanding the basic components of the text and 2) inferring meaning from rhetorical devices, word choice, and text structure. The following question addresses the first of these.

1. **Which of the following best captures the main goal of the passage?**

    A. To bring additional attention to Winogrand, unfairly neglected as an important American photographer
    B. To showcase the diversity of Winogrand's subject matter and the genres he explored
    C. To describe the controversy over the appropriate use of Winogrand's archival color slides
    D. To argue that art lovers and scholars have a right to see all of the work that Winogrand left after his death

The correct answer is C. This question asks you to determine which of the four options presented best captures the main goal of the passage.

To answer this question, you must understand the author's main points and arguments and distinguish these from subordinate points. This question illustrates understanding of basic components of text by asking you to identify the primary goal of the passage.

The answer is correct because most of the passage emphasizes the curator's decision. Note that the passage author does not take a clear position on the controversy (making D incorrect). Instead, the author represents multiple perspectives on the controversy, which is the central concern of the passage.

Foundations of Comprehension Example: Now, let's take a look at a question that tests the second skill in Foundations of Comprehension, which is making assumptions based on the author's inference through the use of rhetorical devices, word choice, and the text structure.

2. **The author's use of the term kinetic immediacy (paragraph 1) to describe Winogrand's photographs most likely refers to the photographs':**

    A. ability to capture the hustle and bustle of the city.
    B. incorporation of roadside scenes.
    C. historically significant details and context.
    D. unique compositional strategies.

The correct answer is A. You are asked to determine which of the four options presented most likely refers to the phrase "kinetic immediacy" as used to describe Winogrand's photographs.

Because of the way the term "kinetic immediacy" is used in the context of the sentence in which it appears, the answer is A. The term refers to Winogrand's "street photographs" of New York City, shot decades ago; the author says that the pictures retain their "kinetic immediacy" over time. So the author suggests that the speed and dynamism of the photos is still present, and this is best captured in option A. Because this question asks you to determine the implication of a term or phrase by considering the context of its use, it's an example of the second skill in Foundations of Comprehension.

Reasoning Within the Text Example: Now we'll move on to a question that addresses the next skill, Reasoning Within the Text. The analysis skill related to Reasoning Within the Text is integrating different components of the text to increase comprehension.

3. **The curator who used the example of Max Brod refusing to destroy the manuscripts of Franz Kafka (final sentence) was most likely implying that:**

    A. the individual rights of an artist are sometimes outweighed by the greater public and artistic good.
    B. the destruction of an artist's work is never warranted.
    C. once a work of art is created, its destruction is almost a crime against humanity.
    D. great artists will always attempt to keep their works from being seen and must be prevented from doing so.

The correct answer is A. This question asks you to integrate different components of the text to increase comprehension, specifically the way the author has framed his or her use of the example of Max Brod refusing to destroy the manuscripts of Franz Kafka. To answer the question, you must determine the function or purpose of this example, determining which point or argument the evidence of Max Brod refusing to destroy the manuscripts is used to support.

The author provides as evidence the curator's point that the artist may not be the ultimate judge of his or her work. Then the author suggests that Brod ignored Kafka's request that Brod destroy Kafka's work, "to the world's benefit." So both points lead to the conclusion that the curator means to suggest that sometimes aesthetic value and the "good" of the "world" may take precedence over an artist's desire or expressed wish. The answer is A because of the way the passage author has framed his or her use of this example.

Reasoning Beyond the Text Example: The final Critical Analysis and Reasoning Skills skill is Reasoning Beyond the Text. This skill includes the following two skills: 1) applying or extrapolating ideas from the passage to new contexts and 2) assessing the impact of introducing new factors, information, or conditions to ideas from the passage.

Let's look at a question asking you to apply or extrapolate information or ideas presented in the passage to new or novel situations.

4. **Someone who agreed with Misrach's defense of his choice to show the color slides would be most likely to also approve of:**

    A. exhibiting works that an artist had donated to a museum for scholarly purposes only.
    B. examining the rest of Winogrand's unprinted photographs and selecting some for display.
    C. requiring that artists clearly state their intentions for display and publication when donating works to a museum.
    D. organizing an exhibition that included all of Winogrand's work whether previously shown and published or not.

The correct answer is B. This question illustrates the first Reasoning Beyond the Text skill because it asks you to begin with an argument presented in the passage—Misrach's defense of his choice to show the color slides—and then apply that understanding to a new situation to see if the new situation is analogous to the idea presented in the passage. To answer the question, you must identify the option that matches Misrach's defense of his choice to show the color slides.

In the final paragraph of the passage, Misrach explains his logic in defense of his choice to show the color slides, including the suggestion that the archive contains some "hidden treasures," and implying that the curator, not necessarily the artist, might select these. Therefore, option B most closely aligns with the principle behind Misrach's defense.

Reasoning Beyond the Text Example: The second skill in Reasoning Beyond the Text involves considering new information presented, integrating this new information into the passage content, and then assessing how ideas in the passage might be affected by this new information.

Here is a question asking you to demonstrate the second skill in Reasoning Beyond the Text.

5. **If it were established with certainty that Winogrand did, as the author suggests, stop shooting in color because of the "difficulty and expense of making color prints and their instability" (paragraph 2), this information would best support which of the following arguments?**

    A. Winogrand would have liked to have his color slides printed once the technology made this feasible.
    B. Winogrand felt that working in color was stylistically inferior to black and white.
    C. The color slides should be viewed as finished products and not printed.
    D. Winogrand would have returned to photographing in color once the technology improved.

The correct answer is D. This question asks you to assess new information—what it would mean if it was established with *certainty* that Winogrand did stop shooting in color because of the difficulty and expense of making color prints and their instability. You need to decide which of the arguments this new information would best support.

This question illustrates the second skill in Reasoning Beyond the Text because it presents a novel scenario (one not discussed in the passage) and asks you to assess how that novel scenario would affect the arguments in the passage.

If Winogrand had stopped shooting in color because of the technical and financial challenges posed by shooting in color, it follows logically that if he could surmount those challenges, he would likely return to shooting in color. The other options involve assumptions that the information in the question does not support. It does not imply anything about Winogrand's feelings about printing color slides or about his preference for black and white over color photography.

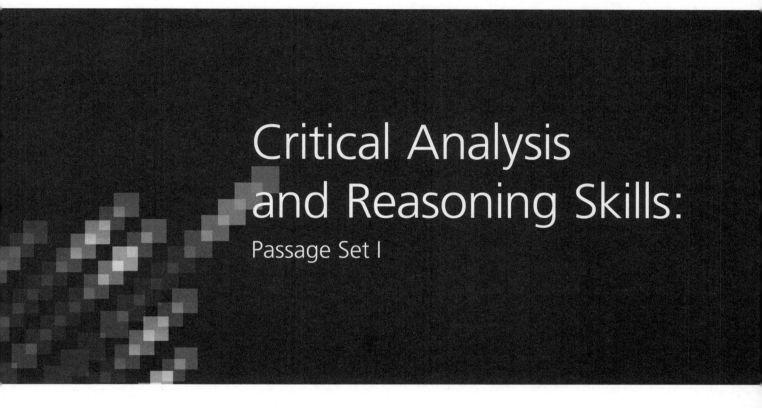

Critical Analysis and Reasoning Skills:

Passage Set I

Sample Test Questions: Critical Analysis and Reasoning Skills

Sample test questions for the Critical Analysis and Reasoning Skills section are provided below.
The answer key appears below each question, along with the skill the question is testing.
These sample questions will give you an idea of what to expect from this section of the exam.

MCAT® is a program of the
Association of American Medical Colleges

Critical Analysis and Reasoning Skills

Passage I: Questions 1–5

From Population Health

Rudolph Virchow, the nineteenth-century German physician, came of age with two dramatic events— a typhoid outbreak in 1847, and the failed revolutions of 1848. Virchow gained two insights from those experiences: 1) the spread of disease has much to do with appalling living conditions; and 2) those in power have enormous means to subjugate the powerless. As Virchow summarized in his famous epigram, "Physicians are the natural attorneys of the poor."

Physicians are advocates for the underprivileged because poverty and poor health tend to go hand in hand. Poverty means bad or insufficient food, unhealthy living conditions, and endless other factors leading to illness. When you examine socioeconomic status (SES)— a composite measure that includes income, occupation, education, and housing conditions—it becomes clear that, starting with the wealthiest stratum of society, every step downward in SES correlates with poorer health.

This "SES gradient" has been documented throughout Westernized societies as the impetus for a variety of health problems. It is not a subtle statistical phenomenon. When you compare the highest versus the lowest rungs of the SES ladder, the risk of some disease varies tenfold.

So what causes this correlation between SES and health? Lower SES may give rise to poorer health, but conversely, poorer health could also give rise to lower SES. After all, chronic illness can compromise one's education and work productivity, in addition to generating enormous expenses.

Nevertheless, the bulk of the facts suggests that the arrow goes from economic status to health—that SES at some point in life predicts health measures later on. Among the many demonstrations of this point is a remarkable study of elderly nuns in the U.S. All had taken their vows as young adults and had spent many years thereafter sharing diet, health care, and housing, thereby controlling for those lifestyle factors. Yet in their old age, patterns of disease, incidence of dementia, and longevity were still significantly predicted by their SES status from when they became nuns, at least half a century before.

So how does SES influence health? The answers that seem most obvious, it turns out, do not hold much water. One such explanation posits that for the poor, health care may be less easily accessible and of lower quality. But that explanation fails for reasons made clearest in the famed Whitehall studies. These studies documented an array of dramatic SES gradients in a conveniently stratified population, namely, the members of the British civil service (ranging from blue-collar workers to high-powered executives). Office messengers, for example, have far higher mortality rates from chronic heart disease than professionals do. Lack of access to medical attention cannot explain the phenomenon, because the U.K. has universal health care.

The next "obvious" explanation centers on unhealthy lifestyles. As you descend the SES ladder in Westernized societies, people are more likely to drink excessively or smoke. They are also less likely to have access to clean water and healthy food. Thus, it seems self-evident that lower SES affects health by increasing risks and decreasing protective factors.

What is surprising, though, is how little of the SES gradient these risk and protective factors explain. It is reasonable to assume that the wealthier a country, the more financial resources its citizens have to buy protection and avoid risk. If so, health should improve incrementally as one moves up the wealth gradient among nations, as well as among the citizens within individual nations. But it does not. Instead, among the wealthiest quarter of countries on earth, there is no relation between a country's wealth and the health of its people.

Source: Adapted from R. Sapolsky, "Sick of poverty." Copyright 2005 Scientific American, Inc.

1. Which of the following facts presented in the passage provides the greatest support for the claim that unhealthy lifestyles do NOT have a substantial effect on the SES gradient?

   A. As one descends the SES ladder in Westernized societies, people are more likely to smoke or drink excessively.
   B. Lower SES affects health by increasing risks and decreasing protective factors.
   C. The wealthier a country, the more financial resources its citizens have to buy protection and avoid risk.
   D. Among the wealthiest quarter of countries on earth, there is no relation between a country's wealth and the health of its people.

2. Based on information in the passage, with which of the following statements about the health of people in the U.S. would the passage author be most likely to agree?

   A. People in the U.S. who are on the lower rungs of the SES ladder are more likely to drink excessively or smoke than people on the higher rungs.
   B. People in the U.S. who are on the lower rungs of the SES ladder have just as easily accessible and equal quality health care as do people on the higher rungs.
   C. People in the U.S. are less likely to have insufficient food or unhealthy living conditions than people in other Westernized societies.
   D. People in the U.S. who are on the highest rungs of the SES ladder generally have better health than similarly situated people in slightly less wealthy Westernized countries.

3. Which of the following study findings would provide the greatest support for the claim that poorer health leads to lower SES?

   A. Children who are born into families lower on the SES ladder are significantly more likely to have poorer health later in life.
   B. Children who are born into families lower on the SES ladder are significantly more likely to be hospitalized more than twice during their first two years of life.
   C. Children who are hospitalized more than twice during their first two years of life are significantly more likely to have a lower income later in life.
   D. Children who are hospitalized more than twice during their first two years of life are significantly more likely to have poorer health later in life.

4. Which of the following would provide a "conveniently stratified population" most similar to the population examined in the Whitehall studies?

   A. Members of a university faculty
   B. Members of a military branch
   C. Members of a monastery
   D. Members of a state legislature

5. Based on the discussion in the fifth paragraph, the fact that the nuns shared lifestyle factors for the past fifty years was most helpful because it enabled researchers to:

   A. predict the nuns' future patterns of disease, incidence of dementia, and longevity.
   B. calculate the nuns' SES at the time of the study.
   C. determine that the variability in the nuns' health in their old age was predicted by their SES when they were young.
   D. learn which component of the nuns' SES contributed the most to their longevity.

Solutions for this passage begin on next page.

1. Which of the following facts presented in the passage provides the greatest support for the claim that unhealthy lifestyles do NOT have a substantial effect on the SES gradient?

   A. As one descends the SES ladder in Westernized societies, people are more likely to smoke or drink excessively.
   B. Lower SES affects health by increasing risks and decreasing protective factors.
   C. The wealthier a country, the more financial resources its citizens have to buy protection and avoid risk.
   D. Among the wealthiest quarter of countries on earth, there is no relation between a country's wealth and the health of its people.

Skill:
Reasoning Within the Text

Key: D
This question asks you to assess evidence and decide whether it supports the claim in the question. According to the final paragraph of the passage, if unhealthy lifestyles had a substantial effect on the SES gradient, then people in wealthier nations, able to "buy protection and avoid risk," should be healthier than those in poorer nations. Option D states that "among the wealthiest quarter of countries on earth, there is no relation between a country's wealth and the health of its people" and thus provides support for the claim that unhealthy lifestyles do NOT have a substantial effect on the SES gradient.

Distractors

A   This option associates unhealthy lifestyle choices with lower SES, which would potentially *support* the claim that unhealthy lifestyles DO have a substantial effect on the SES gradient, so this is incorrect.

B   Again, this option would potentially support the claim that there is a substantial association between unhealthy lifestyles (increased risks and decreased protective factors) and the SES gradient.

C   This option is essentially the inverse of option B and again would support the claim that unhealthy lifestyles DO have a substantial effect on the SES gradient—because it describes people with higher incomes as able to avoid risks and thus avoid unhealthy lifestyles.

TIP: This kind of question makes clear how important it is to read the question carefully. When the question contains a negative word, as it does here, the negative word will be capitalized (or italicized) to help ensure that that you notice it. It is very important to keep that negative phrasing in mind as you read the options.

2. Based on information in the passage, with which of the following statements about the health of people in the U.S. would the passage author be most likely to agree?

A. People in the U.S. who are on the lower rungs of the SES ladder are more likely to drink excessively or smoke than people on the higher rungs.

B. People in the U.S. who are on the lower rungs of the SES ladder have just as easily accessible and equal quality health care as do people on the higher rungs.

C. People in the U.S. are less likely to have insufficient food or unhealthy living conditions than people in other Westernized societies.

D. People in the U.S. who are on the highest rungs of the SES ladder generally have better health than similarly situated people in slightly less wealthy Westernized countries.

Skill:
Foundations of Comprehension

Key: A
This is a relatively straightforward comprehension question. Paragraph 7 provides explicit support for this option: "As you descend the SES ladder in Westernized societies, people are more likely to drink excessively or smoke." Thus, the passage author would be likely to agree with this statement, which applies to the health of people in the U.S. (a Westernized country).

Distractors
B   In paragraph 6, the passage author discusses the U.K., where, because of universal health care, people have equal access to health care regardless of income. In the same paragraph, though, the passage refers to the point that "for the poor, health care may be less easily accessible and of lower quality." Thus, the passage implies that without universal health care, which the U.S. does not have, equal access to health care does not exist, so the author would not be likely to agree with this statement.

C   There is no suggestion in the passage that the U.S. is different from other Westernized countries in these regards, so there is no reason to think that the passage author would agree with this claim.

D   The last paragraph of the passage explicitly refutes this claim when it says, "among the wealthiest quarter of countries on earth, there is no relation between a country's wealth and the health of its people."

TIP: The passage will contain the information you need to answer the question. You do not need to have prior knowledge of the Whitehall studies or the British civil service to arrive at the answer. You do need to read the passage carefully and look at the way that the passage elaborates on the concept of a "conveniently stratified population." The passage discussion of the professional ranks contained within the British civil service should allow you to answer the question.

3. Which of the following study findings would provide the greatest support for the claim that poorer health leads to lower SES?

    A. Children who are born into families lower on the SES ladder are significantly more likely to have poorer health later in life.

    B. Children who are born into families lower on the SES ladder are significantly more likely to be hospitalized more than twice during their first two years of life.

    C. Children who are hospitalized more than twice during their first two years of life are significantly more likely to have a lower income later in life.

    D. Children who are hospitalized more than twice during their first two years of life are significantly more likely to have poorer health later in life.

Skill:
Reasoning Beyond the Text

Key: C
The question asks you to consider which of a series of findings not mentioned in the passage would provide support for a theory that is discussed in the passage (paragraph 4). This option describes a pattern in which children who experience poorer health (frequent hospitalizations) early in their lives are more likely to have lower SES (lower incomes) later in their lives. Thus, this finding would provide the greatest support among the options for the claim that poorer health actually leads to—or causes—lower SES.

Distractors

A   This option does not provide evidence for the claim the question asks about, as it suggests that low SES precedes poor health, rather than the reverse.

B   Again, this option does not provide evidence for the claim the question asks about, as the lower SES precedes the hospitalizations and may even be seen to influence the likelihood of the hospitalizations; in this scenario there has been no opportunity for the poor health of the child to influence SES.

D   This option only describes poor health—in childhood and later in life. It does not bring in SES, so it cannot support the claim that the question asks about.

4. Which of the following would provide a "conveniently stratified population" most similar to the population examined in the Whitehall studies?

A. Members of a university faculty
B. Members of a military branch
C. Members of a monastery
D. Members of a state legislature

Skill:
Reasoning Beyond the Text

Key: B
This question asks you to reason beyond the text. It asks you to consider which population that was not mentioned in the passage would be most similar to an example given in the passage. The passage example of a "conveniently stratified population" is the British civil service. The passage explains that members "rang[e] from blue-collar workers to high-powered executives." This explanation makes clear that in the British civil service, people's occupations and ranks are both hierarchical and clearly defined. A military branch would similarly contain people of different ranks, positions, and salaries and these would be clearly delineated.

Distractors

A Members of a university faculty might differ in discipline—ranging from scientists to historians, for instance—but they would have similar levels of education and roughly similar or comparable incomes, so they would not be stratified to the degree that they are in the Whitehall study.

C Members of a monastery would all presumably occupy similar positions, even with the possibility of some seniority or status differences. Their incomes would be very closely aligned and therefore, they wouldn't differ as do the members of the British civil service, as described in the passage.

D Members of a state legislature perform the same job and are paid by the same state government. Thus, differences in salary and status would be relatively small and probably determined largely by seniority.

5. Based on the discussion in the fifth paragraph, the fact that the nuns shared lifestyle factors for the past fifty years was most helpful because it enabled researchers to:

    A. predict the nuns' future patterns of disease, incidence of dementia, and longevity.

    B. calculate the nuns' SES at the time of the study.

    C. determine that the variability in the nuns' health in their old age was predicted by their SES when they were young.

    D. learn which component of the nuns' SES contributed the most to their longevity.

Skill:
Foundations of Comprehension

Key: C
This is a comprehension question. It asks you to go to a specific section of the passage and derive the author's meaning in that section of the text. The author explains that the nuns "had spent many years...sharing diet, health care, and housing, thereby controlling for those lifestyle factors." In other words, the nuns' shared lifestyles allowed the researchers to exclude lifestyle as a variable and thus to see correlations between the SES status of nuns when they were young and their health as older adults, as described in the last sentence of the paragraph.

Distractors
A   Lifestyle factors could not predict the nuns' future patterns of disease or longevity because the lifestyle factors were the same over 50 years, whereas the patterns they experienced of disease, dementia, and longevity were different (and correlated with childhood SES).

B   The paragraph indicates that researchers were interested in the nuns' SES from before they became nuns, and researchers already had this information. (All of the nuns presumably had the same SES at the time of the study.)

D   The paragraph only discusses SES in general and makes no suggestion that the nuns' shared lifestyle factors allowed the researchers to identify the effects of specific aspects of SES.

Critical Analysis
and Reasoning Skills:

Passage Set II

MCAT® is a program of the
Association of American Medical Colleges

Critical Analysis and Reasoning Skills

Passage II: Questions 6–11

From Ethics

A predetermined covenant of confidentiality characterizes the physician-patient relationship. Possession of contraband in prison is illegal. But suppose that during a routine medical examination, a prison physician notices that Prisoner A has drugs and paraphernalia. Should the physician report the crime, or should confidentiality prevail?

Professional communications between physicians and patients are statutorily protected as confidential. A routine physical examination is part of the confidential communication, like information obtained by taking a medical history and data entered in the patient's health record. Health professionals have an interest in maintaining confidentiality so that patients will feel comfortable in revealing personal but necessary information. Prisoners do not possess full Constitutional rights to privacy, but they generally retain rights to privacy when there is a special relationship between communicants, such as the physician-patient relationship. In fact, respect for confidentiality is particularly important in a prison hospital setting, in which patients feel distrust because physicians are often employed by the incarcerating institution.

Clinical autonomy for health professionals in the prison setting is essential for good medical practice. Physicians working in prisons also retain the privilege of confidential interactions with patients, although the prison authorities may try to pressure doctors to supply information. Even if physicians are employed by the prison, their first responsibility is to their patients. The circumstances in which to give privileged information to prison authorities remains the physician's decision.

The finding that contraband detected during an examination has the appearance of drugs and paraphernalia, like all results of the examination, is privileged information to be treated confidentially. The right to privacy supersedes a duty to report the discovery because there is no imminent threat to others. In contrast, a weapon harbored by a prisoner represents an imminent threat to other prisoners and to prison staff. Thus, upon discovering a sequestered weapon during the course of a routine examination, the physician has a "duty to warn." According to case law, when the physician believes that a significant threat of harm exists, the duty to warn takes precedence over the patient's right to privacy.

The case of Prisoner A raises the issue of the point at which to draw the line between the duty to protect the public and the duty to protect patients' privacy. Although legal guidelines can assist the physician in making the choice, the health professional must rely on a guiding principle of the medical profession: Where no danger to others exists, patients come first.

The possibility of discovering contraband during routine examinations of prisoner patients reinforces the need for informed consent at several stages. First, prisoner patients should be evaluated and treated only after they provide informed consent, unless they are incompetent. Before an X-ray is taken, they should be informed that it can demonstrate metal and other foreign bodies, and their agreement to the procedure should be obtained. Second, if a concealed weapon is discovered during a routine examination, the prisoner patient should be informed that the discovery will be reported and given the opportunity to surrender the weapon to authorities before more forcible means are taken to remove it. If Prisoner A is harboring drugs and a needle, drug use is quite possibly contributing to A's health problem. It is the physician's responsibility to educate A about the potential harm of drug use.

Source: Adapted from C. Levine (Ed.), Cases in Bioethics: Selections from the Hastings Center Report. Copyright 1989 St. Martin's Press.

6. Assume that a prison did not have a policy of obtaining informed consent before a diagnostic procedure, and almost all of the inmates refused to be X-rayed. The author's comments suggest that this situation could reasonably be interpreted as evidence that prisoners:

   A. believe that they have a Constitutional right to privacy.
   B. are less concerned about their health than are nonprisoners.
   C. distrust physicians who are employed by the prison.
   D. feel a need to carry a weapon for self-protection.

7. Suppose that a prisoner under sedation for a medical procedure inadvertently reveals that a weapon is hidden in the prisoner's cell. Passage information suggests that the author would be most likely to advise the physician to report the incident:

   A. only if the prisoner threatened to use the weapon.
   B. only if the prisoner consented to the report.
   C. only if the prisoner subsequently denied that the weapon existed.
   D. regardless of the patient's assertions.

8. The author argues that a routine examination is part of the confidential communication between a patient and a physician and that the clinical autonomy of the physician is essential for good medical practice in prisons. These beliefs imply that:

   A. if the quality of medicine practiced in a prison declines, a physician has violated the confidentiality of a routine examination.
   B. if all physicians in a prison refuse to reveal information about prisoners obtained during routine examinations, the physicians in that prison have clinical autonomy.
   C. if all physicians who conduct routine examinations in a prison respect their patients' confidence, the quality of medicine practiced in the prison is high.
   D. if a physician is required to reveal information about a prisoner obtained during a routine examination, the quality of medicine practiced in the prison suffers.

9. With respect to prisoners, "necessary information" (paragraph 2) probably refers most specifically to a patient's:

   A. past criminal activities.
   B. use of illegal drugs.
   C. intent to harm others.
   D. psychiatric history.

10. Which of the following conclusions about physician confidentiality can be inferred from the passage?

    A. It is more likely to be assumed in a private setting than in a prison.
    B. It is especially important when patients are incompetent to give informed consent.
    C. It is threatened by the use of invasive diagnostic tools such as X-rays.
    D. It is an aspect of a Constitutional right that is lost by prisoners.

11. Which of the following objections, if valid, would most *weaken* the argument made for the special importance of the physician-patient covenant within prisons?

    A. Prisoners understand that X-rays will detect hidden weapons.
    B. Prisoners assume that physicians are independent of the institution.
    C. Prison officials often question physicians about prisoners.
    D. Prisoners often misunderstand their Constitutional rights.

Solutions for this passage begin on next page.

6. Assume that a prison did not have a policy of obtaining informed consent before a diagnostic procedure, and almost all of the inmates refused to be X-rayed. The author's comments suggest that this situation could reasonably be interpreted as evidence that prisoners:

    A. believe that they have a Constitutional right to privacy.
    B. are less concerned about their health than are nonprisoners.
    C. distrust physicians who are employed by the prison.
    D. feel a need to carry a weapon for self-protection.

Skill:
Reasoning Beyond the Text

Key: C
This questions asks you to reason beyond the text. It asks you to use ideas from the passage to analyze a scenario that does not appear in the passage. According to the passage, informed consent discloses to the prisoner the potential risks of the procedure that he or she is about to undergo if he or she consents to the procedure. It also makes clear the rights that the prisoner has if contraband is detected during an examination. Without informed consent (disclosure of risks and rights), if prisoners routinely refused to be X-rayed, this could likely be because they did not trust the physicians working for the prison and did not know what they might do. This point is made clear at the end of paragraph 2, where the author says that "respect for confidentiality is particularly important in a prison hospital setting, in which patients feel distrust because physicians are often employed by the incarcerating institution."

Distractors
A   The passage discusses the fact that the prisoner's Constitutional right to privacy is not complete, but does exist. However, the scenario described in the question, in which patients in prisons without informed consent policies refuse to be X-rayed, does not imply anything about the patient's belief in his or her right to privacy.

B   The passage does not say anything about the degree of concern that either prisoners or nonprisoners feel about their health, nor does it imply that prisoners feel any less concern about their health than does anyone else.

D   The passage suggests that informed consent is a necessity in a prison medical setting, not that there is any reason to assume that most prisoners carry weapons (nor does the passage claim that weapons that are carried in prison are necessarily intended for self-protection).

7. Suppose that a prisoner under sedation for a medical procedure inadvertently reveals that a weapon is hidden in the prisoner's cell. Passage information suggests that the author would be most likely to advise the physician to report the incident:

A. only if the prisoner threatened to use the weapon.
B. only if the prisoner consented to the report.
C. only if the prisoner subsequently denied that the weapon existed.
D. regardless of the patient's assertions.

Skill:
Reasoning Beyond the Text

Key: D
Like the previous question, this question proposes a scenario that does not appear in the passage and asks you to examine that scenario based on information in the passage. The author writes explicitly in paragraph 4 that physicians have a "duty to warn" others of any concealed weapon that they discover or learn about. As the author puts it, "a weapon harbored by a prisoner represents an imminent threat to other prisoners and to prison staff." Regardless of how the physician discovered the potential presence of a weapon, the author would advise the physician that he or she must report the incident.

Distractors
A   The physician's obligation to warn does not contain exceptions, so regardless of whether the prisoner threatened to use the weapon, the author would advise the physician to report it.

B   Again, as the passage presents it, the physician's duty to warn does not contain exceptions, so regardless of whether the prisoner consented to the report, the author would advise the physician to report his or her knowledge of the weapon.

C   The duty to warn supersedes other considerations described in the passage. So the prisoner's denial (or admission) of the existence of the weapon is irrelevant.

TIP: This is an example of a question where some options refer to important points in the passage, but they are irrelevant to the question. Option B, for instance, suggests that the author would advise the physician to report the weapon he or she learned about "only if the prisoner consented to the report." There is an important discussion of "informed consent" at the end of the passage. It could be tempting to assume that since the passage endorses "informed consent," this might be the right answer, and the author would advise the physician to report the weapon only with the prisoner's consent. However, the actual discussion of informed consent in the passage does not imply this. When you see words, phrases, or concepts from the passage among the answer choices, consider their context and the way they are used in the passage.

8. The author argues that a routine examination is part of the confidential communication between a patient and a physician and that the clinical autonomy of the physician is essential for good medical practice in prisons. These beliefs imply that:

    A. if the quality of medicine practiced in a prison declines, a physician has violated the confidentiality of a routine examination.
    B. if all physicians in a prison refuse to reveal information about prisoners obtained during routine examinations, the physicians in that prison have clinical autonomy.
    C. if all physicians who conduct routine examinations in a prison respect their patients' confidence, the quality of medicine practiced in the prison is high.
    D. if a physician is required to reveal information about a prisoner obtained during a routine examination, the quality of medicine practiced in the prison suffers.

Skill:
Reasoning Within the Text

Key: D
This question asks you to reason within information provided in the passage. It asks you to consider logically what assumptions or implications can be derived from the passage author's argument. If clinical autonomy is essential to good medical practice, then an infringement on that clinical autonomy (such as requiring physicians to reveal information obtained during a routine examination—assuming that it did not pose an imminent threat to others) would logically mean that the quality of medical care would be lower than it would be otherwise.

Distractors
A   It is not possible to assume that any decline in quality of medicine is attributable to a lack of confidentiality on the part of physicians.

B   The passage author argues that there are circumstances (such as the physician's discovery of something during an exam that poses a danger to others) where the physician has an ethical obligation to warn others of that potential danger, so simple refusal to reveal information does not translate into clinical autonomy. The author stresses that "the circumstances in which to give privileged information to prison authorities remains the physician's decision."

C   Again, the passage author argues that there are circumstances (such as the physician's discovery of a weapon during an exam) in which the physician has an ethical obligation to warn others of that potential danger. Thus, the passage does not imply that the quality of medicine will always suffer if a physician is required to reveal information obtained during a routine medical examination.

9. With respect to prisoners, "necessary information" (paragraph 2) probably refers most specifically to a patient's:

   A. past criminal activities.
   B. use of illegal drugs.
   C. intent to harm others.
   D. psychiatric history.

Skill:
Foundations of Comprehension

Key: B
This comprehension question asks you to determine from passage context how the passage author uses a particular term. The author writes that "health professionals have an interest in maintaining confidentiality so that patients will feel comfortable in revealing personal but necessary information" during a medical exam. The previous paragraph poses the hypothetical situation that a physician might discover drugs or paraphernalia during a routine medical examination and questions whether reporting this crime or maintaining confidentiality is more important for the physician. The patient's use of drugs would certainly be an important part of his or her medical history (as is also implied at the end of the passage), and the discussion of the need for confidential communication in paragraph 2 most likely refers to the drugs mentioned in the previous paragraph.

Distractors
A   The passage refers to the "personal but necessary information" that a health professional gathers during a medical history. Past criminal activities are not relevant to the medical record that the physician is gathering.

C   The passage refers to the "necessary information" that a health professional gathers during a medical history. While intent to harm others is something that a physician would be obligated to report if he or she discovered it during an examination, it is not what "personal but necessary information" most likely refers to here.

D   Certainly, a psychiatric history could be part of the "personal but necessary" information the physician gathers, but based on the previous paragraph, which poses the hypothetical situation that a physician might discover drug paraphernalia during a routine medical examination, it is more likely that "necessary information" here refers to the use of illegal drugs.

TIP: Read *all* the words in a question carefully and consider them when you evaluate potential answers. Here, the question asks for the option to which the phrase in question "probably refers *most specifically*." This means that even if one option is plausible, it may not be the one to which the phrase applies "most specifically."

10. Which of the following conclusions about physician confidentiality can be inferred from the passage?

   A. It is more likely to be assumed in a private setting than in a prison.
   B. It is especially important when patients are incompetent to give informed consent.
   C. It is threatened by the use of invasive diagnostic tools such as X-rays.
   D. It is an aspect of a Constitutional right that is lost by prisoners.

Skill:
Foundations of Comprehension

Key: A
The author writes that "confidentiality is particularly important in a prison hospital setting, in which patients feel distrust because physicians are often employed by the incarcerating institution" (paragraph 2). The clear implication here is that patients do not assume that they can count on physician confidentiality in a prison setting and by contrast, this would be more likely to be assumed in a private, non-institutional setting.

Distractors
B   While the passage discusses the importance of informed consent, it does not imply that confidentiality is "especially important" in the absence of informed consent.

C   The passage talks about the need for informed consent for prisoners and includes the need for this when X-ray technology is used, but it does not suggest that the X-ray technology *per se* represents a threat to confidentiality.

D   While the passage states that prisoners do not possess full Constitutional rights to privacy, it also says that they "generally retain rights to privacy when there is a special relationship between communicants, such as the physician-patient relationship." So there is no implication that prisoners have specifically "lost" this right.

11. Which of the following objections, if valid, would most *weaken* the argument made for the special importance of the physician-patient covenant within prisons?

    A. Prisoners understand that X-rays will detect hidden weapons.
    B. Prisoners assume that physicians are independent of the institution.
    C. Prison officials often question physicians about prisoners.
    D. Prisoners often misunderstand their Constitutional rights.

Skill:
Reasoning Beyond the Text

Key: B
If prisoners assume that physicians are independent of their institutions, then prisoners would not have reason to distrust physicians in a prison setting, as the passage says they frequently do. The author claims that "respect for confidentiality is particularly important in a prison hospital setting, in which patients feel distrust because physicians are often employed by the incarcerating institution." Therefore, without any reason for that distrust, respect for confidentiality, or the "physician-patient covenant," would be less important. Thus, option B weakens the argument for the special importance of the covenant.

Distractors

A   That prisoners understand that a diagnostic X-ray will detect hidden weapons does not weaken the argument for the importance of the physician-patient covenant. If anything, it points to the need for the prisoner to trust the physician to make diagnostic recommendations that are in his or her interest as a patient.

C   If prison officials often question physicians about patients, this only makes the covenant between the patient and physician more important (as suggested in paragraph 3).

D   If prisoners misunderstand their Constitutional rights, this certainly does not weaken the claim that the covenant between physicians and patients is important.

TIP: You should also read all possible answers before choosing one. Sometimes it can be tempting to zero in on one answer that appears likely before you have looked at the other options. In a case like this one, though, this strategy could leave you with an answer that you haven't compared to the others and may not be the *best* choice.

Critical Analysis and Reasoning Skills:

Passage Set III

MCAT® is a program of the
Association of American Medical Colleges

Critical Analysis and Reasoning Skills

Passage III: Questions 12–16

From Literature

Author of the famous five-part Leatherstocking series, twenty-seven other novels, and a box of historical and miscellaneous works, James Fenimore Cooper remains one of the most innovative yet most misunderstood figures in the history of U.S. culture. Almost single-handedly in the 1820s, Cooper invented the key forms of U.S. fiction—the Western, the sea tale, the Revolutionary romance—forms that set a suggestive agenda for subsequent writers, even for Hollywood and television. In producing and shrewdly marketing fully 10 percent of all U.S. novels in the 1820s, most of them best sellers, Cooper made it possible for other aspiring authors to earn a living by their writings. Cooper can be said to have invented not just an assortment of literary genres but the very career of the U.S. writer.

Despite Cooper's importance, he continues to be profoundly misunderstood, and this is partly his own fault. Although it was becoming common for writers in the early nineteenth century to indulge public curiosity about their lives, the usually chatty Cooper turned reticent when asked for biographical details. Whereas contemporaries, such as Sir Walter Scott and Washington Irving, made prior arrangements for authorized biographies, Cooper refused to follow suit. When nearing death in 1851, he insisted that his wife and children protect his life and his papers from outsiders. His private documents remained out of reach to most scholars until the 1990s.

The biographical problem is only one reason for Cooper's languishing reputation. Another reason is that he's always been the object of strong feelings, pro and con. Almost from the start of his career, Cooper was admired, imitated, recited, and memorized. In his day, he was reportedly the author most widely translated into German, and what has been called "Coopermania" hit France especially hard as early as the 1820s. Yet, from the outset, he was also subjected to various criticisms that, when combined with later politically motivated assaults, have hampered true appreciation of his work. Critics have at times faulted him for his occasional bad grammar, his leisurely pacing, and his general inability to eclipse his greatest contemporary, Sir Walter Scott.

The criticisms were not without merit. But the problems in Cooper's first books need to be understood in their proper context. At least some of Cooper's failings were owing to the very newness of what he was attempting. Robert E. Spiller summed up this point in 1931 by noting that Cooper "always suffered from the crudities of the experimenter."

Cooper was not just a pathbreaking figure in the history of writing in the U.S., or a potent visionary; he was a remarkably representative man. He was as much at home in the salons of New York City or the country houses of the rural Hudson Valley as in the raw frontier villages where his family's life had taken its root and rise. Knowing the country's most characteristic landscapes in ways that few of his contemporaries did, Cooper wrote of them with unexampled authority. He closely followed the War of 1812, partly because his friends fought in it, and partly because so much hinged on its outcome. Cooper thereafter joined in the effort of his most influential contemporaries to forge a new culture for the reaffirmed nation. One might say that Cooper's story is almost incidentally a literary story. It is first a story of how, in literature and a hundred other activities, Americans during this period sought to solidify their political and cultural and economic independence from Great Britain and, as the Revolutionary generation died, stipulate what the maturing Republic was to become.

Source: Adapted from W. Franklin, James Fenimore Cooper: The Early Years. Copyright 2007 by W. Franklin.

MCAT® is a program of the
Association of American Medical Colleges

12. Which of the following best describes an assumption made by the passage author in the first paragraph?

    A. Ten percent of all U.S. novels produced in the 1820s were best sellers.

    B. The most innovative figures in U.S. culture are often the most misunderstood.

    C. Before the 1820s, U.S. writers were unable to earn a living by their writings.

    D. Cooper was the only U.S. author writing during the 1820s.

---

13. Which of the following statements about authors is most strongly implied by information in the second paragraph?

    A. The public is most curious about authors who are reticent when asked about their lives.

    B. Authors who authorize biographies of themselves are likely to be better understood than authors who do not.

    C. Authors did not share biographical details of their lives before the early nineteenth century.

    D. Most authors' papers are not protected from outsiders after the authors die.

---

14. Which of the following people would the passage author most likely consider to be remarkably representative, as this concept is used in the final paragraph?

    A. Someone who has written many stories set in various locations

    B. Someone who has an understanding of a variety of diverse locations

    C. Someone who is well liked by people from different backgrounds

    D. Someone who has written descriptions of many famous landscapes

15. Which of the following situations in the automotive industry is the most analogous to the one described in the fourth paragraph regarding Cooper's early writings?

    A. An automobile manufacturer introduces a new model that quickly becomes the best-selling vehicle in its class.

    B. An automobile manufacturer designs a vehicle that becomes popular with a group of people different from the group the manufacturer had anticipated.

    C. An automobile manufacturer has unexpected mechanical issues with an innovative new vehicle after its release.

    D. An automobile manufacturer offers an extended warranty on its vehicles in an attempt to shed its reputation for poor craftsmanship.

---

16. Which of the following passage assertions is the LEAST supported by examples or explanations in the passage?

    A. "Cooper can be said to have invented not just an assortment of literary genres but the very career of the U.S. writer."

    B. "[Cooper] continues to be profoundly misunderstood, and this is partly his own fault."

    C. "Cooper was not just a pathbreaking figure in the history of writing in the U.S., or a potent visionary; he was a remarkably representative man."

    D. "[Cooper] closely followed the War of 1812, partly because his friends fought in it, and partly because so much hinged on its outcome."

Solutions for this passage begin on next page.

12. Which of the following best describes an assumption made by the passage author in the first paragraph?

    A. Ten percent of all U.S. novels produced in the 1820s were best sellers.

    B. The most innovative figures in U.S. culture are often the most misunderstood.

    C. Before the 1820s, U.S. writers were unable to earn a living by their writings.

    D. Cooper was the only U.S. author writing during the 1820s.

Skill:

Foundations of Comprehension

Key: C

The first paragraph says that "in producing and shrewdly marketing fully 10 percent of all U.S. novels in the 1820s...Cooper made it possible for other aspiring authors to earn a living by their writings." The author clearly implies here, then, that before Cooper's actions in the 1820s, it was not yet possible for writers to earn a living by their writings.

Distractors

A   The paragraph says that Cooper himself produced "fully 10 percent of all U.S. novels in the 1820s, most of them best sellers," but that does not imply there were no other best sellers at the time.

B   Although the author calls Cooper "one of the most innovative yet most misunderstood figures in the history of U.S. culture," this does not suggest that he or she assumes that innovative figures are generally misunderstood.

D   The first paragraph describes the innovations Cooper achieved "almost single-handedly"— that is, on his own—but it does not suggest that there were no other writers writing at the time. If Cooper produced 10 percent of U.S. novels in the 1820s, someone had to be writing the other 90 percent.

TIP: Confine your assumptions to what is said or implied in the passage. Some incorrect answers can trip you up if you are prone to making generalizations that the passage does not support. You would pick the wrong answer here if you assumed, for instance, that because the passage calls Cooper both innovative and misunderstood, innovative figures are generally misunderstood.

13. Which of the following statements about authors is most strongly implied by information in the second paragraph?

    A. The public is most curious about authors who are reticent when asked about their lives.

    B. Authors who authorize biographies of themselves are likely to be better understood than authors who do not.

    C. Authors did not share biographical details of their lives before the early nineteenth century.

    D. Most authors' papers are not protected from outsiders after the authors die.

Skill:
Foundations of Comprehension

Key: B
This comprehension question asks you to understand a point clearly implied, though not stated explicitly, by the passage author. The author argues that the fact that Cooper "continues to be profoundly misunderstood...is partly his own fault." The author then explains that Cooper's contemporaries "made prior arrangements for authorized biographies, [but] Cooper refused to follow suit." The implication here is that those authors who arranged for authorized biographies do not suffer the same fate of being misunderstood that Cooper does, partly as a result of his own actions or inactions.

Distractors

A   The author refers to Cooper's uncharacteristic reticence about his biography, but does not imply that reticence itself creates public curiosity.

C   The passage says that it was "becoming common" for authors to "indulge public curiosity about their lives." This does not imply that no authors shared details before this time.

D   The author says that when he was close to death, Cooper "insisted that his wife and children protect...his papers from outsiders," but this does not mean that others do not protect their papers or that his insistence was necessarily rational.

14. Which of the following people would the passage author most likely consider to be remarkably representative, as this concept is used in the final paragraph?

    A. Someone who has written many stories set in various locations
    B. Someone who has an understanding of a variety of diverse locations
    C. Someone who is well liked by people from different backgrounds
    D. Someone who has written descriptions of many famous landscapes

Skill:
Reasoning Beyond the Text

Key: B
This question asks you to reason beyond the text. It asks you to understand a concept used in the passage and then determine how that concept would apply to people who are not discussed in the passage. Immediately after calling Cooper "remarkably representative," the author writes about the various locations where Cooper felt "at home" (New York City salons, Hudson Valley country houses, frontier villages). The author also talks about Cooper's intimate knowledge of "the country's most characteristic landscapes." All of this suggests that part of what the author means by "remarkably representative" is that Cooper had a wide-ranging knowledge and experience of places in the U.S. Thus, option B, which talks generally about a person with an "understanding of diverse locations," is the most consistent with the passage description of "remarkably representative."

Distractors
A   While this option touches on the "various locations" that the author considers important in being "representative," it deals with writing stories about these locations, while the passage author stresses actual life experience.

C   The passage does not connect being well-liked with being "remarkably representative."

D   Like option A, this option deals with writing—in this case, about landscapes, rather than with knowing and understanding landscapes based on real experience.

15. Which of the following situations in the automotive industry is the most analogous to the one described in the fourth paragraph regarding Cooper's early writings?

- A. An automobile manufacturer introduces a new model that quickly becomes the best-selling vehicle in its class.
- B. An automobile manufacturer designs a vehicle that becomes popular with a group of people different from the group the manufacturer had anticipated.
- C. An automobile manufacturer has unexpected mechanical issues with an innovative new vehicle after its release.
- D. An automobile manufacturer offers an extended warranty on its vehicles in an attempt to shed its reputation for poor craftsmanship.

Skill:
Reasoning Beyond the Text

Key: C
This question asks you to apply ideas from the passage to a scenario outside of the passage. In paragraph 4, the passage author attributes "at least some of Cooper's failings" to "the very newness of what he was attempting." Option C describes an "innovative new" car that has unanticipated problems when it is first released. The option, then, links difficulties or failures to innovation, just as the passage author does with Cooper's early writing.

Distractors

A   This option describes something new that is a runaway success, which is not how the author describes Cooper's early writings.

B   The option discusses the audience for something new and how it departed from what the producer expected; the author's discussion of Cooper's early writings does not focus on questions of audience or suggest that Cooper's audience was different from the one he or his publishers anticipated.

D   This option describes an effort to compensate for a poor reputation by offering the buyer a guarantee. The author doesn't talk about anything like this when he or she talks about Cooper's early writing.

16. Which of the following passage assertions is the LEAST supported by examples or explanations in the passage?

- A. "Cooper can be said to have invented not just an assortment of literary genres but the very career of the U.S. writer."
- B. "[Cooper] continues to be profoundly misunderstood, and this is partly his own fault."
- C. "Cooper was not just a pathbreaking figure in the history of writing in the U.S. . . . he was a remarkably representative man."
- D. "[Cooper] closely followed the War of 1812, partly because his friends fought in it, and partly because so much hinged on its outcome."

Skill:
Reasoning Within the Text

Key: D
This question asks you to reason with information provided in the passage. It asks you to assess the passage author's use of evidence in the text, looking at specific points in the passage to see whether the author provides supporting examples or explanations for them. Option D contains the only assertion among the options that the passage author does not support with any additional discussion or specific examples. He or she simply makes the statement, treats it as true, and moves on to what Cooper did after the War of 1812. (He or she does not, for example, elaborate on what actually "hinged on [the] outcome" of the war.)

Distractors

A The first paragraph describes the important ways in which Cooper "invented" the career of the U.S. writer—largely by making the endeavor financially feasible.

B Paragraph 2 focuses on the ways in which Cooper's reluctance to make his papers available and his refusal to authorize a biography contributed to the public misunderstanding him.

C Paragraph 5 describes in detail the wide-ranging, eclectic experiences and knowledge that made Cooper a "representative" man.

 TIP: In questions like this one, which require you to look for evidence or support for a particular claim, do not assume that all evidence or support for a point will be found *after* the claim. Sometimes examples or support may appear before the claim does, with the claim functioning as a summary or explanatory statement.

Critical Analysis and Reasoning Skills:

Passage Set IV

MCAT® is a program of the
Association of American Medical Colleges

Critical Analysis and Reasoning Skills

Passage IV: Questions 17–23

From Political Science

Party identification in the United States is a relatively uncomplicated measure determined by responses to the following questions:

> Generally speaking, do you usually think of yourself as a Republican, a Democrat, an independent, or what?

> (If R or D) Would you call yourself a strong (R), (D) or a not very strong (R), (D)?

> (If independent) Do you think of yourself as closer to the Republican party or to the Democratic party?

As this self-identification measure of party loyalty is the best indicator of partisanship, political analysts commonly refer to partisanship and party identification interchangeably. Partisanship is the most important influence on political and voting behavior. Many other influences are at work on voters in U.S. society, and partisanship varies in its importance in different types of election and in different time periods; nevertheless, no single factor compares in significance with partisanship.

Partisanship represents the feeling of sympathy for and loyalty to a political party that an individual acquires (probably) during childhood and holds (often) with increasing intensity throughout life. This self-image as a Democrat or a Republican is useful to the individual in a special way. For example, individuals who think of themselves as Republicans or Democrats respond to political information partially by using party identification to orient themselves, reacting to new information in such a way that it fits in with the ideals and feelings they already have. A Republican who hears a Republican party leader advocate a policy has a basis in party loyalty for supporting that policy, quite apart from other considerations. A Democrat may feel favorably inclined toward a candidate for office because that candidate bears the Democrat label. Partisanship may orient individuals in their political environment, but it may also distort their picture of reality.

An underlying partisanship is also of interest to political analysts because it provides a base against which to measure deviations in particular elections. In other words, the individual voter's longstanding loyalty to one party means that, "other things being equal," or in the absence of disrupting forces, he or she can be expected to vote for that party. However, voters are responsive to a great variety of other influences that can either strengthen or weaken their tendency to vote for their usual party. Obvious variations occur from election to election in such factors as the attractiveness of the candidates, the impact of foreign and domestic policy issues, and purely local circumstances. These current factors, often called "short-term forces," may move voters away from their normal party choices.

These ideas can also be used in understanding the behavior of the electorate as a whole. If one added up the political predispositions of all the individuals in the electorate, one would have an "expected vote" or "normal vote." This is the electoral outcome to be expected if all voters voted their party identification. Departures from this expected vote in actual elections represent the impact of short-term forces, such as issues or candidates.

Source: Adapted from W.H. Flanigan and N.H. Zingale, Political behavior of the American electorate. Copyright 1991 by Congressional Quarterly.

17. According to the passage, one drawback of partisanship is that it can:

    A. cause voters to react to political information on the basis of their personal feelings.
    B. distort voters' views of reality.
    C. orient voters in their political environment.
    D. make voters vulnerable to short-term forces.

18. According to the passage, partisanship is of interest to political analysts because:

    A. it provides a base against which electoral fluctuations can be measured.
    B. it helps identify the short-term forces that affect voters' decisions.
    C. it represents a relatively complex measure of party identification.
    D. it reveals the political climate in which an individual voter was reared.

19. According to passage information, which of the following factors would be most likely to cause a voter to choose a candidate from a party other than the voter's party?

    A. A local scandal involving officials of the voter's party
    B. Pressure from a political action committee
    C. Opinions of the voter's family members
    D. Campaign advertising by the opposing party

20. In 1952, despite a substantial Democratic majority among U.S. voters, a Republican president, Dwight Eisenhower, was elected. Given the information in the passage, this result was probably due to:

    A. a wholesale shift in party loyalty among registered Democrats.
    B. low voter interest in the campaign.
    C. personal qualities that made Eisenhower an especially attractive candidate.
    D. a lack of pressing domestic issues facing the country.

21. On the basis of information in the passage, one would generally expect the content of a campaign advertisement attacking an opposing candidate to be received most favorably by:

    A. voters in the party sponsoring the ad.
    B. voters disaffected by the political process.
    C. voters in the party being attacked in the ad.
    D. independent voters.

22. If the information is correct, one could most reasonably conclude that, compared to partisan voters, independent voters:

    A. care less about politics.
    B. take longer to evaluate political information.
    C. are less susceptible to the influence of short-term factors.
    D. exhibit basically the same political behavior.

23. Which of the following best describes the way that the passage author represents the process for measuring the effect of short-term forces on an election?

    A. The author represents this process as accepted by politicians across the political spectrum.
    B. The author represents this process as challenged by some statistical data.
    C. The author represents this process as one that is clearly effective and accurate, without reference to supporting data.
    D. The author represents this process as one that is controversial among political analysts, accepted by some and rejected by others.

Solutions for this passage begin on next page.

17. According to the passage, one drawback of partisanship is that it can:

    A. cause voters to react to political information on the basis of their personal feelings.

    B. distort voters' views of reality.

    C. orient voters in their political environment.

    D. make voters vulnerable to short-term forces.

Skill:

Foundations of Comprehension

Key: B

This is an example of a comprehension question that hews fairly closely to the original text. The end of paragraph 3 says explicitly that while "partisanship may orient individuals in their political environment...it may also distort their picture of reality."

Distractors

A   The passage talks about the partisan "feeling of sympathy...and loyalty" a voter may have, but it doesn't characterize these as specifically "personal," nor does it suggest that these feelings would represent a "drawback" of partisanship.

C   This option makes a true statement about the passage (the end of paragraph 3 points out that "partisanship may orient individuals in their political environment"), but it does not respond to the question. The question asks for a drawback of partisanship, and being "oriented" in a "political environment" is not a "drawback," but a positive aspect of partisanship. The last sentence of paragraph 3 makes this clear when it uses "but" before explaining the drawback of partisanship it emphasizes here.

D   Paragraph 4 talks about circumstances in which "short-term forces" may affect voter behavior, but this is not treated as an outcome of partisanship, but as a deviation from partisan behavior.

TIP: Answering correctly requires that you read the passage carefully enough that you understand *how* a particular point is being used in the text. In this case, the question asks for a "drawback" of partisanship, and so you must evaluate how the author frames the particular points he or she makes about partisanship. Use contextual cues in the passage, like those discussed in option C above, to help you make these judgments.

18. According to the passage, partisanship is of interest to political analysts because:

    A. it provides a base against which electoral fluctuations can be measured.

    B. it helps identify the short-term forces that affect voters' decisions.

    C. it represents a relatively complex measure of party identification.

    D. it reveals the political climate in which an individual voter was reared.

Skill:
Foundations of Comprehension

Key: B
The passage explains that in elections, departures from expected outcomes—the outcomes that party identification would predict—"represent the impact of short-term forces, such as issues or candidates" (final paragraph). The previous paragraph, too, focuses on the way that "deviations in particular elections" can highlight the impact on a particular election on a number of different short-term forces in which political analysts would be interested.

Distractors

A   The passage does say that political analysts are interested in partisanship because "it provides a base against which to measure deviations in particular elections" (paragraph 4). The rest of paragraph 4, however, as well as the final paragraph, are devoted to a discussion of the "short-term" forces that might affect an election and thus explain a fluctuation from the outcome that party identification would otherwise predict. So the passage suggests that measuring the fluctuations is useful because fluctuations point to the effects of "short-term forces."

C   To the contrary, the first sentence calls party identification "a relatively uncomplicated measure."

D   While the passage says that party identification is often formed in childhood, it does not say that one can extrapolate from party identification to discover details about individual voters. Further, political analysts tend to be interested in patterns, not in the histories of individual voters.

TIP: When you read a passage in the Critical Analysis and Reasoning Skills section, think about the overall meaning or goals of the passage as you read. This will help you understand how important a particular point or claim is in the context of the passage. Is it a central point? Is it just a building block to help the author get to the main argument? When you see how the pieces of a passage fit together, you are less likely to be distracted by incorrect answers that overstate the importance of a particular point in the passage.

19. According to passage information, which of the following factors would be most likely to cause a voter to choose a candidate from a party other than the voter's party?

    A. A local scandal involving officials of the voter's party
    B. Pressure from a political action committee
    C. Opinions of the voter's family members
    D. Campaign advertising by the opposing party

Skill:
Foundations of Comprehension

Key: A
Paragraphs 4 and 5 of the passage talk about the impact of "short-term" forces on elections—forces that cause deviations from the expected outcomes that partisanship would predict. Option A represents an example of a "short-term force" that makes the voter's usual party look less attractive at a particular time.

Distractors

B   The passage explains that voters usually evaluate political information in ways that reinforce their partisan leanings. Thus, there is no reason to believe, based on the passage, that pressure from a political action committee would influence a voter to support a candidate from the opposing party. (The option does not say which party is sponsoring the PAC.)

C   The passage mentions that the opinions of a voter's family members (at least during childhood) may help to shape the voter's partisan leanings in the first place, so the passage does not suggest that family members would sway the voter from his or her party affiliation. Or, if the family member did have a different political affiliation from the voter, nothing in the passage suggests that the voter would be swayed by this as an adult.

D   As with option B, passage information suggests that voters evaluate political information in ways that work to reinforce their pre-existing partisan leanings. Thus, campaign advertising from the opposing party likely would be ineffective.

Fifth Edition
The Official Guide to the MCAT® Exam
360
MCAT® is a program of the
Association of American Medical Colleges

20. In 1952, despite a substantial Democratic majority among U.S. voters, a Republican president, Dwight Eisenhower, was elected. Given the information in the passage, this result was probably due to:

A. a wholesale shift in party loyalty among registered Democrats.
B. low voter interest in the campaign.
C. personal qualities that made Eisenhower an especially attractive candidate.
D. a lack of pressing domestic issues facing the country.

Skill:
Reasoning Beyond the Text

Key: C
This question begins with a scenario outside the scope of the passage and asks you to understand or explain it in light of passage information. The question presents the kind of scenario that the passage describes in the fourth and last paragraphs when it talks about particular elections where results deviated from what would have been expected based on partisan affiliations. Paragraph 4 mentions various "short-term forces," which include the "attractiveness of the candidates," among others, that might influence an election.

Distractors
A   Based on the passage discussion of partisanship, such a wholesale shift in party loyalty is highly unlikely.

B   The passage does not discuss low voter interest as a factor that might account for an outcome that deviates from what party affiliations and loyalty would predict.

D   The passage calls the "impact of domestic and foreign policy issues" an example of a "short-term force" that might influence an election, but there is no information in the passage to suggest that a "lack of pressing domestic issues" might influence people to vote against their usual partisan interests.

21. On the basis of information in the passage, one would generally expect the content of a campaign advertisement attacking an opposing candidate to be received most favorably by:

    A. voters in the party sponsoring the ad.
    B. voters disaffected by the political process.
    C. voters in the party being attacked in the ad.
    D. independent voters.

Skill:
Reasoning Beyond the Text

Key: A
Paragraph 3 of the passage says that voters respond to political information in ways consistent with their partisan feelings. A campaign advertisement attacking an opposing candidate, then, most likely would resonate with voters already predisposed to sympathize with the party that made the advertisement and oppose the candidate attacked in the ad. The passage suggests that political information generally works to reinforce existing feelings, not change them.

Distractors

B   The passage does not address voters who are not engaged with the political process.

C   For the same reason that the ad would be most likely to be effective with voters from the party who made the ad, it would be *less* likely to be effective with voters from the party whose candidate the ad attacks. Those voters would be likely to evaluate the ad on the basis of their pre-existing political sympathies rather than respond to or be influenced by the ad.

D   As independent voters are less defined by specific partisan allegiances, the passage discussion of the way that voters generally respond to political information (in terms of their preexisting political sympathies) is less relevant to independent voters. There is no reason to think, based on the passage, that independent voters would be especially receptive to a particular kind of political advertisement.

22. If the information is correct, one could most reasonably conclude that, compared to partisan voters, independent voters:

    A. care less about politics.
    B. take longer to evaluate political information.
    C. are less susceptible to the influence of short-term factors.
    D. exhibit basically the same political behavior.

Skill:
Reasoning Beyond the Text

Key: B
The passage suggests that partisanship, or party affiliation, helps voters orient themselves in a political landscape and also respond to political information. Without the "short-cut" that that orientation likely provides, it would make sense that independent voters—voters without a party affiliation—would take longer to process or evaluate political information.

Distractors

A   There is no suggestion in the passage that partisan voters care more about politics than non-affiliated voters.

C   There is no indication in the passage that short-term forces would be less important for independent voters than for partisan voters (especially as these short-term forces are represented in the passage as forces that may influence voters to act independently of partisanship).

D   This option is strongly at odds with the passage, which talks about the powerful influence of partisanship on voter behavior, so it would be unlikely, in the terms of the passage, for independent voters to show the same political behavior as partisan voters.

23. Which of the following best describes the way that the passage author represents the process for measuring the effect of short-term forces on an election?

    A. The author represents this process as accepted by politicians across the political spectrum.

    B. The author represents this process as challenged by some statistical data.

    C. The author represents this process as one that is clearly effective and accurate, without reference to supporting data.

    D. The author represents this process as one that is controversial among political analysts, accepted by some and rejected by others.

Skill:
Reasoning Within the Text

Key: C
This question asks you to assess the way in which an author presents information and identify the kind of supporting evidence he or she provides. In paragraphs 4 and 5, the author explains the process he or she recommends for measuring the effects of "short-term forces" on an election. The author presents this process as uncontroversial, without citing any other experts or statistical data to support the value of the process. Rather, the author implies that this is a universally accepted process among political analysts and he or she is simply explaining it to the reader.

Distractors

A   The author does not talk about what politicians themselves think about measures of partisanship or how these measures are used to assess short-term forces.

B   The author does not present statistical data to challenge (or support) any claims, explicit or implicit, about the accuracy of this process.

D   While the author does refer to "political analysts" in paragraph 4, he or she does this only to discuss the analysts' use of language about partisanship. The author does not suggest that political analysts differ in their approach to the process he or she describes for calculating the effect of short-term forces on an election.

Critical Analysis and Reasoning Skills:

Passage Set V

MCAT® is a program of the
Association of American Medical Colleges

Critical Analysis and Reasoning Skills

Passage V: Questions 24–30

From Studies of Diverse Cultures

Western culture views the written word as the dominant form of record keeping. Therefore, until recently, Westerners have sometimes considered so-called oral societies to be peoples without history. This could not be further from the truth. Oral societies record and document their histories in complex ways, including through dancing and drumming. Although most oral societies have now adopted the written word for documentation, expression, and communication, many still greatly value the oral transmission of knowledge as fundamental to their cultures and societies.

For example, oral-based knowledge systems are predominant among various Aboriginal peoples in Canada, sometimes called First Nations. Stories are frequently told as evening entertainment to pass along local or family knowledge. Stories are also told more formally, in ceremonies, to validate a person's authority, responsibilities, or prestige.

Some stories are told only during certain seasons, at a particular time of day, or in specific places. Similarly, some stories are meant to be heard only by specific people. Such stories often teach important lessons about a society's culture, the land, and the ways in which members are expected to interact with each other and their environment. The passing on of these stories from generation to generation keeps the social order intact. Oral histories must therefore be told carefully and accurately, often by a designated person who is responsible for keeping the knowledge and eventually passing it on in order to preserve the historical record.

Notwithstanding this emphasis on accuracy, oral narratives are often presented with variations. Narrators may adjust a story to place it in context, to emphasize particular aspects of the story, or to present a lesson in a new light. Multiple tellings create a broader, more comprehensive narrative.

In contrast, written history does not present a dialogue so much as a static record of an authority's singular recounting of a series of events. As readers, we may interpret these writings, but the writing itself remains the same. Oral narratives, on the other hand, do not have to be retold exactly the same way—what is fundamental is whether or not they carry the same message.

The landscape plays an important role in connecting Aboriginal oral histories to lived experiences. As an individual moves through the landscape, oral traditions inform his or her responses to it. In what is now British Columbia, Canada, the Aboriginal people of the Fraser River Valley believe that their deities, known as the creators, turned to stone anyone who misbehaved, resulting in a number of distinct geological formations throughout the territory. The creators were also believed to reward individuals who showed exemplary behavior by turning them into valuable natural resources. On encountering these landmarks, individuals may recall the stories and their embedded lessons and gain insight into them over time.

Despite the complexities of oral traditions, discussions of oral history have sometimes been framed in terms of simplistic binary oppositions. Critics wary of oral history tend to frame oral history as subjective and biased, in comparison to written history, presumed to be rational and objective. In Western contexts, authors of written documents may be received automatically as authorities on their subjects and what is written down taken as fact. Such assumptions ignore the fact that authors of written documents bring their own experiences, agendas, and biases to their work.

Source: Adapted from E. Hanson, "Oral Traditions." Copyright 2009 by First Nations Studies Program, University of British Columbia.

24. According to the passage, Aboriginal cultures use stories to do which of the following?

      I. Entertain children
     II. Convey information
    III. Reinforce community roles

A. I only
B. II only
C. I and III only
D. II and III only

25. Based on the information provided in the passage, the role of stories in oral societies is most like which of the following?

A. Legal precedents, which are used by judges to make determinations about standards and penalties
B. Innovations, which keep a society from becoming dependent on tradition
C. Family rules, casually decreed by parents and easily transgressed by children and teenagers
D. Works of art, intended to showcase the best and brightest of each generation

26. Which of the following statements most supports the information given in the passage?

A. Oral tradition is unreliable.
B. Oral tradition is a collective enterprise.
C. Oral societies develop small vocabularies.
D. Oral societies are more emotional than cognitive.

27. The passage implies that written narratives and oral narratives differ with respect to:

A. the importance of tone.
B. the importance of morals.
C. the locus of the burden of interpretation.
D. the degree of sophistication as it relates to form.

28. Information in the passage suggests that for Aboriginals, features of the landscape serve as:

A. symbols.
B. refuges.
C. sacred shrines.
D. memory triggers.

29. Hypertext narratives published on the internet allow a reader to choose to explore various dimensions of a written text (by clicking a link); the text may be different with each encounter with a reader. How does this statement affect the author's claims in the passage?

A. It supports the author's characterization of written narratives.
B. It questions the author's characterization of written narratives.
C. It is irrelevant to the author's characterization of written narratives.
D. It repeats earlier points about written narratives.

30. The author implies which of the following about written narratives?

A. They are seldom true to the facts they contain.
B. They have subjective elements, just as oral narratives do.
C. They should not be considered authoritative.
D. They typically derive from oral narratives.

Solutions for this passage begin on next page.

24. According to the passage, Aboriginal cultures use stories to do which of the following?

     I. Entertain children
    II. Convey information
   III. Reinforce community roles

  A. I only
  B. II only
  C. I and III only
  D. II and III only

Skill:
Foundations of Comprehension

Key: D
Option II is correct, as the passage says that "stories are frequently told...to pass along local or family knowledge" (paragraph 2), or "convey information," as option II would have it. Option III is also correct, as the author claims that "stories are also told...to validate a person's authority, responsibilities, or prestige" (paragraph 2). Stories also "teach important lessons about . . . the ways in which members are expected to interact with each other" (paragraph 3). These two latter quotations both support the claim that stories work to "reinforce community roles."

Distractors
A   Although the author mentions that stories are told as entertainment, there is no mention in the passage of children in particular, so option I is incorrect.

B   Option II is correct, as discussed above, but so is option III.

C   While option III is correct, option I is not. (Although the author mentions that stories are told as entertainment, there is no mention of children in particular, so option I is incorrect.)

 TIP: With questions in this format, it is especially important to read each answer choice and evaluate it carefully. If you are sure that one answer choice is incorrect, you can then rule out any answers containing that answer choice.

25. Based on the information provided in the passage, the role of stories in oral societies is most like which of the following?

    A. Legal precedents, which are used by judges to make determinations about standards and penalties

    B. Innovations, which keep a society from becoming dependent on tradition

    C. Family rules, casually decreed by parents and easily transgressed by children and teenagers

    D. Works of art, intended to showcase the best and brightest of each generation

---

Skill:

Reasoning Beyond the Text

Key: A

This question asks you to reason beyond the text. It asks you to take information in the passage and apply it to a series of scenarios that are not in the passage to determine which of these is most analogous to passage descriptions. The passage describes the stories in oral societies as working to "teach important lessons about a society's culture...and the ways in which members are expected to interact with each other." Stories also keep "the social order intact." This corresponds to option A, in which legal precedents make clear social "standards" and expectations. It also can be inferred that "penalties" might be part of keeping the social order "intact."

Distractors

B   The stories preserve tradition; there is no implication that they keep the society from becoming dependent on tradition.

C   There is no indication in the passage that the lessons in the stories are either "casually decreed" or "easily transgressed." In fact, the passage represents the stories as an important, meaningful part of Aboriginal cultural tradition.

D   There is no indication in the passage that the stories "showcase the best and brightest of each generation."

26. Which of the following statements most supports the information given in the passage?

    A. Oral tradition is unreliable.

    B. Oral tradition is a collective enterprise.

    C. Oral societies develop small vocabularies.

    D. Oral societies are more emotional than cognitive.

Skill:
Reasoning Beyond the Text

Key: B
The description of oral tradition as "collective" supports the characterization of orality throughout the passage. For instance, in paragraph 4, the author writes, "Multiple tellings create a broader, more comprehensive narrative." This statement, along with the rest of the paragraph, describes a multi-authored, collaborative approach that supports this option. Other paragraphs describe the passing on of the stories from generation to generation, which again is supported by a description of the oral tradition as a "collective enterprise."

Distractors

A   The passage does not say or imply that oral tradition is not reliable.

C   There is nothing in the passage that suggests that oral societies might have smaller vocabularies than other societies. This is the kind of generalization or assumption, in fact, that the passage works to challenge.

D   The author mentions that some critics believe written history is "rational and objective," but that belief is represented in the passage as part of a simplistic and misleading binary opposition, not as a correct description of the difference between oral and written language.

27. The passage implies that written narratives and oral narratives differ with respect to:

    A. the importance of tone.

    B. the importance of morals.

    C. the locus of the burden of interpretation.

    D. the degree of sophistication as it relates to form.

Skill:

Reasoning Within the Text

Key: C

This question asks you to reason with information provided by the passage. It asks you to determine the relationship between two different kinds of narratives, based on passage information about each type; the relationship itself is not explicitly described in the passage. The passage says that "in contrast [to oral narrative], written history does not present a dialogue so much as a static record of an authority's singular recounting of a series of events. As readers, we may interpret these writings, but the writing itself remains the same" (paragraph 5). The implication here is that the reader may interpret a written narrative (without affecting its final shape). In oral narrative, by contrast, the multiple narrators or storytellers bear the burden of interpretation, and are thus free to "adjust a story" as they see fit.

Distractors

A   The passage author does not mention tone in relation to either written or oral language.

B   Although "lessons" (or morals) are mentioned as important to oral narratives, there is no indication that this is not true for written narratives.

D   The passage does not suggest that either written narratives or oral narratives are more formally "sophisticated" than other narratives. The author mentions complexity in the first paragraph in relation to the ways in which oral societies record and document their histories, but there is no suggestion that written narratives are not sophisticated.

28. Information in the passage suggests that for Aboriginals, features of the landscape serve as:

- A. symbols.
- B. refuges.
- C. sacred shrines.
- D. memory triggers.

Skills:
Foundations of Comprehension

Key: D
The author explains that "on encountering…landmarks, individuals may recall the stories and their embedded lessons," suggesting that features of the landscape trigger particular memories for Aboriginals.

Distractors

A   The Aboriginal belief that creators turn to stone anyone who misbehaves is described as a belief in a literal, not symbolic, process.

B   The passage does not say anything to imply that the landmarks provide a place of refuge.

C   The passage author mentions deities, but does not imply that features of the landscape are shrines.

29. Hypertext narratives published on the internet allow a reader to choose to explore various dimensions of a written text (by clicking a link); the text may be different with each encounter with a reader. How does this statement affect the author's claims in the passage?

    A. It supports the author's characterization of written narratives.
    B. It questions the author's characterization of written narratives.
    C. It is irrelevant to the author's characterization of written narratives.
    D. It repeats earlier points about written narratives.

Skill:
Reasoning Beyond the Text

Key: B
This question asks you to reason beyond the text. It describes a situation that is not contained within the passage and asks you to determine how it affects or relates to the author's arguments within the passage. The author writes, "written history does not present a dialogue so much as a static record of an authority's singular recounting of a series of events. As readers, we may interpret these writings, but the writing itself remains the same" (paragraph 5). The scenario described in the question, however, suggests a very different process, as hypertext is different on each encounter with a reader. So the scenario works to question the author's characterization of written language, and this option is correct.

Distractors
A   The scenario described in the question stem does not support the author's suggestion that written narratives are generally static.

C   As discussed in the solution above, the statement is relevant to the author's claims about written narratives.

D   There is no other instance in the passage of a description of a dynamic, changing form of written language, so this statement does not repeat earlier points of the author.

TIP: Just as you do not need outside knowledge to answer questions in this section, you should be especially careful when you *do* have relevant outside knowledge about a topic. In this case, perhaps you write hypertext narratives of your own, or have recently taken a course on digital media. It can be very tempting to use what you know to try to second-guess the information in the passage or in the question. The passages in this section are designed, however, to give you the information and context you need to understand the passage and answer the questions. Be sure that there is support *in the passage* for the choices you make and you are not relying on your own expertise to answer questions.

30. The author implies which of the following about written narratives?

    A. They are seldom true to the facts they contain.
    B. They have subjective elements, just as oral narratives do.
    C. They should not be considered authoritative.
    D. They typically derive from oral narratives.

Skill:
Foundations of Comprehension

Key: B
This comprehension question asks you to examine the text to determine what the passage author implies—and as important, what he or she does not imply—in the text itself. The passage says that those who consider written narratives authoritative "ignore the fact that authors of written documents bring their own experiences, agendas, and biases to their work" (final paragraph).

Distractors
A   Although the author seems critical of the tendency of written narratives to be "received automatically as authorities on their subjects," he or she does not say that they are "seldom" true to the facts.

C   Though the author criticizes the presumption that written narratives are authoritative, he or she does not imply that they should never be considered authoritative.

D   The passage does not indicate that written narratives usually derive from oral narratives.

Chapter 14

Where Can I Find Additional Information About the MCAT Exam?

You can find more information about the MCAT exam at the following websites:

- For prospective examinees: students-residents.aamc.org/applying-medical-school/taking-mcat-exam

- For prehealth advisors and other baccalaureate faculty: students-residents.aamc.org/advisors/mcat-resources-pre-health-advisors

- For medical schools admissions officers and faculty: students-residents.aamc.org/advisors/mcat-resources-pre-health-advisors

Addendum

Periodic Table of the Elements

1 **H** 1.0																	2 **He** 4.0
3 **Li** 6.9	4 **Be** 9.0											5 **B** 10.8	6 **C** 12.0	7 **N** 14.0	8 **O** 16.0	9 **F** 19.0	10 **Ne** 20.2
11 **Na** 23.0	12 **Mg** 24.3											13 **Al** 27.0	14 **Si** 28.1	15 **P** 31.0	16 **S** 32.1	17 **Cl** 35.5	18 **Ar** 39.9
19 **K** 39.1	20 **Ca** 40.1	21 **Sc** 45.0	22 **Ti** 47.9	23 **V** 50.9	24 **Cr** 52.0	25 **Mn** 54.9	26 **Fe** 55.8	27 **Co** 58.9	28 **Ni** 58.7	29 **Cu** 63.5	30 **Zn** 65.4	31 **Ga** 69.7	32 **Ge** 72.6	33 **As** 74.9	34 **Se** 79.0	35 **Br** 79.9	36 **Kr** 83.8
37 **Rb** 85.5	38 **Sr** 87.6	39 **Y** 88.9	40 **Zr** 91.2	41 **Nb** 92.9	42 **Mo** 95.9	43 **Tc** (98)	44 **Ru** 101.1	45 **Rh** 102.9	46 **Pd** 106.4	47 **Ag** 107.9	48 **Cd** 112.4	49 **In** 114.8	50 **Sn** 118.7	51 **Sb** 121.8	52 **Te** 127.6	53 **I** 126.9	54 **Xe** 131.3
55 **Cs** 132.9	56 **Ba** 137.3	57 **La*** 138.9	72 **Hf** 178.5	73 **Ta** 180.9	74 **W** 183.9	75 **Re** 186.2	76 **Os** 190.2	77 **Ir** 192.2	78 **Pt** 195.1	79 **Au** 197.0	80 **Hg** 200.6	81 **Tl** 204.4	82 **Pb** 207.2	83 **Bi** 209.0	84 **Po** (209)	85 **At** (210)	86 **Rn** (222)
87 **Fr** (223)	88 **Ra** (226)	89 **Ac†** (227)	104 **Rf** (267)	105 **Db** (268)	106 **Sg** (271)	107 **Bh** (270)	108 **Hs** (269)	109 **Mt** (278)	110 **Ds** (281)	111 **Rg** (282)	112 **Cn** (285)	113 **Nh** (286)	114 **Fl** (289)	115 **Mc** (289)	116 **Lv** (293)	117 **Ts** (294)	118 **Og** (294)

	58 **Ce** 140.1	59 **Pr** 140.9	60 **Nd** 144.2	61 **Pm** (145)	62 **Sm** 150.4	63 **Eu** 152.0	64 **Gd** 157.3	65 **Tb** 158.9	66 **Dy** 162.5	67 **Ho** 164.9	68 **Er** 167.3	69 **Tm** 168.9	70 **Yb** 173.0	71 **Lu** 175.0
†	90 **Th** 232.0	91 **Pa** (231)	92 **U** 238.0	93 **Np** (237)	94 **Pu** (244)	95 **Am** (243)	96 **Cm** (247)	97 **Bk** (247)	98 **Cf** (251)	99 **Es** (252)	100 **Fm** (257)	101 **Md** (258)	102 **No** (259)	103 **Lr** (266)

About Your Prehealth Advisor

As you explore the resources available to you, consider the ways your prehealth, or health professions, advisor can be of service. He or she can direct you to courses that will help you prepare for the MCAT exam, point you to other premed students (with whom you might want to create a study group), assist you in developing a timeline for applying, and, in general, support you through the medical school admissions process. The following is reprinted with permission from the National Association of Advisors for the Health Professions (NAAHP) to provide you with additional information.

Who are health professions advisors?

Students exploring or planning a career in medicine should seek out the health professions advisor on their campus to assist them. Most U.S. colleges and universities designate an individual as the school's health professions advisor. That person may be a faculty member, often in the sciences, who advises health professions students as well as teaches them, and perhaps even performs scientific research. The health professions advisor may be a member of the academic dean's office who oversees all academic advising at the institution. Another possibility is that the advisor is housed in the school's career center, specializing in advice regarding health careers. The common denominator is that health professions advisors are knowledgeable, supportive individuals whose role is to provide information and guidance as you prepare for your chosen profession.

How can a health professions advisor help you?

Your advisor can help you determine which courses satisfy premedical requirements, how to best sequence them, and how to find tutoring or other academic support if you are having difficulty. An advisor can guide you in incorporating study abroad, a double major, or a senior honors thesis into your course of study and still prepare well for medical school. Your advisor will encourage you to seek experience in the health care field as a way of informing yourself about the profession as well as strengthening your application to medical school. Your advisor will encourage and support you as you try to determine the right career path for yourself, by assessing your own strengths and weaknesses, values, and life's goals. Although it may be possible to choose the proper courses, find meaningful health-related experience, explore your own personal strengths and weaknesses, and negotiate the complexities of the medical school admissions process independently, seeking the advice of your health professions advisor will greatly ease your burden.

Who can be aided by a health professions advisor?

All health professions advisors meet with students individually at their campuses to offer the assistance described above. But while many students applying to medical school are college-age, some are not. Increasingly, advisors work with older or "nontraditional" students who have graduated from their institution or who have come to the school to pursue postbaccalaureate coursework. All students, regardless of age or status, should seek out the health professions advisor where they are currently studying or at their alma mater. Policies differ from school to school, but some students with access to health professions advising are unaware of this valuable resource.

How can your health professions advisor help you decide which medical schools you should consider?

Your health professions advisor is knowledgeable about many aspects of the various medical schools. Each American medical school has a stated mission for its school, and the missions are not all the same. Some schools have a very high commitment to global health. Others are committed to training clinical and laboratory researchers who will be academic faculty at American medical schools. Others have a higher commitment to primary care, and even that commitment may be focused at a given school specifically on rural primary care or inner-city primary care. Therefore, in counseling you about where you might apply to medical school, your health professions advisor will review with you not only your academic record and coursework but also your background and ultimate career goals in helping you select which medical school or medical schools best suit your individual strengths and aspirations.

If your institution does not have a health professions advisor, NAAHP members have volunteered to help those individuals who have no other access to advising. NAAHP can help answer your questions about applying to medical school.
Visit: naahp.org.

Contact: volunteer.advisor@naahp.org

Reprinted with permission from the National Association of Advisors for the Health Professions (NAAHP)